You can build great websites with Drupal.

Our names are Steve Burge and Cindy McCourt, and we're Drupal trainers.

During hundreds of Drupal classes in many cities and countries, we've met lots of different types of Drupal learners:

- Drupal learners come from many different backgrounds. They are accountants, florists, photographers, secretaries, factory workers, stay-at-home parents, and people from all walks of life.

- Drupal learners don't need to know anything about websites. Some Drupal learners are professional web designers, but many others have never built a site before and don't know any website code or jargon.

- Drupal learners don't need any experience. We've trained people who went to work the previous week and found their boss saying, "Surprise! You're running our Drupal site!" They often still wore their look of that very surprise.

- Drupal learners are of all ages. We've taught 15-year old students skipping class all the way up to retirees in their '80s.

If any of those descriptions sound like you, you've picked up the right book.

Using plain English and straightforward instructions, this book will help teach you how to build great websites using Drupal.

THIS BOOK IS ACTIVE

You don't learn to ride a bicycle by reading a book: You learn by actually riding.

You don't learn to drive a car by reading a book: You learn by actually driving.

A book can help and give some advice, but without actually riding a bike or driving a car, you'll never really learn. The same is true with Drupal.

So, throughout every chapter of this book, you're going to be asked to work with Drupal.

THIS BOOK USES SPECIFIC EXAMPLES

After you master the techniques in this book, you can build your own websites for companies, charities, schools, sports, or whatever else you need.

However, this book uses a specific example site. Asking all the readers of this book to build the same site makes it easy for us to give you specific instructions, explanations, and screenshots.

It's not essential that you follow every task provided, but by following the flow of each chapter you can get a good understanding of all the key Drupal concepts.

The example we're going to use is a website about Drupal. You're going to create a site with information about it. The project is called Drupalville. That's going to be the project you use to see how to build and run a Drupal site.

You can also find lots of information, including detailed instructions, updates, and corrections for each chapter at http://ostraining.com/books/d8e.

This book also uses a specific process. Drupal is incredibly flexible and provides you with many options. That is both a strength and a weakness of Drupal. To make things as clear as possible for beginners, we're going to use a specific workflow for building the Drupalville website:

1. **Planning**

2. **Content types**

3. **Fields**

4. **Add content**

5. **Install Modules and Themes**

6. **Views**

7. **Layout Modules**

8. **Finish the Design**

9. **Users**

10. **Site Management**

THIS BOOK WILL LEAVE SOME THINGS OUT

Big books are no fun. They're expensive to buy, heavy to carry, and often written in long, complicated sentences, paragraphs, and chapters that go on and on while the text grows and the words grow longer and more obscure as the author tries to show their verbosity and vocabulary, examining the thesaurus for words that describe, narrate, impress, and fill up space but never quite get to the point so that you end up going back to the beginning of the long confusing text and try to reread, but then you start wondering what's for dinner or what's on TV instead.

Yes, this book will also include some bad jokes.

This book is as small as possible because it leaves things out.

You're going to read that time and time again, but it's worth repeating: This book will leave things out.

You will focus on only the most important parts of Drupal so that you can understand them as easily as possible.

This book is not comprehensive. It does not contain everything you could know about Drupal. It contains only what a Drupal beginner needs to know.

THIS BOOK USES ALMOST NO CODE

You do not need to know any HTML and CSS to use this book. That is a deliberate decision because we want to make this book accessible to ordinary people. We believe you don't have to be a developer to use Drupal.

However, that will disappoint some of you because this book does not discuss designing themes or building modules. If you do know CSS and PHP and want to dive into more advanced topics, there's a lot of advanced training at https://ostraining.com/classes/drupal-8.

THINGS IN THIS BOOK WILL CHANGE

Drupal changes regularly, and so do the extra features and designs that you add on to it.

Everything in this book is correct at the time of writing. However, it's possible that some of the instructions and screenshots may become out-of-date.

Be patient with any changes you find. We will list changes at http://ostraining.com/books/d8e. Please feel free to visit that site, search for updates, and contact us if you find any we haven't listed.

WHAT DO YOU NEED FOR THIS BOOK?

Now that you know a little bit about this book, let's make sure you're ready to follow along.

You need only two things to follow along with the exercises in this book:

- A computer with an Internet connection
- A hosting account or computer where you can install Drupal

Yes, that 's really all you need.

Before you start, you probably need to know something about Drupal. Turn to Chapter 1 and let's get started!

ABOUT THE OSTRAINING BOOK CLUB

Drupal 8 Explained is part of the OSTraining Book Club.

The Book Club gives you access to all of the "Explained" books from OSTraining:

- These books are always up-to-date. Because we self-publish, we can release constant updates.
- These books are active. We don't do long, boring explanations.
- You don't need any experience. The books are suitable even for complete beginners.

Join the OSTraining Book Club today: https://ostraining.com/ books.

Use the coupon "**drupal8explained**" to save 35% on your membership.

ABOUT PANTHEON

This book was made possible by the support of Pantheon.

We host our Drupal sites with Pantheon and love the features and support.

The Pantheon founding team built some of the biggest and most famous Drupal sites in the world. They really know Drupal. Pantheon's goal is to provide the most complete, bulletproof, and creativity-enabling platform for websites.

Pantheon provides you with a built-in development workflow, managed security, and the highest performance possible. Plus, you get expert support from real developers.

Check them out at http://pantheon.io.

ABOUT THE OSTRAINING TEAM

Stephen Burge has split his career between teaching and web development. In 2007, he combined the two by starting to teach web development. His company, OSTraining, now teaches Drupal classes around the world and online. Stephen is originally from England, and now lives in Florida.

Cindy McCourt is an experienced Drupal trainer, who coaches clients side-by-side to build internal Drupal capacity while planning and developing their Drupal solutions. She specializes in user experience planning, configuration, and code strategizing, site building and project management.

This book also would not be possible without the help of the OSTraining team.

Thanks to Daniel Pickering and Valentin Garcia for their work on the Breeze theme that we use in this book.

Thanks to my wife Stacey. She has saved me from many mistakes over the years, and many terrible typos in this book.

WE OFTEN UPDATE THIS BOOK

This is version 1.4 of Drupal 8 Explained. This version was released on September 27, 2017.

Drupal 8 Explained was first released in March, 2017.

We aim to keep this book up-to-date, and so regularly release new versions to keep up with changes in Drupal.

If you find anything that is out-of-date, please email us at books@ostraining.com. We'll update the book, and to say thank you, we'll provide you with a new copy.

ADVANTAGES AND DISADVANTAGES

We often release updates for this book. Most of the time, frequent updates are wonderful. If Drupal makes a change in the morning, we can have a new version of this book available in the afternoon. Most traditional publishers wait years and years before updating their books.

There are two disadvantages to be aware of:

- Page numbers do change. We often add and remove material from the book to reflect changes in Drupal.

- There's no index at the back of this book. This is because page numbers do change, and also because our self-publishing platform doesn't have a way to create indexes yet. We hope to find a solution for that soon.

Hopefully, you think that the advantages outweigh the disadvantages. If you have any questions, we're always happy to chat: books@ostraining.com.

ARE YOU AN AUTHOR?

If you enjoy writing about the web, we'd love to talk with you.

Most publishing companies are slow, boring, inflexible and don't pay very well.

Here at OSTraining, we try to be different:

- **Fun**: We use modern publishing tools that make writing books as easy as blogging.
- **Fast**: We move quickly. Some books get written and published in less than a month.
- **Flexible**: It's easy to update your books. If technology changes in the morning, you can update your book by the afternoon.
- **Fair**: Profits from the books are shared 50/50 with the author.

Do you have a topic you'd love to write about? We publish books on almost all web-related topics.

Whether you want to write a short 100-page overview, or a comprehensive 500-page guide, we'd love to hear from you.

Contact us via email: books@ostraining.com.

ARE YOU A TEACHER?

Many schools, colleges and organizations have adopted Drupal 8 Explained as a teaching guide.

This book is designed to be a step-by-step guide that students can follow at different speeds. The book can be used for a one-day class, or a longer class over multiple weeks.

If you are interested in teaching Drupal, we'd be delighted to help you with review copies, and all the advice you need.

Please email books@ostraining.com to talk with us.

Sample course outlines, descriptions, and learning outcomes are available at: https://ostraining.com/books/d8e/classroom.

SPONSORING AN OSTRAINING BOOK

Is your company interested in sponsoring an OSTraining book?

Our books are some of the world's best-selling guides to the software they cover.

People love to read our books and learn about new web design topics.

Why not reach those people? Partner with us to showcase your company to thousands of web developers.

We have partnered with Acquia, Pantheon, Nexcess, GoDaddy, InMotion, GlowHost and Ecwid to provide sponsored training to millions of people.

If you want to learn more, visit https://ostraining.com/ sponsor or email us at books@ostraining.com.

THE LEGAL DETAILS

DRUPAL 8 EXPLAINED

STEPHEN BURGE

Cindy McCourt

OSTraining

CONTENTS

CHAPTER 1.

DRUPAL EXPLAINED

Before you start using Drupal, let's give you some background on Drupal itself.

WHAT IS DRUPAL?

Drupal is web-publishing software.

It's designed for people to publish content online: news, blogs, photos, products, documents, events, or 1,001 other things.

Because it enables you to manage your content, you'll often hear it called a "Content Management System" or CMS for short.

In recent years, it's been used for more sophisticated applications. People are starting to build Drupal sites that power things such as mobile apps and in-flight entertainment on airplanes.

WHO STARTED DRUPAL?

It was created by Dries Buytaert in 2000. At that time, Dries was a student in Belgium. He was living in a tiny dorm room but was able to get access to one of the first high-speed connections in the country.

The first thing Dries set up after getting online was a messaging system, so he could chat with friends. That tiny messaging system has slowly grown into the Drupal we use today.

Dries continues to lead the way for Drupal. Dries works at http://acquia.com, which is the largest company in Drupal. You can recognize him instantly by his spiky hair.

WHO RUNS DRUPAL?

Drupal is run by volunteers. However, many of the volunteers also work for businesses that provide Drupal development services.

They and their clients benefit from the code created by the Drupal community and in return, they contribute, keeping the project life-cycle spinning and growing.

HOW MUCH DOES DRUPAL COST?

Drupal is free. Yes, 100% free.

Drupal is free to use, free to download, free to use on your sites, and free to use on your customers' sites.

There are also thousands of free features available. You can find designs that people have created and are giving away. You can also find free shopping carts, calendars, photo galleries, and much more.

However, there are companies that make a living by selling services and products for Drupal. For example, if you need somewhere to host your site or someone to help you build it, you will probably need to pay.

WHAT DOES "DRUPAL" MEAN?

Yes, Drupal is an unusual name.

Why was it chosen? Dries chose the name Drupal because the domain name was available. That sounds like a joke, but it's partially true.

The name went through three variations:

- First, Dries, the founder of Drupal, originally wanted to call the project "dorp," which is Dutch for village.
- Second, when he went to register the domain name, he typed "drop" by accident and so registered drop.org.
- Finally, Dries released his software as "Drupal," which is a misspelling of the Dutch word "druppel," which means drop.

Drupal is often mispronounced. The correct way to say it is "Droo-puhl".

The "drop" meaning of Drupal influenced the mascot, which is shown below. The overall mascot looks like a drop. The two eyes in the middle were originally designed as two drops to look like the infinity symbol. The design looked so much like a face that a nose and mouth were added.

HOW MANY VERSIONS OF DRUPAL ARE THERE?

In this book, you use Drupal 8. Still, you may encounter at least two different versions of Drupal:

- **Drupal** 7 was released in 2011. Some websites still use it. However, with the release of Drupal 8, Drupal 7 support is now limited.

- **Drupal 8** was released in 2015 with significant improvements to the way Drupal data and code is managed. The community is busy converting their Drupal 7 modules into features supported in Drupal 8. So if you don't see the Drupal 8 feature you want, it might still be in development.

Previously, it was very difficult to move between different Drupal versions. However, with Drupal 8, things changed. The Drupal developers promise that it will be very easy to move from Drupal 8 to Drupal 9 and other, future releases.

The Drupal community works hard to keep the new user interface similar to the last version. If you are used to using a previous version of Drupal, getting started with Drupal 8 should be fairly straightforward.

Learning Drupal actually is like learning to drive. You learn to drive in one type of car, but after you understand how to do it, you can quickly adapt to driving any other type of car. If you learn one version of Drupal, you can quickly adapt to any other version.

WHY SHOULD YOU CHOOSE DRUPAL?

- **Drupal is easier.** We can't promise that your Drupal experience will be 100% frustration-free. There will be some moments when you're stuck and feel baffled. However, Drupal is easier to use than many other options for creating websites.

- **Drupal is quicker.** Drupal provides you with many ready-built features. If you want a new site design, or wish to add a calendar or shopping cart to your site, you can often do it with just a few clicks. It may take a few days or even weeks to build a great Drupal site, but you can develop and launch more quickly than with many alternatives.

- **Drupal is cheaper.** Building a Drupal site is unlikely to be completely cost-free. You may have purchased this book or other training, and you might need to hire an expert. A good Drupal site can cost between a few dollars and hundreds of thousands of dollars. However, it costs you nothing to get into Drupal, whereas commercial alternatives to Drupal often cost hundreds of thousands of dollars before you even start.

- **Drupal has more options.** If you'd like extra features on your Drupal site, http://drupal.org is the place to go. It currently lists more than 35,000 modules that provide you options in building your solution. You can do many things with Drupal without writing a line of code. However, you may have to hire a developer if you have unusual or specific requirements.

WHO USES DRUPAL?

Everyone from non-technology savvy bloggers who just want to post stories about their commentary to corporations that span the world uses Drupal to power their web presence. And, let's not forget the governments that run the world's countries, non-profits that support the people, and educational organizations. The list goes on and on. Below are just a few examples we hope will inspire you.

Governments: Drupal is used by many national government sites. International organizations such as the United Nations and the European Union use Drupal, and so do governments from the United States, the U.K. and Portugal to Indonesia, Sri Lanka, and Mongolia. The next image shows the Drupal-powered website for the German government at http://deutschland.de.

Media: Drupal powers many TV, entertainment, and news websites and can handle large amounts of traffic. Leading newspapers in many other countries use Drupal. The Economist is a historic and widely read British publication. Its website, http://economist.com, is built in Drupal.

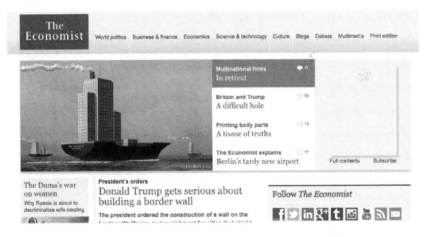

Education: Drupal is popular in education with everyone from large universities to small schools using it. One of the most famous is Harvard University: http://harvard.edu.

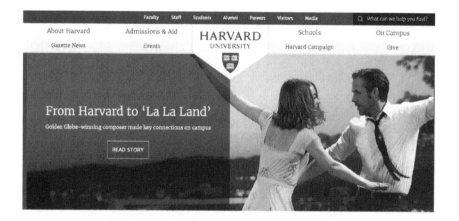

Business: Many successful organizations around the world use Drupal. Some of the most famous are Pfizer, Puma, Whole Foods, and General Electric, whose Drupal website at http://ge.com is below.

Entertainment: Sony and Warner have both adopted Drupal for many of their artists. If you visit the websites for oldies like Led Zeppelin and Eric Clapton or new acts like Lady Gaga and Bruno Mars, you'll find them running on Drupal. Visit http://ladygaga.com for Drupal in action.

You can see a more detailed list of sites built with Drupal at http://drupal.com/showcases.

WHAT'S NEXT?

In this chapter, you learned important information about Drupal.

The next step is to get you thinking about and planning your Drupal site.

Are you ready?

If you are, turn to the next chapter, and let's begin.

CHAPTER 2.

DRUPAL PLANNING EXPLAINED

Before you build any website, it's important to plan.

However, it's difficult for you to plan a Drupal site at the moment because you have little or no experience with Drupal.

So, in this chapter, we're going to suggest some things you should plan for before you begin building a Drupal site.

We're also going to recommend a workflow that will help you carry out your plan successfully.

At the end of this chapter, you should be able to:

- Recognize what's involved in a website plan.
- Recognize what's involved in a project management plan.
- Recognize what's involved in a development plan.
- Recognize what's involved in a maintenance plan.
- Start to think about the website, project management, development and maintenance plans for the site we'll build in this book.

DIFFERENT TYPES OF PLANNING

Planning means different things to different people. Your role in the project, your experience, and your skills all influence your approach to planning.

- If you are a project manager, your thoughts might go directly to scheduling and budgets.

- If you are a designer, your first thoughts might lean more toward how each page of the site will look.

- If you are a content manager, content development workflows might come to mind followed quickly by how the content will be organized on the site.

- If you are a developer, your idea of a plan might be which development methodology you want to use or which strategies are best for implementing the design created by the designer and content strategist.

There are many things to consider when you plan. For example, if the schedule is tight and the budget is low, the desired visual design might not be possible. You might need to accept a look and feel produced by a free theme (that bit of code, colors, and images that define the look of your site).

Another example: if you do not have the appropriate skills on your development team, you might need to change your requirements, sacrifice a cool feature or wait to add your custom feature when time, skills, and budget allow.

There are general guidelines for planning; however, each plan must be customized to your situation. Luckily, Drupal's modular architecture allows you to select the building blocks that support your needs, thus allowing you to create a custom solution without custom code.

To plan a Drupal site, you need four types of plans:

1. Website
2. Project Management

3. Development
4. Maintenance

Let's consider a brief introduction of each type of plan.

For a more detailed view into planning Drupal websites, check out Cindy's other book called *Drupal: The Guide to Planning and Building Websites*. Its current version talks about Drupal 6 and 7, but the principles apply to a site built with Drupal 8 as well.

TYPE #1. DRUPAL WEBSITE PLANS

This plan focuses on defining the content and functional requirements, as well as the design (visual, structural, layout, and interaction) aspects of the site. The website plan conveys what you want from your site after it is built. It influences the schedule, required budget, and skills, and provides a way to manage expectations for all involved. The more detailed the plan, the higher probability that you will get the site you want, assuming all things equal.

A website plan commonly includes a requirements document and a design. Depending on the project management methodology you choose, the level of detail associated with the website plan may vary. You may start out with a big-picture sketch and later, as you build each section of your site, you add the finer details that make your site exactly what you need.

No matter your project management methodology, you need to consider requirements, which include, but are not limited to the following:

- **Content**: Types of content required
- **Communication:** Strategies the site needs to support messages between users and your team
- **Navigation**: Strategies that will support visitors finding the content they need

- **Features**: Various types of functionality that add value to users' experiences and to support tracking
- **Roles and Permissions**: From anonymous visitors to site administrators, answer the question, "Who can do what?"
- **Performance**: Expectations based on projected use
- **Security**: Content access, site access, server access, and security code updates are the top considerations

And you need to consider design, which includes but is not limited to:

- Wireframes that describe the layout of the homepage, the landing pages, and the different types of content as they appear on a desktop computer, a tablet, and a phone (don't worry, Drupal has themes that will magically change your pages to fit in mobile devices)
- Interaction plan describing the behavior of the objects included in the wireframes (e.g., click here for a pop-up ad)
- Style guide used to ensure consistency in color, fonts, layout, imagery, branding, etc.
- Theme region plan required to support the layout strategies assumed in the wireframes (Chapters 9 and 10, Themes Explained and Blocks Explained, will help you with this)
- Graphic rendering of the finished pages (also known as comps)

TYPE #2. DRUPAL PROJECT MANAGEMENT PLANS

For this type of plan, you should consider the resources required to meet the website plan and the maintenance plan. Below are some questions to ask yourself. You might not know the answers to the questions right now, but hopefully, you will have a better understanding after you complete this book.

- What skills will you need?
- In what order will the website planning and development tasks be accomplished?
- When can the site be launched?
- How much will it cost?
- How will you monitor progress?
- How will you manage expectations if a requirement or design feature cannot be met as originally requested?

These are only some of the questions that fall into the realm of project management. With these questions, you can start a discussion with those involved in the website project, whether you are the client, the developer, or the designer.

In short, the project management plan can include one or more of the following:

- Schedule
- Budget
- Skills
- Expectations
- Assumptions

TYPE #3. DRUPAL DEVELOPMENT PLANS

Development plans are a source of much discussion among people who build websites. The important thing to remember is the word development. The next thing to remember is development shouldn't go forward without a website plan, something that conveys to the developers what you want or need, how it is to look, what processes it needs to support, and so on.

Content: For instance, the development plan can document your content strategy. If your website plan included the requirement to add events and a wireframe or image that showed the event, the development plan might be:

- Two content types: Event and Sponsor
- Four separate fields: Name of event, Description, Date and Time, and Sponsor

However, it could be as simple as one content type called event, and the description field would contain the other details (this is a very HTML way of doing things).

Implementation: Another aspect of a development plan is when each strategy will be implemented. For instance, will each section of the site be implemented one at a time? Or will aspects of each site section be implemented, thus implementing all sections at the same time but in varying degrees of detail?

In the end, the development plan should convey what is needed to implement the requirements and design contained in the website plan, as well as meet the project management expectations regarding schedule and budget. For example, development plans can include one or more of the following:

- A list of different types of content along with their data fields, features, and user permissions
- A list of features needed on your site together with the modules required to provide those features
- A coding strategy for implementing the design of your site
- A development methodology that conveys how the developers will assemble and code your site
- A test plan that covers each aspect of testing, including integration, regression, security, usability, and accessibility

TYPE #4. DRUPAL MAINTENANCE PLANS

Maintenance tasks are typically performed after the site is officially launched, but that doesn't mean you start planning your maintenance when the site is about to go live. At least three types of maintenance tasks need to be planned pre-launch:

- Routine monitoring maintenance
- Planned update maintenance
- Site management

The way you plan to perform each type of maintenance can influence development strategies. For instance, if you plan to maintain the content on your site by allowing specific people to manage specific types of content, the development team needs to be aware of that and provide the necessary roles and permissions.

Another insight into maintenance to consider is your ability to update your site code. You might need a hosting plan that will do it for you. Or, you might need a dedicated developer, especially if you have custom features on your site.

Ask yourself:

- Do I have the skills to step in where the development team left off?
- Do I have the budget to maintain that custom feature after the site is live?
- Do I have the resources to manage the content posts of multiple users?

Planning the production of a website should go hand-in-hand with the maintenance of the said site.

Now that we've seen the four general types of plans, let's use them for the Drupalville site in this book.

OUR DRUPALVILLE WEBSITE PLAN

As mentioned earlier, we're going to build a site called Drupalville.

By the end of this book, the plan is for our site to look like the following image:

The site we're going to build in this book has multiple types of content. Here's a list of the types of content that we'll add to our site:

- News articles
- Online book
- Audio and videos

- Static content

- Documentation

- Information about Drupal companies

- Events with a map

- Discussion forums

- Information about useful Drupal websites

- Information about useful Drupal user groups

The site we're going to build will also have these types of communication:

- The content on the screen communicates the *message*.

- Drupal's default emails communicate account settings actions.

- Comments are allowed for users to respond to the content.

- Social media links provided can help visitors to share pages of the site with others.

- Contact form so that users can reach the administrators on the site.

We're going to provide the following to help visitors navigate the site:

- Menus

- Dynamically generated lists of content that can be filtered

The content, communications, and navigation requirements previously listed hint to many of the features planned for the site. The following list reinforces what has already been implied and adds additional features. The list could be quite extensive if you include all the default functionality on the site, but given it is a Drupal site, that isn't always necessary.

- Sharing capability: Functionality that enables users to post site content to social media sites and email it to friends
- Forum management: Functionality that organizes forums and their displays
- Polls: Functionality that manages the availability and access to the polls
- Contact Forms: Enable users to submit inquiries
- Search: Enables users to search site content
- Site map: Helps major search engines to scroll and index the site content
- Automated custom URLs: Automatically generates human-friendly URLs
- Google Analytics: Provides various data regarding the site traffic
- Search Engine Optimization features: Help ensure that the site pages conform to major search engines guidelines.

There will be several different groups of users with roles on the site:

- Anonymous visitors who can only look at the site
- Authenticated users who can log in, post comments, and join the discussion forums
- Bloggers who can write blog posts
- Company editors who can manage the Drupal company listings
- Moderators who can manage forum topics
- Administrators who have free reign to do anything on the site

To help you visualize what our Drupalville site can look like at the end of this book, here are some of the key landing pages you will be building. Note that we're using sample data, so the text is in Latin and the images are automatically generated.

- **Resources:** An overview of the Drupal information that people can use on this site:

Resources

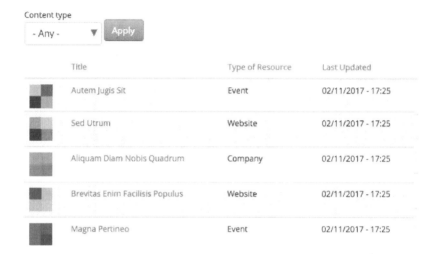

- **Companies**: A grid showing Drupal companies with their logos:

Companies

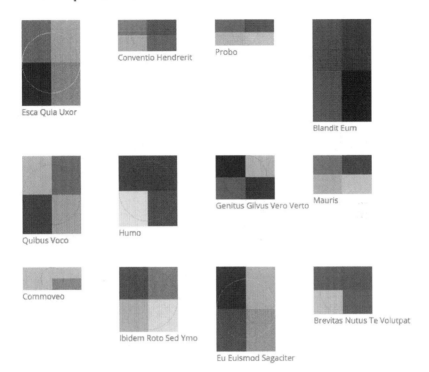

Esca Quia Uxor

Conventio Hendrerit

Probo

Blandit Eum

Quibus Voco

Humo

Genitus Gilvus Vero Verto

Mauris

Commoveo

Ibidem Roto Sed Ymo

Eu Euismod Sagaciter

Brevitas Nutus Te Volutpat

- **Events**: Displayed in a calendar layout:

February 2017

Previous «   Next »

Sun	Mon	Tue	Wed	Thu	Fri	Sat
29	30	31	1	2	3	4
5	6	7 Autem Consequat Genitus Tue, 02/07/2017 - 12:00	8	9 Quidem Quidne Thu, 02/09/2017 - 12:00	10	11 Loquor Sit Tego Sat, 02/11/2017 - 12:00
12	13	14	15	16	17	18
19	20	21	22	23	24	25
26	27	28	1	2	3	4

Previous «   Next »

- We're also going to be building slideshows, contact forms, content archives, discussion forums and much more.

OUR DRUPALVILLE PROJECT MANAGEMENT PLAN

Project management plans aren't usually conveyed in four bullet points, but here is a quick summary of what we'll need to complete this book's project successfully:

- **Schedule**: You'll build this site at your own pace. Someone working quickly may finish this book in two days or less. Someone without so much free time can build the site successfully, but more slowly.

- **Budget**: Zero. You won't need to spend any money to build the site for this book.

- **Special Skills**: Zero. You'll learn everything you need to know to build the site.
- **Expectations**: Your first Drupal site does not come with very complicated expectations. Your Drupalville site won't be the most beautiful Drupal site in the world.

OUR DRUPALVILLE MAINTENANCE PLAN

Because the site we're creating in this book is only designed to help you learn, we don't necessarily need an ongoing maintenance plan. At the end of this book, you have two options:

- You can delete the Drupalville site that we've built.
- You can maintain the Drupalville site using the techniques shown in the chapter called "Drupal Site Maintenance Explained".

WHAT'S NEXT?

Now that we've discussed planning, you're ready to build your first Drupal site.

Turn to the next chapter, and let's learn how to install a Drupal site so we can start building.

CHAPTER 3.

DRUPAL INSTALLATIONS EXPLAINED

This chapter shows you where and how to install Drupal. When you finish, you should have a Drupal site that you can use throughout this book. That is where you can practice everything else you do in upcoming chapters.

At the end of this chapter, you should be able to:

- Choose the best place to host Drupal.
- Choose the best way to install Drupal.
- Install Drupal automatically.
- Install Drupal manually.
- Get help if you're stuck with installing Drupal.

HOSTING YOUR DRUPAL SITE EXPLAINED

Drupal is not like many other software programs. It can't just run on any computer. It requires a server to run successfully. That means you normally have the choice of installing Drupal in one of three places:

- A local server on your computer.
- A generic PHP web server.
- A web server hosted by Drupal specialists.

Choosing the best place to install Drupal is important, so here is an explanation of the difference between the three options.

A LOCAL SERVER ON YOUR COMPUTER

We generally don't recommend that Drupal beginners use a local server.

It can be tempting to choose this route. More advanced users find several useful advantages to working on their own computers:

- **Working offline**: You can work without an Internet connection.
- **Privacy**: Your Drupal site will be safe and private, accessible only to people who can access that computer.
- **Free**: There are no fees to pay.

However, there are also several important disadvantages to using your computer:

- **Extra installations needed**: You need to download and configure special software for your computer.
- **Difficult to get help**: You can't easily show it to other people and ask for help.
- **Only one computer**: You can access it only from the computer you used to install it.
- **Need to move to launch**: When you're ready to make your site public, you need to move everything to a web server and adjust for any differences between the two locations.

Because of these disadvantages, installing on your computer can present significant obstacles for a beginner. Do not take this route until you have more experience.

However, if you do feel comfortable overcoming these obstacles, you can find instructions on how to install Drupal on your computer at https://ostraining.com/books/d8e.

A GENERIC PHP WEBSERVER

Unlike your computer, a web server is specifically designed for hosting websites so that they are easy to visit for anyone who's online.

If you work for a company, it might provide a server. However, many people need to rent space from a hosting company.

Drupal servers must be able to normally run PHP because that is the language Drupal is written in. It's also best to have MySQL available because it is the type of database Drupal normally uses. These are the minimum versions needed:

- **PHP**: 5.5.9 or above
- **MySQL**: 5.5.3 or above

Linux servers also require Apache, a type of web server software. The minimum version for that is 1.3 and above. You can find more details on Drupal's technical requirements at https://drupal.org/docs/8/system-requirements/web-server.

To run Drupal, Apache has long been the favorite choice. Microsoft is working hard to make Drupal run as smoothly as possible on IIS servers. However, for now, Apache is still the most popular alternative, although Nginx is a fast-growing option.

Most hosting companies now support Drupal, but it's worth choosing carefully. Some hosting companies are much better than others. Here is some advice on picking your host:

- Search http://drupal.org/forum for other people's experiences with that host.

- Contact the hosting company's customer support and ask what it knows about Drupal. One of our training students actually called the phone numbers of several hosts and timed their responses. After all, in an emergency, you don't want to be on hold for an hour or to be talking to someone that knows nothing about Drupal.

A WEBSERVER HOSTED BY DRUPAL SPECIALISTS

You just saw that you can install Drupal on almost any server that has PHP and MySQL installed. However, you can also host on servers that are fine-tuned for Drupal. One service is Pantheon, whose website is at https://pantheon.io. Pantheon sponsors this book, and we use it for many of our Drupal projects.

There are many advantages to choosing Drupal-specific hosting services:

- They are managed by Drupal experts who know exactly what Drupal sites need to run well.
- They can keep your web server up to date, which greatly increases security. Some also keep your Drupal site up to date for you.
- They provide extra features that make it easier to install, manage and maintain a Drupal site.

WHAT DO WE RECOMMEND FOR HOSTING DRUPAL?

Although you can install Drupal in other ways, we recommend one of three methods:

- Install Drupal on Pantheon, or a Drupal-specific hosting service.
- Install Drupal automatically on a web server.
- Install Drupal manually on a web server.

If you use one of these three methods, it will be easier to follow along with this book.

We're going to explain these three different options in the next three parts of this chapter.

OPTION #1. INSTALL DRUPAL ON PANTHEON

Do you remember in Chapter 1, we said that many large government sites were built in Drupal? Well, one of the most famous Drupal sites is http://whitehouse.gov. Some of the team members behind that project are also responsible for Pantheon Hosting.

Pantheon offers a complete set of tools to build, launch, and run Drupal sites. They also offer you a free account that you can use to host your site for this book.

- Start by visiting https://pantheon.io, and you'll see the site below.

- Click the "Get Free Account" button, and you will be able to register.

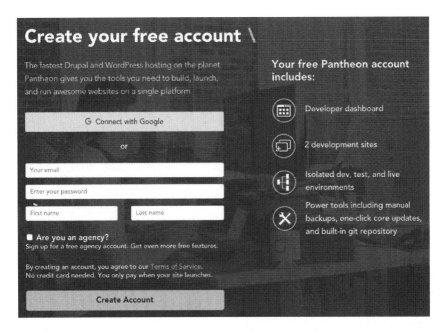

- After you register with Pantheon, you will see a welcome screen, as in the next image.

- Click the "Create New Site" button to proceed.

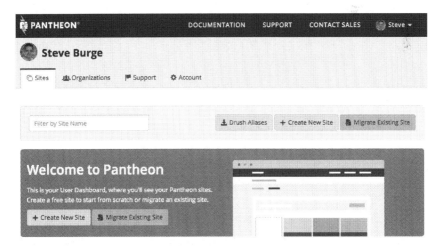

- Choose a name for your Drupal site. In this book, we're going to build a site called "Drupalville", so that would make a good site name.

- Click the "Continue" button.

On the next screen, choose "Deploy Drupal 8" from amongst the other alternatives, as shown below.

- On the following screen, you'll see a message saying "Complete!"
- Click the "Visit your Pantheon Site Dashboard" button to continue.

Deploying Drupal 8

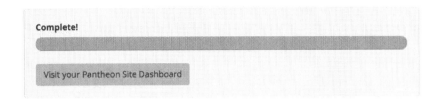

You will now see the dashboard for your Pantheon site. Click the "Visit Development Site" button.

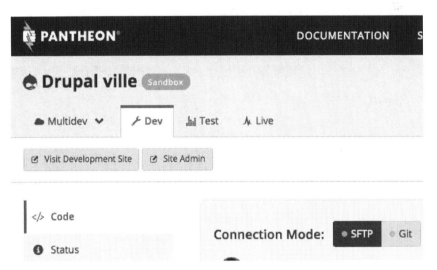

- You will now be taken to the installation screen for your Drupal 8 site. The first step in the installation process is simple: You just need to choose the language for your site.

- Click "Save and continue".

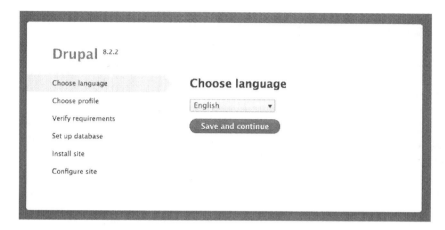

- On the next step, "Select an installation profile", you don't need to change anything here.

- Click "Save and continue", as shown below.

The next step is when you enter any information for your site. Be sure to make a careful note of the email, username, and password that you enter:

- **Site name**: Enter Drupalville here. This is what people see when they get emails from your site. For example, the email will say, "Thank you for Registering at Drupalville".

- **Site email address**: This will be used for emails sent from the site.

- **Username**: This is the username you use on your site.

- **Password**: This is the password you use to log in. Please don't use "admin" here! Don't use "password," "1234," or "iloveyou" either. There are plenty of good free password generators available if you do a quick look on your favorite search engine.

- **E-mail address**: Enter an email address that you want to use for your personal account on the site.

When you have entered all your details, click "Save and continue".

SITE INFORMATION

Site name *

Site email address *

Automated emails, such as registration information, will be sent from this address. Use an address ending in your site's domain to help prevent these emails from being flagged as spam.

SITE MAINTENANCE ACCOUNT

Username *

Several special characters are allowed, including space, period (.), hyphen (–), apostrophe ('), underscore (_), and the @ sign.

Password *

Password strength:

Confirm password *

Passwords match:

Email address *

- If you entered your information successfully, you will now see a new website!

Because you installed Drupal on Pantheon, you have automatically been logged in. Look at the horizontal admin bar, and you'll see your username, which in this case is "steve". We're going to be talking more about this admin bar in future chapters.

However, your site is now ready. You can go straight to the next chapter and start building your Drupal site.

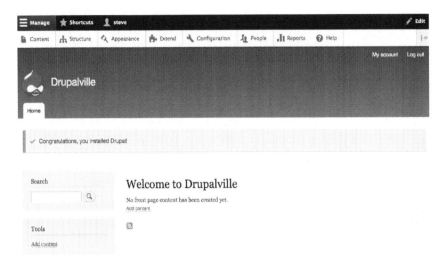

OPTION #2. INSTALL DRUPAL AUTOMATICALLY

Automatic installers are often called "One Click" installers. Actually, "One Click" is a bit of an exaggeration. Installing Drupal this way takes approximately five clicks.

There are many different versions of automatic installers. In this chapter, we'll use one of the most popular versions, which is called Softaculous. Your hosting company may offer an alternative such as Fantastico, which looks a little different but works in a similar way.

Here is the process to install Drupal automatically:

- Log in to your web hosting account. Each hosting account looks a little different, but there are often many similarities.

- Find the Softaculous button and click it. You can find it by looking for the box of software logos, as in this next image.

Softaculous

- View the Softaculous Control Panel.
- If you can't see the Drupal logo, click on the link called, "Portals/CMS".
- Click on the Drupal logo.

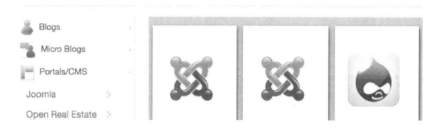

- You now see a screen with a brief introduction to Drupal.
- Click the blue "Install" button to proceed.

Drupal

★★★★☆ Version : **8.2.2, 7.51, 6.38, 8.2.2 + demo data** Release Date : 02-11-2016

| Install | Overview | Features | Screenshots | Demo | Ratings | Reviews | Import |

Drupal is an open-source platform and content management system for building dynamic web sites offering a broad range of features and services including user administration, publishing workflow, discussion capabilities, news aggregation, metadata functionalities using controlled vocabularies and XML publishing for content sharing purposes.

Equipped with a powerful blend of features and configurability, Drupal can support a diverse range of web projects ranging from personal weblogs to large community-driven sites.

Drupal is free, open, and available to anyone under the GNU/GPL license.

Install Now   My Apps

Enter your new site details. Softaculous now asks for the details of your new site. Here's what you need to know:

- **Chose the version you want to install**: Select the latest version of Drupal 8.

- **Choose Protocol**: As this is a test site, you can choose http instead of https.

- **Choose Domain**: You can leave this to the default setting.

- **In directory**: You can leave this blank if you'd like the site to be accessible directly via your domain, for example, http://www.drupal8explained.com. The recommended alternative for learning with this book is to use a subdirectory. For example, as you build a site about Drupalville, you can place the site in a /drupalville/ subdirectory. If you do this, it's not difficult to move your site if you later want to make it accessible directly via your domain. So, go ahead and enter "drupalville" into this field.

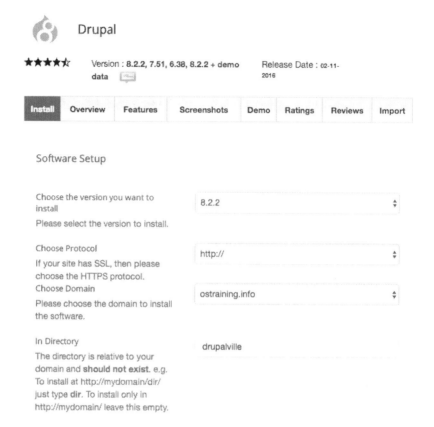

Further down the screen, there are more settings:

- **Site Name**: This is the main name for your site and will appear at the top-left corner of the site.
- **Admin Username**: Enter the username you want to use when logging in.
- **Admin Password**: This is the password you use to log in. Don't use "admin" here also! Don't use "password," "1234," or "iloveyou" either. A good combination of numbers, punctuation, and uppercase and lowercase letters is vital.
- **Admin Email**: Enter your email address here. If you forget your password, this is where it will be sent.

Enter those details in the screen shown below:

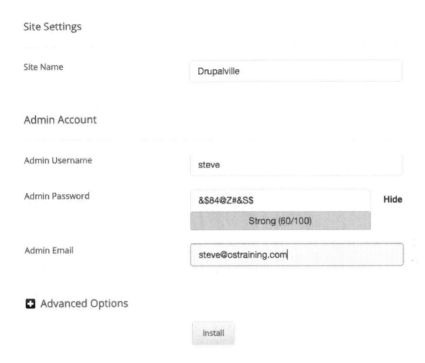

- Confirm your installation details and click "Install".
- You will now see a confirmation screen saying that Drupal was installed.

Congratulations, the software was installed successfully

Drupal has been successfully installed at :
http://ostraining.info/drupalville
Administrative URL : http://ostraining.info/drupalville/user/login

We hope the installation process was easy.

NOTE: Softaculous is just an automatic software installer and does not provide any support for the individual software packages. Please visit the software vendor's web site for support!

Regards,
Softaculous Auto Installer

In the previous image, you can see two links are showing.

- The full URL to your site.

- The full URL to the login screen for your Drupal site.

Click the "The full URL to your site" link. You will now see a new website.

- Try logging into your new site. You can log in using the "Log in" link in the top-right corner of the site.
- Log in using the username and password you created earlier.

Log in

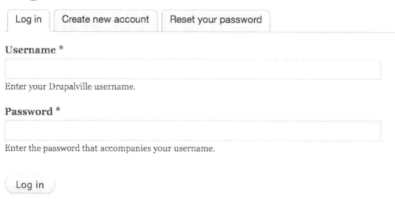

If you entered your username and password correctly, you'll now see a black and gray administration menu across the top of your site.

Congratulations! You can now go straight to the next chapter and start building your Drupal site.

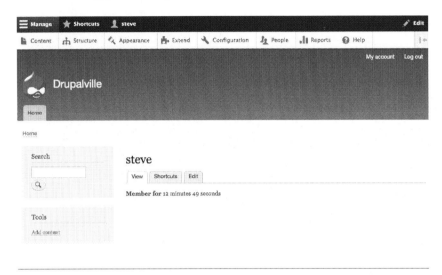

OPTION #3. INSTALL DRUPAL MANUALLY

This final option is more difficult than the other two but does give you the opportunity to get hands-on with many aspects of your Drupal site.

An old-fashioned HTML website consists only of one part: files. It doesn't need anything else to run.

However, a Drupal website is a little different because it consists not only of files, but it also includes a database to store all the site's information. In the other two options, all of this was taken care of for you. In this option, you must set up both the files and the database and then connect them together.

The process of installing Drupal manually is like this:

- Create a database.

- Download the Drupal files, and upload them to your web server.

- Complete the Drupal installation by connecting the database and files together.

The first step is to create a database to store all the unique information about your site.

A database is basically a group of tables with letters and numbers stored in its rows and columns. Think of it as several spreadsheets. There's a spreadsheet with all the articles you write. There's another for all of the users who register on your site. The database makes it easy for Drupal to handle large amounts of data. If a new article or user is added, Drupal just needs to add an extra row to the appropriate spreadsheet. Drupal uses a particular type of database known as MySQL.

Now let's go ahead and set up a database for your new Drupal site.

Login to your web hosting account. Each hosting account looks a little different, but there are often many similarities. In this example, we're using cPanel, shown below.

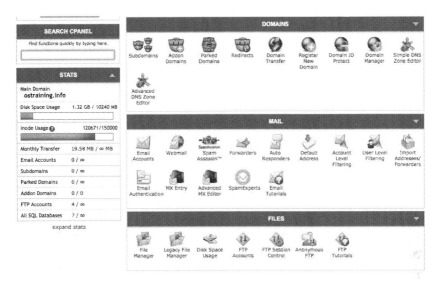

- Find the button that says "MySQL Databases" and click it. The button has the MySQL name and the blue dolphin logo, as shown below.

MySQL®
Databases

Now, let's create a new database.

- Choose a name that is relatively easy to remember, and click "Create Database". Be sure to write this name down and note that it's likely to have your hosting account name before it. In the image below, the new database is called ostrain2_drupalville.

Create a New Database

New Database: ostrain2_ drupalville

Create Database

The next step is to create a user account so that you can access the database. Without password protection, anyone might log in and see your site's important information. Here's what you need to choose:

- **Username**: Enter a short username here, different from anything you've used before. This example uses "steve". The username is a little confusing because your hosting account name is added also, so, in the image below, your full username will be ostrain2_steve.

- **Password**: Some versions of CPanel can help you choose a password that is difficult to guess. If you set your own choice, use a combination of numbers, punctuation, and uppercase and lowercase letters so that the password is hard to guess.

- Be sure to record both your username and password safely. You need them again soon.

Now that you've made your choices, you can finish creating the user:

- Click "Create User".

- You will see a message saying the user has been created successfully.

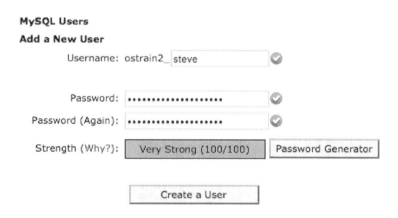

Next, you need to allow your new user to log in to the database.

- There will be an area on the screen called "Add a User to Database".
- Choose your database name and then your username.
- Click "Add", as shown below.

The final step in this process is to decide what your new user can and cannot do with the database.

- Give your user "All permissions" so that your Drupal site can make whatever changes it needs to the database.
- Click "Make Changes" to finish the process.

MySQL Account Maintenance

Manage User Privileges

User: **ostrain2_steve**
Database: **ostrain2_drupalville**

☑ **ALL PRIVILEGES**	
☑ ALTER	☑ ALTER ROUTINE
☑ CREATE	☑ CREATE ROUTINE
☑ CREATE TEMPORARY TABLES	☑ CREATE VIEW
☑ DELETE	☑ DROP
☑ EVENT	☑ EXECUTE
☑ INDEX	☑ INSERT
☑ LOCK TABLES	☑ REFERENCES
☑ SELECT	☑ SHOW VIEW
☑ TRIGGER	☑ UPDATE

Make Changes

Now that you have the database ready, you can upload the Drupal files. These contain all the code and images that Drupal needs to run.

- Go to http://drupal.org/download.
- Click the blue "Download Drupal" button.

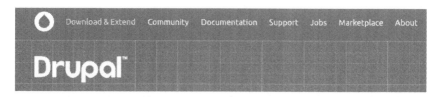

Download & Extend

Download

Download Drupal 8.2.5   Try a hosted Drupal demo

- You now see a page with information on the latest version of Drupal 8.
- Click the green "Download tar.gz" or "Download zip" buttons. The only major difference is that the zip files may not open on non-Windows computers unless you have special software installed.

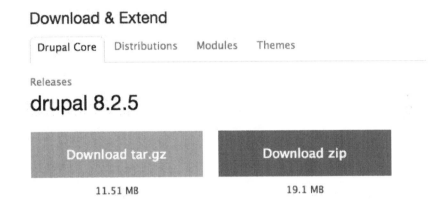

You will now see a file downloaded to your desktop. You need to uncompress this file.

- On a Windows computer, you can right-click the file and choose "Extract Here".
- On a Mac, you can right-click on the file, choose "Open With", and then choose Archive Utility.

When that's complete, you should have a folder on your desktop looking like Figure 3.19. The folder should have a name similar to drupal-8.2.5.

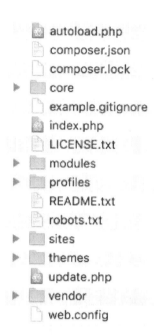

autoload.php
composer.json
composer.lock
core
example.gitignore
index.php
LICENSE.txt
modules
profiles
README.txt
robots.txt
sites
themes
update.php
vendor
web.config

You're now going to start the process of moving your files on to your web server.

- Open your FTP software. One useful example is Filezilla, which can be downloaded from https://filezilla-project.org/.

- Log in to the FTP account for your server.

- Browse to the folder where you want to install Drupal. Often this is the root directory, which often has a name such as /public_html/, /www/ or /htdocs/.

- Open the folder that just downloaded to your desktop and select all the files.

- Move all the files, via your FTP software, into the folder where you're installing Drupal. With Filezilla, this is as simple as dragging-and-dropping the files. Uploading might take from 5 to 30 minutes or more depending on the speed of your Internet connection.

Now that files are uploaded, we're going to connect them to

the database. Before going any further, let's double-check your database information. Here's what you need:

- **Hostname**: This is often localhost, but some hosting companies, such as GoDaddy, have a different hostname. You can find it in your hosting account or by contacting customer support.
- **Username**: The username for your database.
- **Password**: The password for your database.
- **Database name**: The name of your database.

Got all that? Great! Then let's wrap up your Drupal installation.

Start your browser and visit the URL where you uploaded the files. You should see an installation screen like the one below. This is the first step in Drupal's easy-to-use installation manager.

- Choose the language for your Drupal site.
- Click "Save and continue".

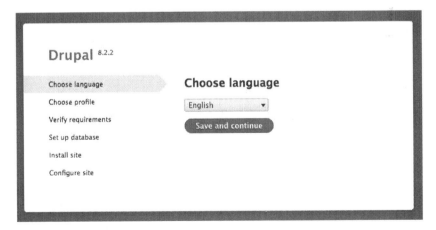

- On the next step, "Select an installation profile", you don't need to change anything here.
- Click "Save and continue", as shown below.

The next step will verify that your server is ready to use Drupal 8. If Drupal makes any suggestions here, you can fix them. Some suggestions will be important enough that you can't proceed. Other suggestions are not so important, and you can click "continue anyway".

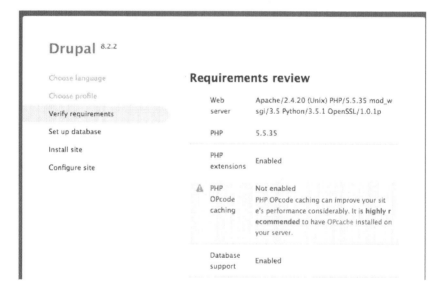

Now we connect our files to the database. You need the details you collected when you created the database earlier.

- **Database type**: Leave this on the default setting, unless you are using SQLite.

- **Database name**: Enter the details you collected earlier.
- **Database username**: Enter the details you collected earlier.
- **Database password**: Enter the details you collected earlier.

Click "Save and Continue" when you finish. If you made a mistake, Drupal sends you back to try again.

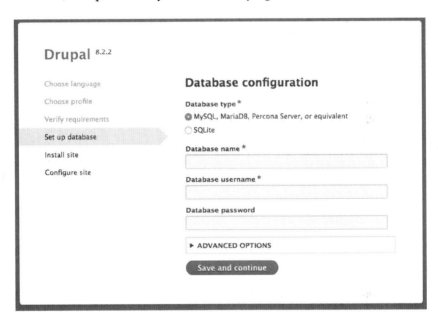

The final step is when you enter specific information to customize your site. Be sure to make a careful note of the email, username, and password that you enter:

- **Site name**: Enter Drupalville here. This is what people see when they get emails from your site. For example, the email will say, "Thank you for Registering at Drupalville".
- **Site email address**: This will be used for emails sent from the site.
- **Username**: This is the username you use on your site.
- **Password**: This is the password you use to log in. Please don't use "admin" here also! Don't use "password," "1234," or

"iloveyou" either. There are plenty of good free password generators available if you do a quick look on your favorite search engine.

- **E-mail address**: Enter an email address that you want to use for your personal account on the site.

When you have entered all your details, click "Save and continue".

SITE INFORMATION

Site name *

Site email address *

Automated emails, such as registration information, will be sent from this address. Use an address ending in your site's domain to help prevent these emails from being flagged as spam.

SITE MAINTENANCE ACCOUNT

Username *

Several special characters are allowed, including space, period (.), hyphen (-), apostrophe ('), underscore (_), and the @ sign.

Password *

Password strength:

Confirm password *

Passwords match:

Email address *

- If you entered your information successfully, you will now see a new website!

Because you installed Drupal manually, you have automatically been logged in. Look at the horizontal admin bar, and you'll see your username, which in this case is "steve". We're going to be talking more about this admin bar in future chapters.

However, your site is now ready. You can go straight to the next chapter and start building your Drupal site.

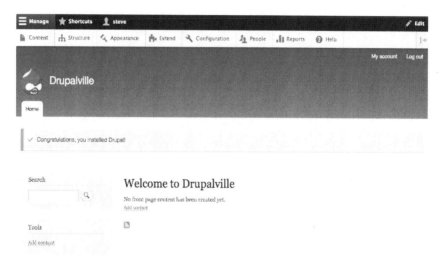

GETTING HELP WITH INSTALLATIONS

There are at least four places you should go to for help if you get stuck at any point during this chapter:

- **The Drupal forum**: It's almost guaranteed that someone has experienced the same Drupal installation problem as you and has asked about it on http://drupal.org/forum/1/. It's a great place to search for solutions and ask for help.

- **The Drupal docs site**: There's an installation manual available for Drupal 8 at https://drupal.org/docs/8/install.

- **Your Hosting company**: If you chose to work with a hosting company, their support will be able to help.

- **Drupal 8 Explained**: http://books.ostraining.com has video tutorials and more to help with your installation. There's also a Drupal support service available for members.

WHAT'S NEXT?

You now have a Drupal site ready to use.

In the next chapter, you will tour your new site and see how to navigate the Drupal interface.

Are you ready? Turn to the next chapter and let's get going.

CHAPTER 4.

DRUPAL ADMINISTRATION EXPLAINED

This chapter explains the basic concepts of your Drupal site. When you finish, you'll understand how to navigate around your site and how administrators manage your site.

At the end of this chapter, you should be able to:

- Describe the different screens in the administrator area of your Drupal site.
- Recognize the difference between the administrator and visitor areas of your Drupal site.

NAVIGATING YOUR DRUPAL SITE

At the end of the last chapter, "Drupal Installations Explained," you installed your new Drupal site. Congratulations! You're now ready to explore your Drupal site.

- If you haven't done so, log in to your Drupal site using the username and password you chose during the installation.

Across the top of the site, you now see a horizontal menu with a black section and a white section. In this book, we are going to refer to this menu as the administration menu. This menu is the most important part of your site. Almost everything you want to change and modify on your site can be accessed from here.

The links in this menu are logically organized. The links on the left-hand side are used much more frequently than the links on the right-hand side.

"Content" and "Structure" are the two links you will click most often. The "Configuration", "People", "Reports", and "Help" links are used less frequently. These contain settings and maintenance functions and documentation.

There is also another level to the menu. In the black area, you will see "Manage", "Shortcuts", and a link with your name. You are currently looking at the "Manage" tab. This "Manage" tab contains almost all of Drupal's functionality and is where we will be working throughout this book.

- Click "Shortcuts" and observe the menu below is replaced with two links. These are default links to administrative functions most frequently performed. You might have your own, and you can add them to this list.

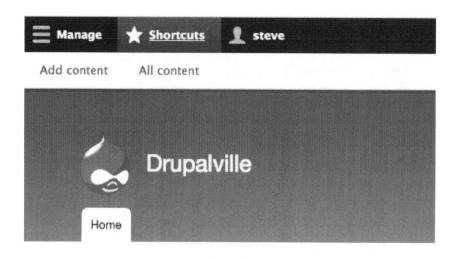

- If you have a part of the site that you visit often, click the star next to the page title. The empty star will become a gold star so you know that it is saved as a shortcut.

- Click your name. You'll see links related to your account such as "View profile", "Edit profile" and "Log out".

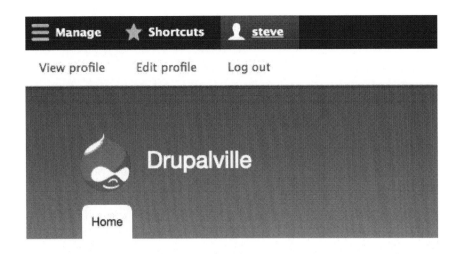

This menu can be moved around if you don't like having it on the top of your site:

- Look in the top-right corner of the site for the bar and arrow icon. Click this link.

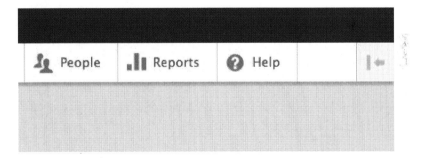

- Your menu will now move to the left-hand side of your site.

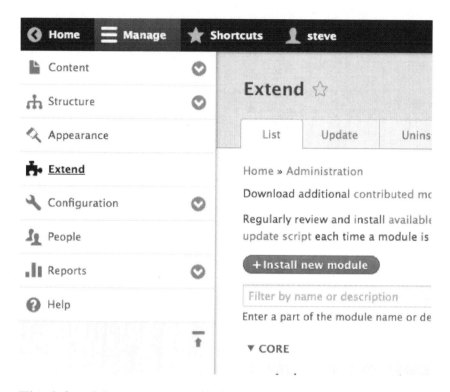

This left-sidebar position will also appear if you're using Drupal on a small screen.

Some people prefer using the menu in this position. However, we've seen some people move the menu accidentally and wonder what happened, so we wanted to explain that it is actually a useful Drupal feature!

You can click the arrow and bar icon again to get the menu back to the top of the site.

THE CONTENT SCREENS

Let's start our tour of Drupal's dashboard with the "Content" link. This is the link you'll be using most often in this book, and when building your Drupal site.

- Click the "Manage" link and then the "Content" link. This screen gives you a list of all the content that has been added to your site. At the moment, that's a grand total of zero content items.

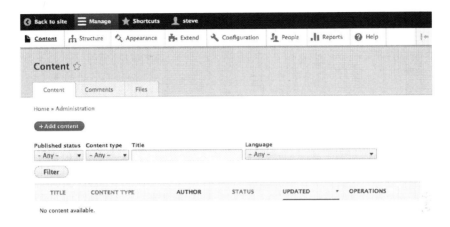

However, if you have a lot of content, you can use the filters at the top of the page to find content easily:

- The "Published status" filter allows you to find published or unpublished content.

- The "Content type" filter allows you to find particular types of content. Chapter 5 explains the difference between an Article and a Basic page.

- The "Title" filter allows you to search the titles of your content.

Also under the "Content" menu link, you can manage the comments and files on your site.

- Click the "Comments" tab. You'll see an area with "Published comments" and another with "Unapproved comments".

You can use tabs like this often during this book. In addition to the main administration menu, these tabs are a common method of navigation in Drupal.

- Click the "Files" tab. You'll see an area that is ready to show the details of all images, PDFs and other files that you upload.

This "Content" area is the most important section in the entire site. After all, you are using a Content Management System (CMS). Everything you do with Drupal in this book is designed to help you add content to your website.

THE STRUCTURE SCREENS

Now let's take a look at another very important area of your Drupal site.

- Click the "Structure" link. You'll see a list of 8 different features from "Block layout" to Views".

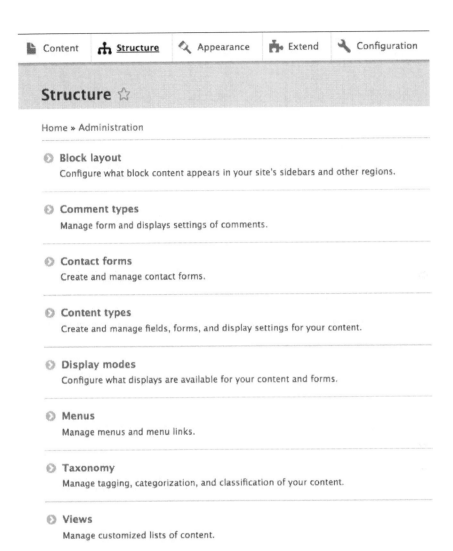

The short explanation of this Structure screen is that it contains the fundamental building blocks of your site.

The long explanation of this Structure screen will take several chapters. You explore these areas in chapters called "Drupal Blocks Explained", "Drupal Content Explained", "Drupal Menus Explained," and more. During the book, you also add several links to this page.

For now, notice that there are short explanations under each link. For example:

- **Block layout**: Configure what content appears in your site's sidebars and other regions.

- **Content types**: Create and manage fields, forms, and display settings for your content.

- **Menus**: Manage menus and menu links.

- **Taxonomy**: Manage tagging, categorization, and classification of your content.

THE APPEARANCE SCREENS

The next link contains the design settings for your site.

- Click the "Appearance" link in the administration menu.

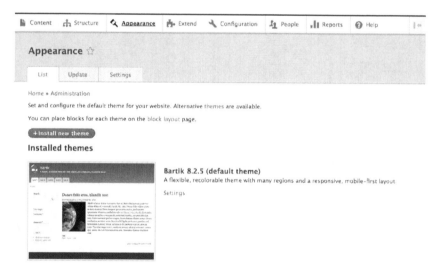

The Appearance screen contains the design for your site. Designs are provided by themes.

Bartik is the theme used by your site at the moment. Bartik is the theme that visitors currently see. It is responsible for the blue-and-white color scheme, plus your site's layout.

Seven is the theme used for your administrator area. You will see Seven every time you click a link in the administration menu.

Seven 8.2.6 (administration theme)
The default administration theme for Drupal 8 was designed with clean lines, simple blocks, and sans-serif font to emphasize the tools and tasks at hand.

Settings | Set as default

Besides Bartik, Drupal provides you with one other default option for the front of your site: Stark. That theme is currently in the "Uninstalled theme" area.

Uninstalled theme

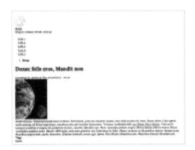

Stark 8.2.6

An intentionally plain theme with no styling to demonstrate default Drupal's HTML and CSS. Learn how to build a custom theme from Stark in the Theming Guide.

Install | Install and set as default

The chapter, "Drupal Themes Explained," shows you how to modify and replace your theme.

THE EXTEND SCREENS

The next link allows us to enable and disable the features on our Drupal site.

- Click the "Extend" link in the administration menu.

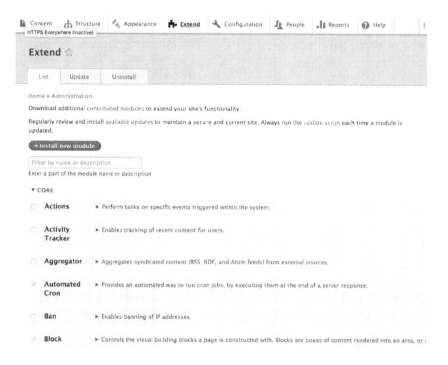

This area contains all the features on your Drupal site. Drupal calls these features, "Modules". Each module has a description beside it showing what it does.

The group of modules at the top of this screen is called "Core". These modules are sorted alphabetically, so the list starts with Actions and ends with Views UI.

Further down this screen are more groups of modules. For example, there's a "Multilingual" group. Enable these modules, and you'll be able to translate your site into multiple languages.

▼ MULTILINGUAL

☐ **Configuration Translation**   ► Provides a translation interface for configuration.

☐ **Content Translation**   ► Allows users to translate content entities.

☐ **Interface Translation**   ► Translates the built-in user interface.

☐ **Language**   ► Allows users to configure languages and apply them to content.

You can add more modules via the "Install new module" link in the top-left corner. You see how to install new modules in Chapter 6.

For now, take a look at one module in detail. The Comment module is shown in the image below.

This area is full of information and useful links:

- **Check box**: Is this module working? If you uncheck this box, comments will be instantly turned off for your whole site.

- **Version**: The module's version number. This will increase while you use Drupal because new versions will be released with improvements and bug fixes. You see how to update to those new versions in the chapter, "Drupal Site Management Explained."

- **Requires** and **Required by**: This area tells you if the Comment module needs other modules to operate. This area also tells you if the Comment module is needed by other modules to function.

- **Help**: If you are unsure how to use a module, click this link for a more detailed explanation.

- **Permissions**: This takes you to the Permissions area so you can decide who is able to use this module.

- **Configure**: If there are any settings for this module, you can find them by clicking this link.

THE CONFIGURATION SCREENS

- Click the "Configuration" link on the administration menu.

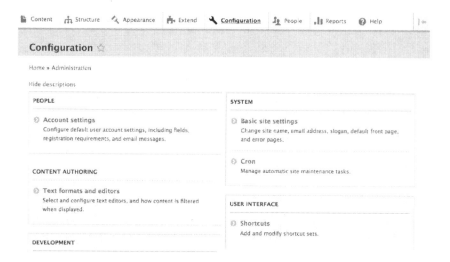

This area has the configuration settings for the main features of your site. As you add more features to your site (and remember, you do that by adding modules), this area becomes larger.

Often these settings are the same that you can get to from the "Configure" link we saw in the "Extend" area.

This book doesn't have a whole chapter dedicated to this Configuration area, but we are going to visit it often, especially when setting up new features.

THE PEOPLE SCREENS

- Click the "People" link in the administration menu. You'll now see a screen with a list of all your site's registered users. Right now, this should just be you.

As with the Content area, there are filters at the top to help you search for users.

There also actions to help you manage users.

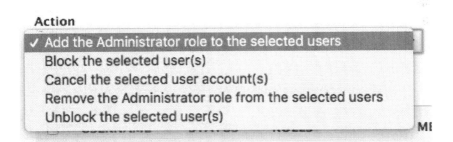

This People area is similar to the Content area in other ways too. There are tabs across the top of the screen. The "Permissions" and "Roles" tabs allow you to closely control who can do what on your site. The chapter called "Drupal Users Explained," goes into this area in detail.

Permissions ☆

| List | Permissions | Roles |

Home » Administration » People

Permissions let you control what users can do and see on your site. You can define a specific set of permissions for each role. (See the Roles page to create a role.) Any permissions granted to the Authenticated user role will be given to any user who is logged in to your site. From the Account settings page, you can make any role into an Administrator role for the site, meaning that role will be granted all new permissions automatically. You should be careful to ensure that only trusted users are given this access and level of control of your site.

Hide descriptions

THE REPORTS SCREENS

* Click the "Reports" link on the Administration menu.

This area contains reports about the health of your site. Here you can find out whether there are any problems with your site, whether your site needs updating, what people are searching for when using your search box, and similar useful information.

The chapter, "Drupal Site Management Explained", explains more about this area.

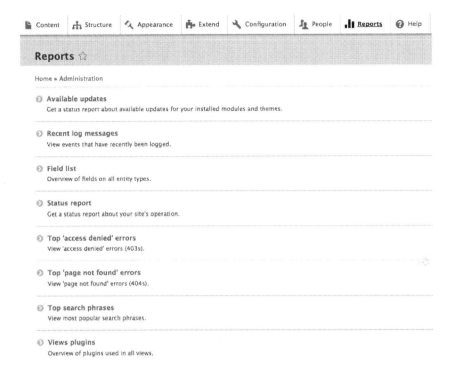

THE HELP SCREENS

- Click the "Help" link on the Administration menu. You'll see links to documentation on all the different areas of your site.

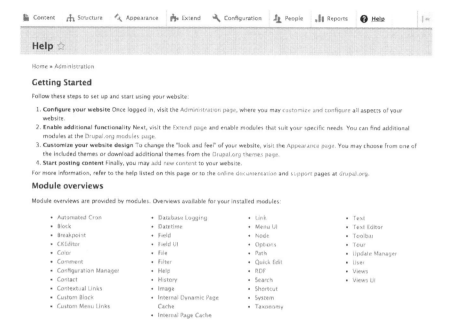

This Help area is something that can become more useful as you become more experienced.

When you first use Drupal, some of the terminology on this screen can be confusing. However, by the end of this book, you will hopefully understand the large majority of these terms.

THE ADMINISTRATION AND VISITOR AREAS EXPLAINED

This chapter ends by showing you the difference between Drupal's administration and visitor areas.

- In the top-left corner of your site, click the "Home" link. In some situations, this will also appear as "Back to site".

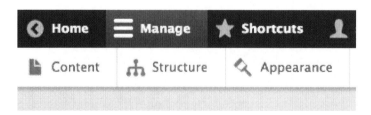

You can now see your site's frontpage. Your site now appears as it did at the beginning of this chapter.

- Click your name in the administration menu.
- Click "Log out".

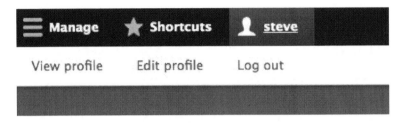

- You will now see what people see if they visit your site without a registered account.

How can you, the administrator, tell if you are logged in? The easiest way to tell is that you can see the black-and-white administrator menu when logged in.

When you start with Drupal, it's sometimes confusing to understand what is visible to visitors and what is visible only to administrators. There are some ways around this.

The simplest solution is to have two browsers open. In one

browser, you can log in as the administrator of your site. In the other browser, don't log in and you can see your site as a visitor would.

Chapter 13, "Drupal Users Explained", recommends a more advanced feature called Masquerade, which enables you to see your site through the eyes of any visitor.

WHAT'S NEXT?

You've now had a tour of Drupal's administrator area. You've had a brief look at all the important screens in your site. Now it's time to start using Drupal.

As mentioned earlier, we recommended that you use the Drupal workflow to build your first sites. This workflow helps overcome much of the confusion that beginners encounter.

In Chapter 2, you covered the first steps in the Drupal workflow: Planning. Now you are ready to take the next step: Content types.

1. **Planning**

2. **Content types**

3. **Fields**

4. **Add content**

5. **Install Modules and Themes**

6. **Views**

7. **Layout Modules**

8. **Finish the Design**

9. **Users**

10. **Site Management**

CHAPTER 5.

DRUPAL CONTENT EXPLAINED

The most important thing on your website is the content.

Drupal itself is called a Content Management System, and the most important way that Drupal helps you manage content is with content types.

In this chapter, we're going to explore the content types available on a new Drupal site.

We're also going to show you how to create and edit your own content types.

At the end of this chapter, you should be able to:

- Add content.
- Find content.
- Create an Article.
- Create a Basic page.
- Enable more content types.
- Create new content types.
- Edit content types.
- Describe the purpose of a content type.

CONTENT TYPES EXPLAINED

There is one important thing to think about before using Drupal content: Different types of content require different features.

Your site might contain many different content types, from news, blogs, and events to opinion polls, e-commerce products, staff member profiles, and more. Each of those is a different content type and needs different features.

When you first install Drupal, it gives you an Article and a Basic page content type.

Drupal 8 also provides two other content types ready for you to enable and use: Book and Forum. Each content type has unique features and serves a unique purpose on the site.

In addition to the content types that Drupal provides, you can also create your own. For instance, imagine you want to sell products on your site. You can create a Product content type. This unique content type can feature photos of the product, its price, and shipping information. You probably don't want to add a price and shipping information to your organization's news stories, so you can create a separate News content type. Perhaps your site is going to help your team run events. You can create an Events content type and include a date and a location. The possibilities are endless.

DEFAULT CONTENT TYPES

The best way to learn about content types is to start using them. Let's start with the two default content types: Article and Basic page.

Articles are where you can post your news and topical information. In our Drupalville site, we will use articles to publish news and information about Drupal 8.

We're going to start simply and walk through the process of creating an Article. After you are familiar with the style of the content form, you can speed up the process and explore more options.

- Make sure you're logged into your Drupal site.
- Click "Shortcuts".
- Click "Add Content".

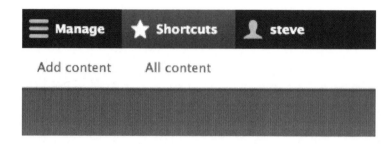

You now see a screen with two options: Article and Basic Page.

You can see that Drupal 8 explains an Article in this way: "Use articles for time-sensitive content like news, press releases or blog posts."

- Click "Article".

You can now see the Create Article screen. This is one of many input forms you will use to post content to your site. You'll be coming back here time and time again throughout the book.

There are only two fields that are essential to enter: Title and Body. We're going to focus on those two fields and explain other fields later.

Enter these details:

- Title: **Welcome to Drupalville**
- Body: **Welcome to Drupalville. This is a great place to spend time!**

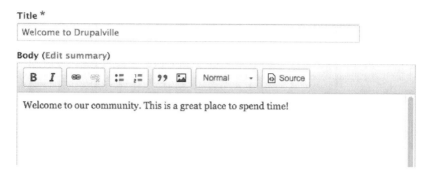

- Scroll to the bottom of the page, and click "Save and publish".

- You can now see your first Drupal article live on your site.

Notice the comment form below your article. Let's give the comments a test. Enter these details:

- Subject: **Yes, let's get started**

- Comment: **I'm excited to see how this site turns out**

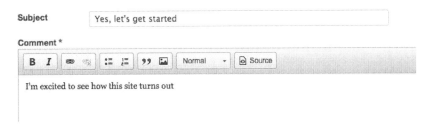

Add new comment

Subject Yes, let's get started

Comment *

I'm excited to see how this site turns out

- Click "Save" under the comment. Your article will now have a comment underneath:

Welcome to Drupalville

View Edit Delete

Submitted by steve on Sun, 01/29/2017 - 15:46

Welcome to our community. This is a great place to spend time!

Add new comment

Comments

new

steve

Sun, 01/29/2017 - 15:56

Permalink

Yes, let's get started

I'm excited to see how this site turns out

Delete Edit Reply

That was easy, right? You've just published your first Drupal article. Now do it again. This time, we are going to create an article about the Drupal logo:

- Go to https://drupal.org/about/media-kit/logos. Right click one of the Drupal logos. Save the logo to your computer. We have also included a copy of the logo in the files for this class at http://ostraining.com/books/d8e. The logo is known as the "Druplicon".
- In your Drupal site, go to "Shortcuts" then "Add content".
- Click "Article".

Enter the following information:

- Title: **Have You Seen The Drupal Logo?**
- Body: **The Drupal logo is designed to look like a drop of water.**
- Tags: **Drupal, logo, druplicon**

Tags are one way that Drupal organizes content. We're going to cover them in more detail in Chapter 6.

Now upload your logo to the article:

- Find the "Image" field.
- Click "Choose File".
- Browse for, and select the Drupal logo saved to your computer.
- You can now see a thumbnail of the logo, as shown below.
- Enter a brief description into the required "Alternative text" field. This text shows to search engines and people who may be partially sighted and can't see images clearly.

Image

Alternative text *

The Drupal logo

This text will be used by screen readers, search engines, or when the image cannot be loaded.

druplicon-small.png (12.16 KB)   Remove

Here's what your article will look like before publishing:

Title *

Have You Seen The Drupal Logo?

Body (Edit summary)

| B | I | ⊖ | ⊛ | ⠿ | ⠿ | ⠿ | ⠿ | Normal | ▾ | ⊕ Source |

The Drupal logo is designed to look like a drop of water.

body p

Text format Basic HTML ▾   About text formats ⍰

Tags

Drupal, logo, druplicon

Enter a comma-separated list. For example: Amsterdam, Mexico City, "Cleveland, Ohio"

Image

Alternative text *

The Drupal logo

This text will be used by screen readers, search engines, or when the image cannot be loaded.

druplicon-small.png (12.16 KB)   (Remove)

- Click "Save and publish". You'll see your article published, with your content and image.

Have You Seen The Drupal Logo?

Let's make some changes to that article.

- Click the "Edit" tab at the top of the article.

Have You Seen The Drupal Logo?

Now you can format your content:

- Try formatting, "The Drupal logo is designed to look like a
  drop of water." Use the Bold and Italic buttons on the HTML
  editor bar.

Body (Edit summary)

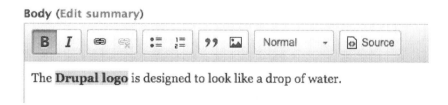

There are other formatting buttons available:

- Try using the bullet options.

- Try using the Quotation marks:

- Try using the Heading options:

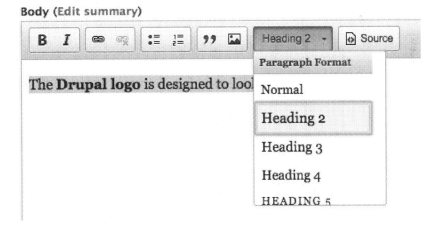

Let's also use the link feature.

- Write "Click here to download the Drupal logo".
- Select that text.
- Click the link icon.

Body (Edit summary)

The **Drupal logo** is designed to look like a drop of water.

Click here to download the Drupal logo.

- Enter this URL into the pop-up window: https://www.drupal.org/about/media-kit/logos.
- Click "Save".

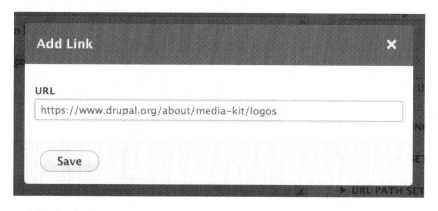

- The linked text will now be underlined.

Body (Edit summary)

The **Drupal logo** is designed to look like a drop of water.

Click here to download the Drupal logo.

You can also insert images into the Body area. In general, we don't recommend doing this. You will have a much more flexible site if you use image fields. However, particularly for very small sites, adding an image through this button is a valid option.

- Click the picture icon.
- You can browse for, and upload an image, just as you did earlier.

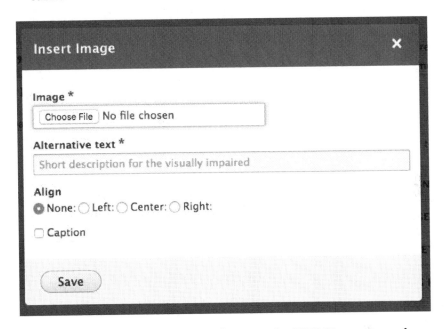

- Finally, you can click "Source" to see the HTML version of this content:

- Click "Save and keep published" at the bottom of the page.
- You can now see a new tab at the top of the article: "Revisions". Every time you make a change, Drupal will automatically save a copy of your content.
- Click "Revisions".

Have You Seen The Drupal Logo?

View	Edit	Delete	Revisions

- You will see a screen with a link to the original version of your content. If you update this content multiple times, this list will get longer and longer. You can click "Revert" to roll back to a particular version.

Now that you've created two Articles, you can see what the other default content type looks like. Let's create an "About Us page" on your Drupalville site. This time we'll use an alternative path to add content.

- Click "Manage".
- Click "Content". Notice that your two articles appear on this screen.
- Click the blue "Add content" button.

- Click "Basic page". Notice the description of this content type, "Use basic pages for your static content, such as an 'About us' page".

Enter these details:

- Title: **About Us**
- Body: **Drupalville is a great resource for everything you want to know about Drupal. It has information about events, sites, companies, and more.**

- Click "Save and Publish" at the bottom of the page. Now that you've finished your first Basic page, your screen will look like the image below.

About Us

Drupalville is a great resource for everything you want to know about Drupal. It has information about events, sites, companies, and more.

Notice anything missing? What did you have on Articles that you don't have on your Basic page?

The Article has the title, author name, the publishing date, an image, body, tags, and comments.

The Basic page has only the title and body.

- Click the "Home" link on the website's main menu.

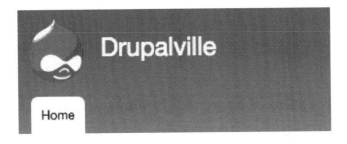

Your site's homepage will look like the image below. What's missing? Your Basic Page again. The Articles are there but the Basic Page is missing.

What do we learn from this? The Article and Basic page have very different features. Articles are specifically designed for topical content, and Basic pages are designed for static content that rarely changes.

Let's create a menu link so that our "About Us" page is easy to find.

- Click "Content".
- Click "Edit" in the "About Us" row.

- Click the "Menu Settings" tab on the right-hand side.
- Check the "Provide a menu link" box.

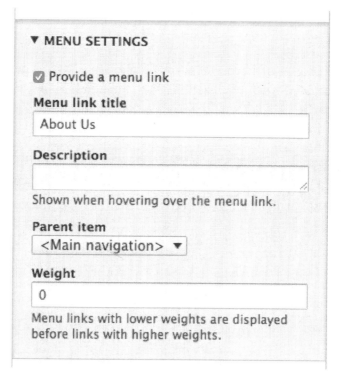

- Click "Save and keep published".
- Click "Back to site" in the top-left corner. You can now see a menu link to your About Us page.

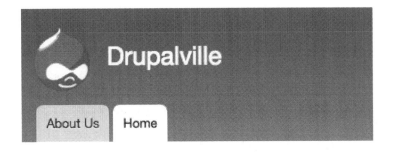

By default, menus are ordered alphabetically. You learn how to change the order of menu links in Chapter 8, "Drupal Menus Explained".

Let's recap. Drupal comes with two content types: Article and Basic page.

Why does Drupal come with two content types? Because different types of content require different features.

We recently spoke with a student who admitted not updating his About Us page since 2000. It certainly would be embarrassing if visitors saw 2000 as the publishing date for that page. So, Basic pages do not show the publishing date.

On the other hand, if you have topical news and use an Article, you probably need the publishing date. It's important to know if the information in the Article is fresh or out-of-date.

Repeat after us, "Different types of content require different features."

In the next part of this chapter, you see how to add more content types and more features.

ENABLING EXTRA CONTENT TYPES

You've seen that Drupal provides two default content types: Article and Basic page. There are also more content types available but not yet enabled. Now see how to enable those extra content types.

On your site, let us assume that you want to encourage visitors to post questions and respond to other visitor questions, so your plan includes a discussion forum. You can find a great example of a discussion forum using Drupal at http://drupal.org/forum.

Forum posts are content in exactly the same way as the Article and Basic page. The Forum module simply organizes the content into a discussion forum layout.

Drupal provides a forum content type, but it is disabled by default. Let's see how to enable the Forum content type for our site.

- Click "Extend" in the administration menu.
- Check the box next to Forum.

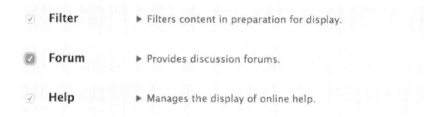

- Scroll to the bottom of the page, and click "Install".

Now we can use exactly the same processes you used when creating an Article and a Basic page:

- Go to "Shortcuts", then "Add content".
- Click "Forum topic".

Enter the following information:

- Subject: **How did you discover Drupal?**

- Forums: **General discussion**
- Body: **What's your Drupal story? Me: I started using it very recently at work, but I'm loving it!**

- Click "Save and publish". Your forum topic should look like the image below:

How did you discover Drupal?

To be honest, this topic looks very similar to the Article you created at the beginning of the chapter. Where is the discussion forum posts?

- On the left side of your screen, you will see a block labeled Tools.
- Click the "Forums" link.

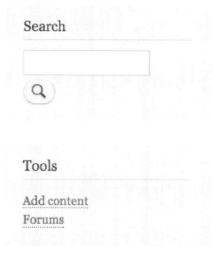

Search

Tools

Add content

Forums

General discuss

| View | Edit |

How did you discove

Submitted by steve on Sun, 01/29/

Forums

General discussion

What's your Drupal story? Me

You now see your forum post organized into a discussion forum layout.

Forums

+ Add new Forum topic

Forum	Topics	Posts	Last post
General discussion	1	1	By steve 2 minutes 27 seconds ago

- Click on "General discussion" and you will see the post you wrote.

General discussion

+ Add new Forum topic

Topic	Replies	Last reply ▼
How did you discover Drupal? By steve 8 minutes 42 seconds ago	0	n/a

At this point, you can add additional Forum topics but they will all appear under General discussion.

If you want a more elaborate organization for your topics, follow these steps:

- Click "Structure" in the administration menu. Can't see it? Remember to click on "Manage" first.
- Click Forums.

There are two things to know here:

- **Container**: This includes the top level categories such as Drupal or Sports. Containers do not actually contain forum topics.
- **Forum**: This includes the subcategories such as Drupal Installation, Drupal Design and Drupal Support or Tennis, Golf, and Football.

Now see how that works in practice. First, we'll create a container:

- Click "Add container".
- Container name: **Drupal**
- Click "Save".

Now, let's add the forums:

- Click "Add forum".
- Name: **Drupal Installation**
- Parent: **Drupal**

- Click "Save".
- Click "Add forum".
- Name: **Drupal Design**
- Parent: **Drupal**
- Click "Save".
- Click "Add forum".
- Name: **Drupal Support**
- Parent: **Drupal**
- Click "Save".
- Click "Add forum".

Your forum organization should now look like this:

NAME	OPERATIONS
⊹ Drupal	edit container
⊹ Drupal Design	edit forum
⊹ Drupal Installation	edit forum
⊹ Drupal Support	edit forum
⊹ General discussion	edit forum

Finally, let's make it easy for people to find our forums. Let's create its menu link.

- Go to "Structure", then "Menus".
- Click "Add link" in the "Main navigation" row.

Main navigation	Site section links	Edit menu
		Add link

- Menu link title: **Forum**
- Link: **/forum**

- Click "Save".

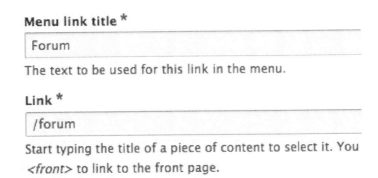

Menu link title *

Forum

The text to be used for this link in the menu.

Link *

/forum

Start typing the title of a piece of content to select it. You
<front> to link to the front page.

- Click "Back to site".
- Your Forum menu link and content is now visible:

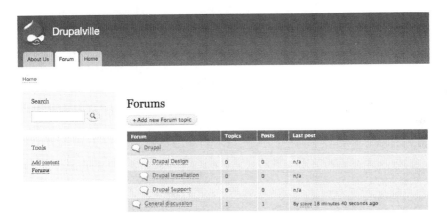

Now let's turn our attention to Book, the last of the four content types available with Drupal by default.

We're going to create a Drupal User Manual as a section for your site. As the name suggests, a user manual is an organized set of pages. For an example of an online book created using Drupal's Book module, visit https://www.drupal.org/documentation/build. Click through the pages using the navigation links at the bottom of the page content. You can see that content is organized using navigational links.

- The links organized vertically at the bottom lead to pages at the same level in the documentation.
- The "Up" link takes you to a higher level in the documentation.

‹ Site Building Guide   up   Types of Contributed Themes ›

To add a manual like this to your site, you need to enable the Book module; then you can create some pages for your book. Follow these steps:

- Click "Extend".
- Check the box next to Book in the module list.
- Click "Install".
- Click "Shortcuts", then "Add Content".
- Click "Book page".

Enter the following information:

- Title: **Drupal User Manual**
- Body: **Welcome to the Drupal manual provided by Drupalville.**
- Menu settings: Check the "Provide a menu link" box.
- Book outline: Select "Create a new book" in the Book dropdown. This is where you tell Drupal that the page you are creating is the page that defines the book.

- Click "Save and publish". Your book page should look like the image below:

Drupal User Manual

The Book module is called Book for a reason. The Book is designed to link content together like the table of contents in a book. The process ends with a series of pages with parent-and-child relationships. For example, book pages are parents to chapter pages. In turn, chapter pages are parents to topic pages. In this next activity, you create child pages to the book you just defined. Now let's create the first chapter:

- Click "Add child page". You can see this link in the bottom right corner of the image above.

Enter the following information:

- Title: **Chapter 1: How to Install Drupal**
- Body: **This part of the Drupal User Manual will show you how to install Drupal.**

- Book Outline > Book: Drupal User Manual
- Book Outline > Parent Item: Drupal User Manual

- Click "Save and publish".
- Click "Add child page".

Enter the following information to create a child page for your documentation:

- Title: **How to Install Drupal Automatically**
- Book Outline > Book: Drupal User Manual
- Parent Item > Book: Chapter 1: How to Install Drupal
- Click "Save and publish" for the current book page.
- Click "Up".
- Click "Add child page".

Enter the following information:

- Title: **How to Install Drupal Manually**
- Book Outline > Book: Drupal User Manual
- Parent Item > Book: Chapter 1: How to Install Drupal

Save that page and click "Up". You'll now see that Chapter 1 is starting to take shape.

If your pages don't end up where you want them, you can move them around quite easily. Let's give it a try.

- Click the "Outline" tab on one of your book pages.
- Click "reorder an entire book" at the end of the top sentence.
- Click "Edit order and titles" for your Drupal book.
- Find the + symbol next to each page. If you click, hold and drag the + symbol, you can rearrange the pages up, down, in, and out.

Let's recap. Drupal comes with two content types: Article and

Basic page. If you enable two modules disabled by default, you can also use these content types: Forum topics and Book pages.

Why does Drupal come with four content types? Because different types of content require different features.

In the final part of this chapter, we're going to see how to add new content types and customize the ones you already have.

CUSTOM CONTENT TYPES

Now that you are familiar with several types of content, you can create custom content types.

In your Drupalville site, you're going to create content types called Event, Website, User Group, and Company. Before diving in and creating them, let's review a brief description of each custom content type defined when planning our site.

- **Event**: This content type will be used to post Drupal related events such as the annual DrupalCons and regional Drupal Camps, and more.

- **Website**: This content type will be used to post sites that provide information, tutorials, modules, or themes for Drupal.

- **User Group**: This content type can be used to post sites for local groups that meet to talk and learn about Drupal.

- **Company**: This content type can be used to post businesses that provide Drupal-related services.

CREATING THE EVENT CONTENT TYPE

Let's create your first custom content type: Event.

- Click "Manage", then "Structure".

- Click "Content types". You see that all the content types used so far are now available here.

- Click "Add content type" in the top-left of the screen.

Take a moment and compare the "Add content type" link and the "Add content" link you have used previously. These links are often confused. "Add content type" is creating the framework that holds your content. "Add content" is creating the content itself.

You now see a screen like the one below.

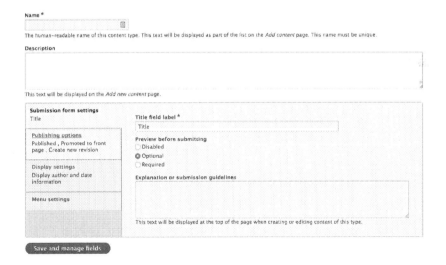

Enter the following information:

- Name: **Event**

- Description: **This is where we enter information about Drupal events around the world.**

Although the description is private and won't be made public, please try to use it. The name of the content type might seem obvious when you create it and remain so for the life of the project. However, we have been on several projects where the name was not so obvious 6 months later. Thus, try to clearly explain the purpose of the content type.

Further down the screen, there are four areas with options to configure your content type. Look at them one-by-one. However, at this point we're going to recommend just one change:

- Title field label: Change this to **Event Name**.
- Click "Save and manage fields".

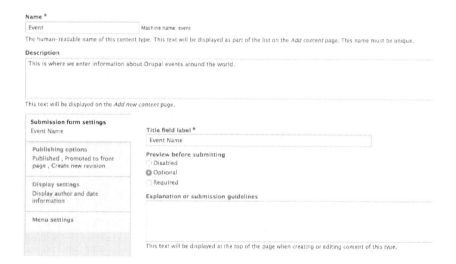

Now we'll test out our new content type.

- Click "Shortcuts", then "Add content".
- Click "Event".

Enter the following information:

- Event Name: **DrupalCon Baltimore**
- Body: **DrupalCon Baltimore is the large Drupal event in North America for 2017.**

Save your Event, and this is what you'll see:

DrupalCon Baltimore

Submitted by steve on Sun, 01/29/2017 - 19:27

DrupalCon Baltimore is the large Drupal event in North America for 2017.

2. CREATING THE WEBSITE CONTENT TYPE

Now create your second custom content type: Website. This gives your visitors information about useful Drupal sites.

- Go to "Manage", then "Structure", then "Content types".
- Click "Add content type".

Enter the following information.

- Title: **Website**
- Description: **This is where you enter information about useful Drupal websites and resources.**
- Title field label: **Website Name**

Save the content type. Now, we'll add a Website example.

- Click "Shortcuts", then "Add content".
- Click "Website".

Enter the following information:

- Website Name: **Drupal.org**
- Body: **Drupal.org is the official homepage of Drupal. Here you can find documentation, support, downloads, and much more.**

Save this content, and the image below shows what you will see.

Drupal.org

| View | Edit | Outline | Delete | Revisions |

Submitted by steve on Sun, 01/29/2017 - 19:35

Drupal.org is the official homepage of Drupal. Here you can find documentation, support, downloads, and much more.

3. CREATING THE USER GROUP CONTENT TYPE

Now create your third custom content type: User Group. This gives your visitors information about useful Drupal User Groups.

- Go to "Manage", then "Structure", then "Content types".
- Click "Add content type".

Enter the following information.

- Title: **User Group**
- Description: **This is where you enter information about Drupal User Groups around the world.**
- Title field label: **User Group Name**

Save the content type. Now, we'll add a User Group example.

- Click "Shortcuts", then "Add content".
- Click "User Group".

Enter the following information:

- User Group Name: **The Atlanta Drupal User Group**
- Body: **This is where people in Atlanta, Georgia meet to discuss Drupal.**

Save this content, and the image below shows the end result.

The Atlanta Drupal User Group

View | Edit | Outline | Delete

Submitted by steve on Sun, 01/29/2017 - 19:42

This is where people in Atlanta, Georgia meet to discuss Drupal.

By now, you might be thinking, "Yes. Yes. I know. However, every content page I create is the same." We understand the frustration you are likely feeling at this point. Hang in there, it gets better. Right now, we are simply laying the foundation for Chapter 6, where we will add new fields to these content types, making them unique and worth the effort.

CREATING THE COMPANY CONTENT TYPE

Finally, let's create one more content type. This time we'll just give you the details.

Here's the information for the content type.

- Title: **Company**
- Description: **This is where you enter information about Drupal companies.**
- Title field label: **Company Name**

Here's the information for your first Company content:

- Company Name: **Pantheon**
- Body: **Pantheon is a hosting company that does a great job of hosting Drupal sites.**

Pantheon

| View | Edit | Outline | Delete |

Submitted by steve on Sun, 01/29/2017 - 19:48

Pantheon is a hosting company that does a great job of hosting Drupal sites.

EDITING CONTENT TYPES

If you want to change any of the settings for any of your eight content types, here is what you do:

- Go to "Structure", then "Content types".
- Click the down arrow next to the Manage field button associated with the content type you want to change. Click "Edit".

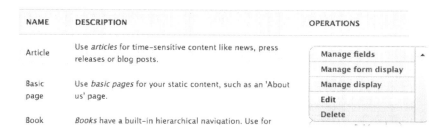

NAME	DESCRIPTION	OPERATIONS
Article	Use *articles* for time-sensitive content like news, press releases or blog posts.	Manage fields ▲
		Manage form display
Basic page	Use *basic pages* for your static content, such as an 'About us' page.	Manage display
		Edit
		Delete
Book	*Books* have a built-in hierarchical navigation. Use for	

WHAT HAVE WE LEARNED?

Now recap what you've learned during this chapter:

- Content types are crucial for setting up content on your Drupal site. Why? Because different types of content require different features. This will become even more evident in Chapter 6.

- Drupal comes with two content types enabled by default: Basic Page and Article.
- Drupal also comes with modules that can add two more content types: Book page and Forum topic.
- You can create your own custom content types.
- You can edit existing content types.

You now have eight different content types on your site. Each of those eight has a customized set of features. You started with two default content types, enabled two more content types, and now added four custom content types.

Click "Add Content", and you can now see all eight content types with a description of what they do.

Article

Use *articles* for time-sensitive content like news, press releases or blog posts.

Book page

Books have a built-in hierarchical navigation. Use for handbooks or tutorials.

Company

This is where you enter information about Drupal companies.

Event

This is where we enter information about Drupal events around the world.

Forum topic

A *forum topic* starts a new discussion thread within a forum.

Basic page

Use *basic pages* for your static content, such as an 'About us' page.

User Group

This is where you enter information about Drupal User Groups around the world.

Website

This is where you enter information about useful Drupal websites and resources.

WHAT'S NEXT?

At the moment, our Drupalville site looks like the image below. Don't worry if your site doesn't match this exactly. If you understand the concepts that we covered in this chapter, you can move on to Chapter 6.

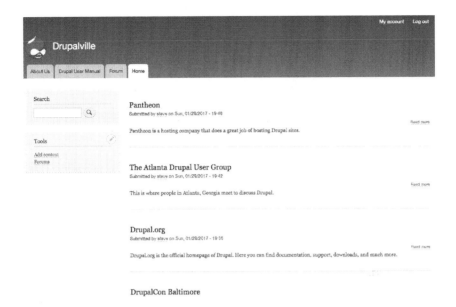

At the moment our new content types still look almost identical. There's little to distinguish between Event, Website, User Group, and Company.

What do we need to do to make our content types more interesting and useful?

- We need to add specific information for each content type.

- We need to add dates and locations to our Events.

- We need to add screenshots and site information to our Websites.

- We need to add meeting locations and organizer details to our User Groups.

- We need to add company logos and addresses to our Companies.

That's what we are going to do in Chapter 6. We're going to make your content types more interesting by using Fields. Fields are the next step in our Drupal workflow.

1. **Planning**

2. **Content types**

3. **Fields**

4. **Add content**

5. **Install Modules and Themes**

6. **Views**

7. **Layout Modules**

8. **Finish the Design**

9. **Users**

10. **Site Management**

CHAPTER 6.

DRUPAL FIELDS EXPLAINED

In the previous chapter, we explored content types, and you created Articles, Basic Pages, Events, Sites, User Groups, and Companies.

The limitation we found at the end of Chapter 5 is that there were few or no differences between those content types.

In this chapter, we start to see how to make your content types unique, interesting, and useful.

At the end of this chapter, you should be able to:

- Add different types of fields to a content type.
- Share a field across multiple content types.
- Manage the display of fields in the full content view and teaser.
- Describe Taxonomy and how Drupal categorizes content.

DIFFERENT FIELD TYPES

Fields provide almost unlimited possibilities for adding information to your content.

Let's start by considering the fields included in Drupal 8.

You have already seen four fields:

- Title
- Body
- Image
- Taxonomy (the field we used in Chapter 5 when we entered Tags for the article about the Drupal logo)

There are many more available:

- Text (5 different types)
- Boolean
- Comment
- Date
- Email
- Link
- Number (3 different types)
- List (for numbers and text)
- Content Reference
- User Reference
- Other Reference (too many to list here)

There is also one field that is not enabled by default: Telephone. It can be installed using the same process used to install the Forum and Book modules.

Also, there are fields contributed by the community of Drupal developers. We will consider those in Chapter 7, Modules Explained.

We currently have four content types from Chapter 5 that need to be made more useful and interesting. Those content types are

Website, Event, Company, and User Group. To be more useful, they need more information. They need fields.

FIELDS FOR THE WEBSITE CONTENT TYPE

We are going to add four new fields to the Website content type:

- Screenshot
- Comments
- Is this an Official Drupal Site?
- Website Link

Additionally, we're going to rename the Body field so that it is more descriptive.

Editing a Field: Website Description

When you created a content type, you weren't given an opportunity to choose the label of the Body field. Let's rename the field so it has a more appropriate label for our Website content type.

- Go to "Manage", then "Structure", then "Content types".
- Click "Manage fields" next to Website.
- Click "Edit" next to Body.

LABEL	MACHINE NAME	FIELD TYPE	OPERATIONS
Body	body	Text (formatted, long, with summary)	Edit ▾

- Change the label from **Body** to **Website Description.**

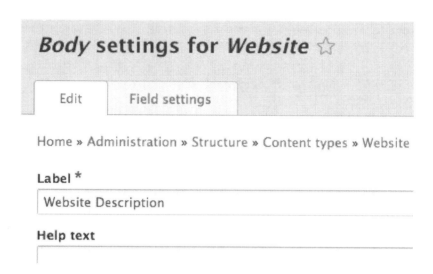

- Click "Save settings" at the bottom of the page.

Note that the Label has changed but not the Machine Name.

LABEL	MACHINE NAME	FIELD TYPE	OPERATIONS
Website Description	body	Text (formatted, long, with summary)	Edit ▼

Let's take a moment to consider the machine name. You will see this throughout Drupal. For instance, a machine name was defined for you when you created your new content types in Chapter 5. You might not have noticed the option to edit the machine name of your content, but it was there.

Name *

| Content Type Name| | 🔒 | Machine name: content_type_name [Edit]

The human-readable name of this content type. This text will be displayed as part

Description

This text will be displayed on the *Add new content* page.

A machine name is used for all sorts of technical purposes in Drupal. For example, the data for this field is stored in a database table that uses the machine name. This is why you can't change the machine name after you've created it.

Reusing a Field: Screenshot

Our next step will be to re-use an existing field.

We've seen that the Article content type has an image field. You used it to upload the Drupal logo. That image field is available for you to reuse on other content types if you choose. Or you can create another image field. How do you decide? Let's see.

Below you can see the "Field settings" for the image field from the Article content type. Notice the warning: "There is data for this field in the database. The field settings can no longer be changed." So, if these settings do not meet your needs, you simply create a new image field.

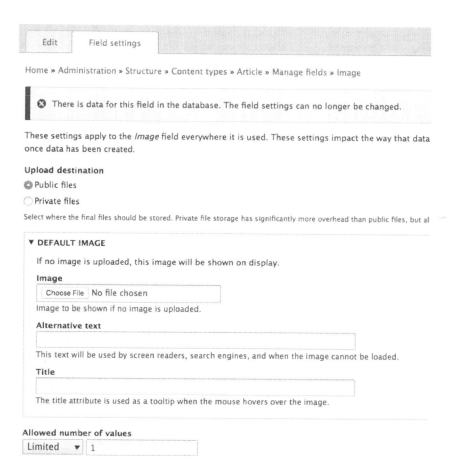

Because you don't need to customize the field settings, you can reuse the existing Image field. Here's how to do it:

- Go to "Manage", then "Structure", then "Content types".

- Click "Manage fields" next to Website.

- Click the "Add field" button.

- Select **Image: field_image** from the "Re-use existing field dropdown".

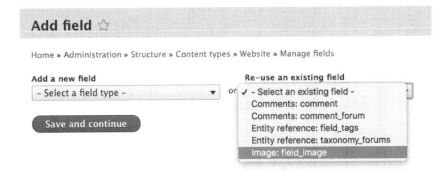

- Click "Save and continue".
- Label: **Screenshot**
- Click "Save and continue".

- Help text: **Upload a screenshot of the home page for this site.**
- You can read through the other settings, but we'll return to some of these later.
- Click "Save settings".
- Check that your new Screenshot field is visible:

LABEL	MACHINE NAME	FIELD TYPE	OPERATIONS
Screenshot	field_image	Image	Edit ▾
Website Description	body	Text (formatted, long, with summary)	Edit ▾

Reusing a Field: Comments

Next, we need to create the Comments field for our Website content type. If you want to include comments, you need to add the feature as if you are adding a field.

- Make sure you are on the Manage Fields page for the Website content type.
- Click the "Add field" button.
- Click the "Re-use existing field" drop-down and select **Comments: comment**.
- Click "Save and continue".
- Keep the default settings.
- Click "Save settings".
- Check that your new field is visible:

LABEL	MACHINE NAME	FIELD TYPE	OPERATIONS
Comments	comment	Comments	Edit ▾
Screenshot	field_image	Image	Edit ▾
Website Description	body	Text (formatted, long, with summary)	Edit ▾

Adding a Field: Official Website

Now let's explore how to create new fields.

This field enables the content author to show whether the site is an official Drupal site. The Boolean field option would be perfect for this because it provides an either/or choice. A Boolean field is an excellent option for choices such as Yes/No and True/False.

For the Official site field, the site will be listed as either an official site (true) or not an official site (false). Let's add this field.

- Make sure you are on the Manage Fields page for the Website content type.
- Click the "Add field" button.
- Add a new field: **Boolean**
- Label: **Official Website**

- Click "Save and continue".
- Allowed number of values: keep as **1**.
- Click "Save field settings".
- Scroll down and enter **This is an official Drupal website** and **This is not an official Drupal website**.

- Click "Save settings".
- Notice the new field is now added to the list.

LABEL	MACHINE NAME	FIELD TYPE	OPERATIONS
Comments	comment	Comments	Edit ▾
Official Website	field_official_website	Boolean	Edit ▾
Screenshot	field_image	Image	Edit ▾
Website Description	body	Text (formatted, long, with summary)	Edit ▾

Adding a Field: Website Link

Our last field we need to add for the Website Content Type is a link. Let's create a link so people can visit the website we're recommending.

- Click the "Add field" button.
- Add a new field: **Link**
- Label: **Website Link**

Click through the settings, and you'll end up with another new field.

LABEL	MACHINE NAME	FIELD TYPE	OPERATIONS
Comments	comment	Comments	Edit ▾
Official Website	field_official_website	Boolean	Edit ▾
Screenshot	field_image	Image	Edit ▾
Website Description	body	Text (formatted, long, with summary)	Edit ▾
Website Link	field_website_link	Link	Edit ▾

TESTING THE FIELDS FOR THE WEBSITE CONTENT TYPE

In Chapter 5, when you created the Website content type, you added Drupal.org as an example. In order to test that we've set up the 4 new fields correctly, let's add a second and also very useful Drupal site.

- Go to "Shortcuts", then "Add content".

- Click "Website".

Complete the content type form with the following:

- Website Name: **simplytest.me**
- Description: **This is wonderful site allows you to quickly create a demo site for any Drupal module or theme.**
- Screenshot: If you are comfortable creating your own screen shots, you can visit http://simplytest.me and capture a screen shot. Otherwise, you can download a screenshot at http://ostraining.com/books/d8e.
- Official site: Check this box.
- Website link: Enter http://simplytest.me for the URL and **Click here to visit Simplytest.me** for the Link text.

Click "Save and publish" to see your new content. At the moment, the fields are not logically arranged. For example, the Comment field should be at the bottom of the page. Later in this chapter, we'll show you how to fix that problem. However, for now, we can move on to adding fields for Company content type.

simplytest.me

View | Edit | Outline | Delete

Submitted by steve on Sun, 01/29/2017 - 21:43

This wonderful site allows you to quickly create a demo site for any Drupal module or theme.

Screenshot

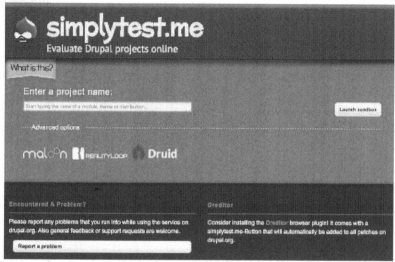

Add new comment

Subject

Comment *

B I | ⚓ ✕ | ≔ ≕ | ” 🖼 | Format · | 🄱 Source

Text format Basic HTML ⬍   About text formats ⓘ

Save   Preview

Official Website
This is an official Drupal website
Website Link
Click here to visit Simplytest.me

FIELDS FOR THE COMPANY CONTENT TYPE

The Company content type reuses several fields created on other content types and adds one more type of field. Using the same processes you have used so far, we're going to set up the following fields:

- **Body**: Company Description
- **Image**: Company Logo
- **Term reference**: Tags
- **List (Text)**: Services
- **Link**: Company Website
- **Comments**: Comments

Let's set up those fields.

Editing a Field: Company Description

- Go to "Manage", then "Structure", then "Content types".
- Click "Manage fields" next to Company.
- Click "Edit" next to Body.
- Change **Body** to **Company Description**.
- Save your changes.

Reusing a Field: Company Logo

- Make sure you are on the Manage Fields page for the Company content type.
- Click the "Add field" button.
- Select **Image: field_image** from the "Re-use existing field dropdown".
- Enter **Company Logo** for the Label.
- Click "Save and continue".
- Help: **Upload a logo for the company.**

- Save this field, and check that your two fields are in place:

LABEL	MACHINE NAME	FIELD TYPE	OPERATIONS
Company Description	body	Text (formatted, long, with summary)	Edit ▾
Company Logo	field_image	Image	Edit ▾

Reusing a Field: Tags

- Click "Add field" for the Company content type.

- Select **Entity reference: field_tags** from the "Re-use existing field dropdown".

- Enter **Tags** for the Label.

- Click "Save and continue".

- Check the box next to "Create referenced entities if they don't already exist" under "Reference method". This means that any new tags will be automatically created if a user types them in.

- At the bottom of the page, check "Tags" under "Available Vocabularies".

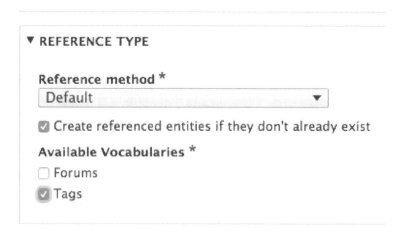

- Save this field, and check that your three fields are in place:

LABEL	MACHINE NAME	FIELD TYPE	OPERATIONS
Company Description	body	Text (formatted, long, with summary)	Edit ▾
Company Logo	field_image	Image	Edit ▾
Tags	field_tags	Entity reference	Edit ▾

Adding a Field: Services

- Click "Add field" for the Company content type.

- Select **List (text)**.

- Enter **Services** as the field label.

- Click "Save and continue".

- On the next screen, enter the various topics that a Drupal site can address. In this example, we entered Development, Design, Hosting, Training, and Support. Each topic is on a new line.

- Select **Unlimited** for "Allowed number of values". Unlimited turns the select list into a series of checkboxes.

Allowed values list

```
Development
Design
Hosting
Training
Support
```

The possible values this field can contain. Enter one valu
The key is the stored value. The label will be used in disp
The label is optional: if a line contains a single string, it

Allowed HTML tags in labels: <a> <b> <big> <code> ·
<li> <p>
 <img>

Allowed number of values

Unlimited ▼

Save field settings

- Click "Save field settings".

- Help: **Check the services provided by the company.**

- Save this field, and check that your four fields are in place:

LABEL	MACHINE NAME	FIELD TYPE	OPERATIONS
Company Description	body	Text (formatted, long, with summary)	Edit ▼
Company Logo	field_image	Image	Edit ▼
Services	field_services	List (text)	Edit ▼
Tags	field_tags	Entity reference	Edit ▼

Reusing a Field: Company Website

Link, under General (handwritten)

Let's re-use the field that you created earlier. By now you should be familiar with the process. Here are the details:

p.124 (handwritten)

- Enter **Company Website** as the field label.
- Keep the default settings.
- Click in the "Help" field and enter **Enter the company website URL.**
- Scroll down and select "External links only" under Allowed link type.
- Save this field, and check that your five fields are in place:

LABEL	MACHINE NAME	FIELD TYPE	OPERATIONS
Company Description	body	Text (formatted, long, with summary)	Edit ▾
Company Logo	field_image	Image	Edit ▾
Company Website	field_website_link	Link	Edit ▾
Services	field_services	List (text)	Edit ▾
Tags	field_tags	Entity reference	Edit ▾

Reusing a Field: Comments

We're going to re-use the existing Comments fields. There's no need to change any settings. Your goal in this step is to add a sixth field, as in the image below:

LABEL	MACHINE NAME	FIELD TYPE	OPERATIONS
Comments	comment	Comments	Edit ▾
Company Description	body	Text (formatted, long, with summary)	Edit ▾
Company Logo	field_image	Image	Edit ▾
Company Website	field_website_link	Link	Edit ▾
Services	field_services	List (text)	Edit ▾
Tags	field_tags	Entity reference	Edit ▾

TESTING THE FIELDS FOR THE COMPANY CONTENT TYPE

In Chapter 5, we used Pantheon as an example. Now add a new Company, using all your new fields.

- Go to "Shortcuts", then "Add content", then "Company".

Complete the content type form with the following:

- Company name: **OSTraining**
- Body: **OSTraining is the company that created this book, Drupal 8 Explained.**
- Tags: **Books, Training, Drupal**
- Services: **Training**
- Logo: You can download the OSTraining logo from http://ostraining.com/books/d8e.
- Website URL: **http://OSTraining.com**

When you publish your new Company, it should look like this:

OSTraining

View   Edit   Outline   Delete

Submitted by steve on Mon, 01/30/2017 - 11:15

OSTraining is the company that created this book, Drupal 8 Explained.

Company Logo

Tags
Books, Training, Drupal

Services
Training
Company Website
Click here to visit OSTraining

Add new comment

Subject

After using your Company content type, you might feel that some of the fields could be improved. For example, there are at least two possible improvements to the Services field:

- You want to make sure that all companies fill in the Services field.

- You want to add "Marketing" to the Services list.

It is possible to go back to edit fields and make these changes.

- Go to "Structure", "Content types", and click on "Manage fields" for the Company content type.

- Click "Edit" next to Services.

- Below the Help field, check the box that says "Required field".

Required field

▼ **DEFAULT VALUE**

The default value for this field, used when creating new content.

Services

- None -
Development
Design
Hosting

- Click the "Field settings" tab.

- Add **Marketing|Marketing** to the "Allowed values list". This syntax may be a little confusing. The text on the left is stored in the database. The text on the right is the human-readable version that people will click on.

- Click "Save field settings".

Allowed values list

Development|Development
Design|Design
Hosting|Hosting
Training|Training
Support|Support
Marketing|Marketing

end

FIELDS FOR THE EVENT CONTENT TYPE

Now that you have created fields for two new content types, you will be feeling more comfortable with the process. We're going to give you less detailed instructions for the next content type.

Here are the fields for your Events content type:

- **Body**: Event Description

- **Image**: Event Logo
- **Link**: Event Website
- **Comments:** Comments
- **Decimal**: Event Price
- **Date**: Event Date
- **Entity reference**: Event Sponsors

Let's go and set up those fields one-by-one.

Editing a Field: Event Description

- Change the label from **Body** to **Event Description**.

Reusing a Field: Event Logo

- Re-use the existing Image field.
- Enter **Event Logo** for the Label.

Reusing a Field: Event Website

- Re-use the existing Link: field_website_link field.
- Enter **Event Website** for the Label.
- Select "External links only".

Reusing a Field: Comments

- Re-use the existing Comments field.

Adding a Field: Event Price

There are three types of number fields provided by default: Integer, Float, and Decimal. You need a field for the price of your event.

An Integer field enables only whole numbers, so if you use that you cannot enter 9.95 for your price. You would have to enter 9 or 10.

The Float field and Decimal give you the option to have a decimal. The difference is that a Float field is generally used for numbers where exact precision is not so important. The name Float comes from "floating point", which is a super-geeky way of writing decimals. In over twenty years combined experience with Drupal sites, we've never seen Float used. You can ignore it!

However, the Decimal field is useful and a perfect fit for recording the price of events.

- Click "Add field".
- Select "Number (decimal)".
- Enter **Event Price** for the label.
- On the next screen, keep the default settings.
- Enter **$** in the "Prefix" field. This dollar sign appears in front of the field.
- When you save this field, check that your content type looks like the image below:

LABEL	MACHINE NAME	FIELD TYPE	OPERATIONS
Comments	comment	Comments	Edit ▾
Event Description	body	Text (formatted, long, with summary)	Edit ▾
Event Logo	field_image	Image	Edit ▾
Event Price	field_event_price	Number (decimal)	Edit ▾
Event Website	field_website_link	Link	Edit ▾

Adding a Field: Event Date

- Click "Add field".
- Select "Date".

- Enter **Event Date** for the Label.
- On the next screen, choose **Date only** for the "Date type".

Adding a Field: Event Sponsors

With this next field, we're going to make it easy to show the sponsors of an event. Anyone adding an event can automatically link to the companies listed in the Company content type.

- Click "Add field".
- Select "Content".
- Enter **Event Sponsors** for the label.
- On the next screen, select **Unlimited** for "Allowed number of values".
- Check **Company** under "Content types".

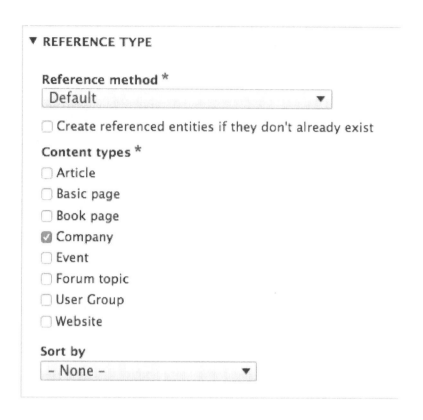

- When you save this field, check that your content type looks like the image below:

LABEL	MACHINE NAME	FIELD TYPE	OPERATIONS
Comments	comment	Comments	Edit ▾
Event Date	field_event_date	Date	Edit ▾
Event Description	body	Text (formatted, long, with summary)	Edit ▾
Event Logo	field_image	Image	Edit ▾
Event Price	field_event_price	Number (decimal)	Edit ▾
Event Sponsors	field_event_sponsors	Entity reference	Edit ▾
Event Website	field_website_link	Link	Edit ▾

TESTING THE FIELDS FOR THE EVENT CONTENT TYPE

In Chapter 5, when you created the Event content type, you

created a content item for DrupalCon Portland. Now that you've added all your extra fields, go back and add another event.

- Title: **DrupalCon Vienna**
- Event Description: **Drupal holds a big conference in North America every year, and it also holds one in Europe. In 2017, the European DrupalCon location is Vienna.**
- Event Logo: You can download this from https://ostraining.com/books/d8e/files/.
- Event Website: **https://events.drupal.org/vienna2017**
- Event Price: **$450.00**
- Event Date: **September 25, 2017**
- Event Sponsors: **Pantheon, OSTraining**

After you save this Event, your content should look like the image below.

DrupalCon Vienna

View | Edit | Outline | Delete

Submitted by steve on Mon, 01/30/2017 - 11:54

Drupal holds a big conference in North America every year, and but it also holds one in Europe. In 2017, the European DrupalCon location is Vienna.

Event Logo

Event Website
Click here to visit DrupalCon Vienna's website

Add new comment

Subject

Comment *

B *I* | :≡ ≡: 99 🖼 | Format ⌄ | 🔲 Source

Text format Basic HTML ⌵   About text formats ℹ

Save | Preview

Event Price
$450.00
Event Date
Mon, 09/25/2017 - 12:00
Event Sponsors
Pantheon
OSTraining

MANAGE DISPLAY EXPLAINED

So far in this chapter, we've added many fields. However, the fields are not displaying in a logical order. For example, with the Event content type, the Comments appear squashed on the right of the page. Why is this happening? The fields are being displayed in the order they were added.

There are some modules that can control the display of fields, and we'll talk about those later in the book. Using the Drupal core, we have two ways to control the display of fields:

• Manage form display

• Manage display

Manage Form Display

This option allows you to change the way that fields appear on the content creation pages.

We are going to change the way this looks given the tools provided by default in Drupal 8.

- Go to "Structure", "Content types".
- Click "Manage form display" for the Event content type.

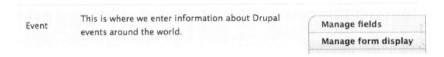

- This screen shows the fields you created, plus some other data such as the "URL alias" and "Authored on".

FIELD	WIDGET		
⊹ Event Name	Textfield ▾	Textfield size: 60	☼
⊹ Authored by	Autocomplete ▾	Autocomplete matching: Contains Textfield size: 60 No placeholder	☼
⊹ Authored on	Datetime Timestamp ▾		
⊹ Promoted to front page	Single on/off checkbox ▾	Use field label: Yes	☼
⊹ Sticky at top of lists	Single on/off checkbox ▾	Use field label: Yes	☼
⊹ URL alias	URL alias ▾		
⊹ Event Description	Text area with a summary ▾	Number of rows: 9 Number of summary rows: 3	☼
⊹ Event Logo	Image ▾	Preview image style: Thumbnail (100×100) Progress indicator: throbber	☼
⊹ Event Website	Link ▾	No placeholders	☼

We can rearrange these fields so they appear in a different order when creating new events.

- Notice the + sign to the left of the field label.
- Click, hold and drag the + sign. This allows you to move the field up and down the list.
- Try moving the Event Date field to the top of the page, under Event Name.

- Try moving "Event Sponsors" up to the same part of the screen.

You can also hide some data:

- Try moving "URL alias", "Sticky at top of lists" and "Promoted to the front page" into the Disabled area at the bottom of the screen.

Disabled

✛ URL alias	– Hidden – ▾
✛ Sticky at top of lists	– Hidden – ▾
✛ Promoted to front page	– Hidden – ▾

- Click "Save".
- Go to add new Event to your site, and you'll see that the content creation form has changed. The fields you moved to the top are more easily visible:

- Also, the "URL Path Settings" and "Promotion Options" boxes have vanished from options on the right-hand side.

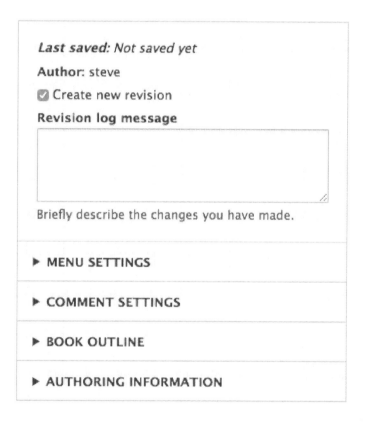

Manage Display

Now that we have changed what content creators see, let's look at how visitors will see these fields. Remember how the comments were squashed up on the events page, as with DrupalCon Vienna? Let's fix that now.

- Go to "Structure", "Content types".
- Click "Manage display" for the Event content type.

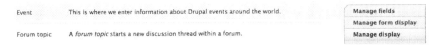

- Drag-and-drop the Comments field to the bottom of the page.
- Drag-and-drop the Event Logo field to the top but under Links.

This is how your Manage display screen will look.

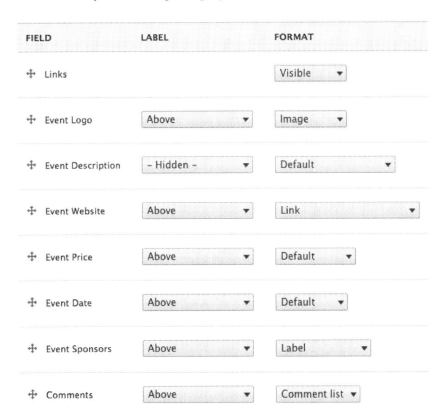

Links, in this instance, refer to the View, Edit, Outline, Delete, Revisions tabs that appear at the top of the content.

You will notice that the title field is not available in this list. In order to change the location of the title field, you will need to extend Drupal's functionality with a module. We will explore such options in Chapter 12, Layout Modules Explained.

We can change not only the order of the fields but also how they display. For example, we change the date format.

- Click the cog on the right-hand side of the Event Date row.

- You can now change the Time zone and the Date format.

- For this example, choose **HTML Date** and click the "Update" button.

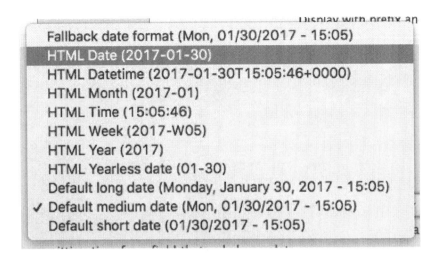

Fallback date format (Mon, 01/30/2017 - 15:05)
HTML Date (2017-01-30)
HTML Datetime (2017-01-30T15:05:46+0000)
HTML Month (2017-01)
HTML Time (15:05:46)
HTML Week (2017-W05)
HTML Year (2017)
HTML Yearless date (01-30)
Default long date (Monday, January 30, 2017 - 15:05)
✓ Default medium date (Mon, 01/30/2017 - 15:05)
Default short date (01/30/2017 - 15:05)

You can use a similar process to make sure all the Event logos are a similar size.

- Click the cog on the right-hand side of the Event Logo row.

- Change the "Image style" to Large. This will force all logos to show at about 220 pixels wide and 220 pixels high.

- Click the "Update" button.

We can also hide the labels. Many of the labels, such as "Event Logo" are so obvious that they don't need to be displayed. Some other labels just take up too much room.

- Click the "Label" dropdown for Event Logo and change it to **Hidden**. The Visually Hidden option allows for the label to be seen by screen readers but is hidden from the screen viewed by sighted individuals.

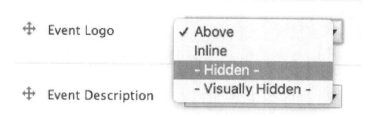

- For the following four fields, change the "Label" dropdown from **Above** to **Inline**. This will save space by putting each label on the same row as the data.

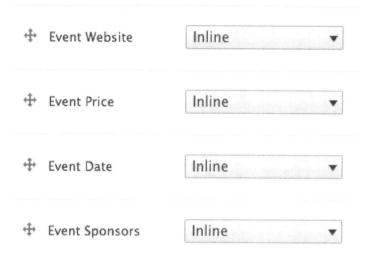

- Click "Save".
- Go to "Shortcuts", then "All content" and click on "DrupalCon Vienna". This is now your new Events layout should appear.

DrupalCon Vienna

View | Edit | Outline | Delete

Submitted by steve on Mon, 01/30/2017 - 11:54

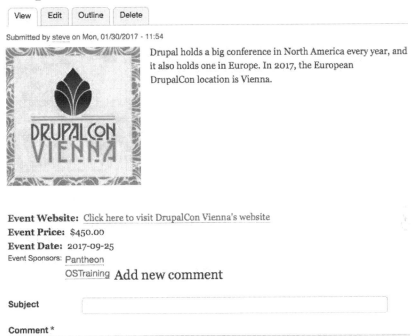

Drupal holds a big conference in North America every year, and it also holds one in Europe. In 2017, the European DrupalCon location is Vienna.

Event Website: Click here to visit DrupalCon Vienna's website
Event Price: $450.00
Event Date: 2017-09-25
Event Sponsors: Pantheon
OSTraining **Add new comment**

Subject

Comment *

B | I | ⊕ | ⧉ | ⋮≡ | ⋮≡ | 99 | 🖾 | Format ▾ | ⊠ Source

This is not a perfect layout for our Event content type, and on a real site we would make more changes to both "Manage form display and "Manage display", but this is a good start.

One thing to note: some changes are beyond the scope of this chapter.

- **Field positioning**: The Event Logo wants to float next to the Event Description, and the "Add new comment" text is out-of-place. This is managed at the CSS level of the Theme. We will look at Themes in Chapter 10, Themes Explained.

- **Fonts**: The fonts and bold settings are also different for the Event Sponsors field. Again, CSS changes need to be made if you want to stay with the default theme.

There's one more thing to talk about before we move on. This is something that often confuses Drupal beginners.

- Click "Home" in the main menu.
- On your site's frontpage, DrupalCon Vienna looks like the image below. If you click on "DrupalCon Vienna", you see the full layout that we just created.

DrupalCon Vienna

Submitted by steve on Mon, 01/30/2017 - 11:54

Read more   Add new comment

Drupal holds a big conference in North America every year, and it also holds one in Europe. In 2017, the European DrupalCon location is Vienna.

Why does the content look different on the frontpage? Because it is possible to show Drupal content in different formats on different pages.

- Go back to the Manage Display screen for the Event content type.
- Notice at the top of the page, there's a "Default" and "Teaser" tab.

Home » Administration » Structure » Content types » Event

- The "Default" tab controls what displays on the main content page.

- The "Teaser" tab controls what displays on the frontpage.

Let's see this in action:

- Click the "Teaser" tab.
- Move the "Event Logo" out of the "Disabled" area.
- Change the "Image style" to 100×100.
- Change the logo's Label to "Hidden".

- Click "Save" and go back to your site's frontpage.
- Notice that the Teaser version of your Event content has now been updated with the logo:

DrupalCon Vienna

Submitted by steve on Mon, 01/30/2017 - 11:54

Read more   Add new comment

Drupal holds a big conference in North America every year, and it also holds one in Europe. In 2017, the European DrupalCon location is Vienna.

In Drupal's terminology, Default and Teaser are examples of View modes. There is a whole area of Drupal dedicated to these under "Structure", then "Display modes", then "View modes".

You can also access View modes by clicking "Custom Display Settings" at the bottom of our current screen. If you wanted to, you could display the Event content type different in the "Print" display, in "RSS" feeds, and in search results.

Disabled

No field is hidden.

▼ CUSTOM DISPLAY SETTINGS

Use custom display settings for the following view modes
- ☐ Full content
- ☐ Print
- ☐ RSS
- ☐ Search index
- ☐ Search result highlighting input
- ☑ Teaser

Manage view modes

Save

FIELDS FOR THE USERS GROUPS CONTENT TYPE

We have one more content type to configure. Here are the fields for your User Group content type:

- **Body**: User Group Description

- **Link**: User Group Website

- **Text**: Meeting Location

- **Content Reference**: Organizers

Now set up those fields one by one. This time you can simplify the instructions even further. If you get stuck, look back to earlier sections in this chapter, and you'll see how to do these tasks.

- Edit the Body field and change the label from Body to **User Group Description**.

- Reuse the Link field and give it the label **User Group Website**. Don't forget to set the Allowed link type to External links only.
- Create a Text (plain) field and give it the label **Meeting Location**.

Similar to adding the Content reference field to the Event content type, this time you will add a User reference. The site user will be the group organizer.

- Click "Add field"
- Select "User" from the Add a new field dropdown.
- Enter **Organizers** for the label.
- On the next screen, select **Unlimited** for "Allowed number of values".
- Click Save field settings.
- Uncheck the option "Include the anonymous user". We want real users associated with the group.
- Select **Name** under "Sort by".

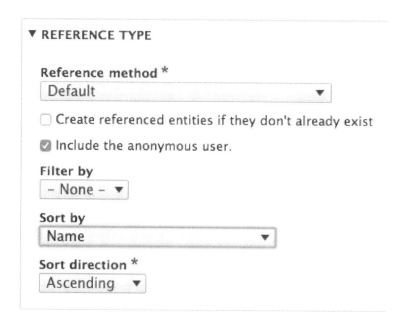

In Chapter 5, when you created the User Groups content type, you created a content item for the Atlanta group. Now that you've added all your extra fields, go back and add another user group.

Complete the content type form with the following:

- User Group Name: **Washington D.C. Drupal**

- User Group Description: **This group is for everyone living in the Washington D.C. metro area who's interested in Drupal.**

- Link URL: http://groups.drupal.org/washington-dc-drupalers

- Organizers: Choose yourself because you are the only current user.

- Address: Stetson's Famous Bar & Grill, 1610 U St, Washington, District of Columbia, 20009

As a final touch, improve the display of the fields:

- Go to the Manage display page for User groups.

- Set all the Labels to **Inline**, except for Description, which should remain set to **Hidden**.

- Use the crosses on the left of the screen; reorganize the fields so that they match as shown below.

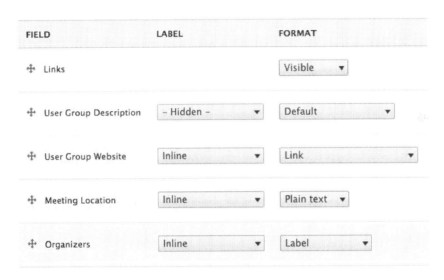

- Visit your content and it should now look like the image below.

Washington D.C. Drupal

Now you have one more task to complete your User Groups:

- Go and find your own local User Group. You might be in North America, Europe, Asia, Africa, or Australasia, but there is a good chance you'll find a Drupal User Group meeting near you. You can use a search engine or look on http://groups.drupal.org.

- Find the website, location, and information for your local user group and add it to your site via the User Group content type.

TAXONOMY EXPLAINED

Of all the fields available in Drupal, one is more frequently used, misused, explained, and misunderstood than any other: Term Reference.

Terms are part of Drupal's Taxonomy system. Taxonomy is Drupal's organizational system.

Each Taxonomy can contain multiple Vocabularies, the containers used to hold Terms. Here's an example of a Vocabulary and Terms that we could use to organize content about films.

Without realizing it, you've actually been using Taxonomy throughout this book. Whenever you have used the Tags field, you have used Taxonomy.

Because Taxonomy is so important, we're going to explain it in more detail than any other field. We show you how Tags works and then show you how to build your own ways to organize content.

Understanding the Term Reference Field: Terms

Let's start by looking at the Taxonomy screens.

- Go to "Manage", "Structure", then "Taxonomy".

- You'll see that Tags and Forums Vocabularies are listed on the page.

Notice that Drupal has a good explanation: "Taxonomy is for categorizing content. Terms are grouped into vocabularies. For example, a vocabulary called "Fruit" would contain the terms "Apple" and "Banana"."

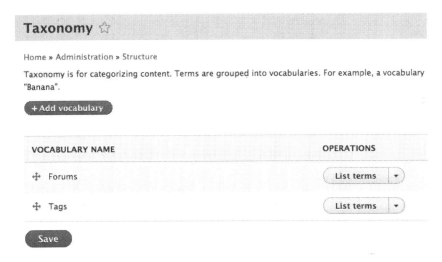

- Click "List terms" next to Tags, and you'll see the tags that you've entered so far.

NAME
✛ Books
✛ Drupal
✛ druplicon
✛ logo
✛ Training

Note: Drupal uses the word "Term" for the words you see in the image. "Tags" is only being used for this one vocabulary. If you are HTML savvy, please know these are not meta tags and will not impact your site's search engine optimization.

So, here's a quick recap:

- **Taxonomy**: This is the name given to the whole system of organizing content in Drupal.
- **Vocabulary**: This is the name given to a group of terms.
- **Terms**: These are the keywords and phrases that actually categorize your content.
- **Term reference field**: This is how your terms are connected to your content.

Now see an example of how this can work with your content types.

You can improve your Companies content type. You can allow

your companies to categorize themselves according to which language they speak.

Here's what you need to set up:

- **Vocabulary**: Languages
- **Terms**: English, Spanish, German, French, Chinese, and so on
- **Term reference field**: The field will be called "Languages Spoken" and attached to your Companies content type.

Why use a Term reference field, rather than List (Text)? There are at least a couple of good reasons, including:

- Taxonomy is more closely integrated with other parts of Drupal and will allow us to do more with this data, as we'll see later.
- Taxonomy is designed to handle a larger number of items. There are about 6,500 languages in the world, and if we entered all of those, a List (Text) field would not be able to handle them all.

The figure below shows a visual overview of that categorization, and the next steps walk you through the process.

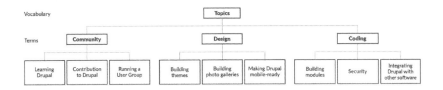

Creating the Vocabulary

- Go to "Structure", then "Taxonomy".
- Click "Add vocabulary".
- Name: **Languages Spoken**

- Description: **This is where companies can show the languages their staff speak**
- Click "Save".

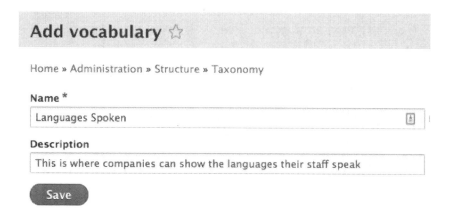

- On the next page, click "Add term".
- Name: **English.**
- Click "Save".

Repeat these steps for the remaining languages:

- Spanish
- German
- Italian
- French

- Chinese

- Japanese

Add as many as you like.

- When you're finished adding Languages, go to "Structure", "Content types".

- Click "manage fields" next to Company.

- Click "Add field".

- Select **Taxonomy term** from the "Add new field dropdown".

- Label: **Languages Spoken**

- Allowed number of values: **Unlimited**

- Check the box for **Languages Spoken** under "Available Vocabularies".

After saving this field, we can now control how the user adds languages.

- Click on the "Manage form display" tab.

- Scroll down to Languages Spoken and select **Check boxes/ Radio buttons** for its Widget.

- Click "Save".

Why did we choose check boxes? The default Autocomplete Widget is great for times when you want your users to select a term already in the list if they happen to enter it, but it also allows them to add new terms. However, it's also a guessing game as to the languages that can be selected. Check boxes allow the users to see all the available choices, and they allow users to easily choose more than one language.

- Go to "Shortcuts", "All content".
- Locate a Company that you have already created and click "Edit" in that row.
- You can now choose the languages spoken inside this company. If you want to remove the N/A option, go back to edit this field and make sure it is "Required".

So, that's the process that you can use for categorizing content in Drupal. However, Taxonomy can be much more flexible than you've seen so far.

Arranging Terms in a Simple Hierarchy

In this first example, we created terms but did not organize them. In this next example, let's see how terms can be structured into a hierarchy.

Let's add some terms to the Event content type. These terms enable Event organizers to show what topics will be covered during an event. Here's the plan for this task:

Vocabulary: Topics

Terms:

- Community:

  ◦ Learning Drupal

  ◦ Contributing to Drupal

  ◦ Running a User Group

- Design:

  ◦ Building themes

  ◦ Building photo galleries

  ◦ Making Drupal mobile-ready

- Coding:

  ◦ Building modules

  ◦ Security

  ◦ Integrating Drupal with other software

Term Reference field: The field will be called What Topics Will Be Covered? and attached to your Event content type.

Let's go through the process of setting up this vocabulary.

- Go to "Structure", then "Taxonomy".
- Click "Add vocabulary".
- **Name**: What Topics Will Be Covered?
- Click "Save".
- Click "Add term".
- Name: **Community,** and then click "Save".
- Name: **Learning Drupal,** and then click "Save".

- Name: **Contributing to Drupal,** and then click "Save".

- Name: **Running a User Group,** and then click "Save".

- Repeat that process for these four terms: Design, Building Themes, Building Photo Galleries, Making Drupal Mobile-Ready.

- Repeat that process for these four terms: Coding, Building Modules, Security, Integrating Drupal with Other Software.

- Go to "Structure", then "Taxonomy", and click "List terms" next to What Topics Will be Covered?

- You'll see a list of all your terms:

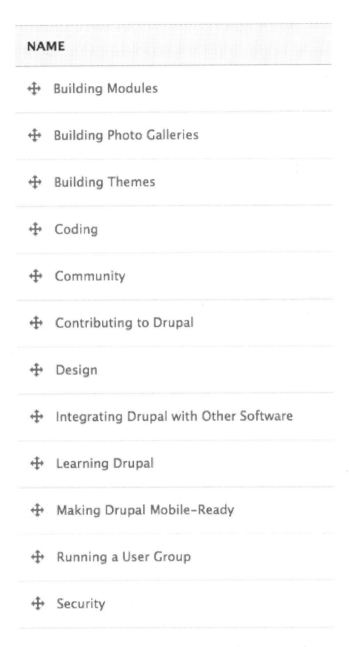

NAME
✛ Building Modules
✛ Building Photo Galleries
✛ Building Themes
✛ Coding
✛ Community
✛ Contributing to Drupal
✛ Design
✛ Integrating Drupal with Other Software
✛ Learning Drupal
✛ Making Drupal Mobile-Ready
✛ Running a User Group
✛ Security

- Now you can use the arrows next to each term to drag-and-drop each term. Your aim is to organize your terms to match your original plan.

NAME
✛ Community
✛   Learning Drupal
✛   Contributing to Drupal
✛   Running a User Group
✛ Design
✛   Building Themes
✛   Building Photo Galleries
✛   Making Drupal Mobile-Ready
✛ Coding
✛   Building Modules
✛   Integrating Drupal with Other Software
✛   Security

Now we can add these terms to the Event content type.

- Go to "Structure", "Content type", and then click "Manage Fields" next to Event.

- Select **Taxonomy term** from the "Add new field dropdown".

- Label: **What Topics Will Be Covered?**

- Allowed number of values: **Unlimited**

- Check the box for **What Topics Will Be Covered?** under "Available Vocabularies".

- After saving this field, click "Manage form display" and change the output of the field to **Check boxes/radio buttons**.

Go to "Find content" and click "edit" next to any of the events you've added. You can now choose to add the topics covered by that event.

What Topics Will Be Covered?

- ☐ Community
- ☐ -Learning Drupal
- ☑ -Contributing to Drupal
- ☑ -Running a User Group
- ☐ Design
- ☑ -Building Themes
- ☐ -Building Photo Galleries
- ☐ -Making Drupal Mobile-Ready
- ☐ Coding
- ☑ -Building Modules
- ☐ -Integrating Drupal with Other Software
- ☐ -Security

Arranging Terms in a Complex Hierarchy

So far you've seen three ways in which terms can be organized:

- **Tags**: The terms are completely unorganized with no hierarchy.

- **Languages Spoken**: The terms are ordered with no hierarchy.

- **What Topics Will Be Covered?**: The terms are ordered and in a simple hierarchy where many terms are organized under parent terms.

There is a fourth option: You can have a complex hierarchy where one term has multiple parents.

Now you can see an example of how this might work. Let's assume that the terms Building Themes and Making Drupal Mobile-Ready need to be added again, only this time, under another parent term.

Our new term list will look like this:

- Community:

  - Learning Drupal

  - Contributing to Drupal

  - Running a User Group

- Design:

  - Building themes

  - Building photo galleries

  - Making Drupal mobile-ready

- Coding:

  - Building modules

  - Building themes

  - Making Drupal mobile-ready

- Security

- Integrating Drupal with other software

Now see how you can organize terms in this way:

- Go to "Structure", "Taxonomy".

- Click "List terms" next to What Topics Will Be Covered?

- Click "Edit" next to Building themes.

- Click "Relations".

- Using your cursor, you can select more than one parent term. Depending on the type of computer you use, you may also need to touch a key such as Shift or Command. In the example shown below, we're selecting both Design and Coding.

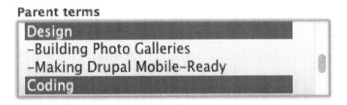

Save this new setting and you can see that Building Themes is now underneath two terms.

Design

Building Themes

Building Photo Galleries

Making Drupal Mobile-Ready

Coding

Building Modules

Building Themes

- Try and repeat that process for Making Drupal mobile-ready.

There are two potential disadvantages to this process.

- **Drag-and-drop organization**: The drag-and-drop feature will not work any longer. You must rearrange all the terms by clicking Edit, Relations and selecting a parent.

- **Content Overlap**: If your intent is to distinguish between content related to coding and building themes versus designing the theme, you have not accomplished that. The Building Themes term will, if clicked by a user, return all content under design and coding associated with building themes.

You might be thinking, "Well, I will just make two Building Themes terms."

You could do that, but, you will introduce a usability issue. Imagine that you are a visitor to a site and you see two links for Building Themes because both instances of Building Themes were assigned to content. Which one do you select? Do you want to have to click on both to see the different options?

If you choose to create a new instance of Building Themes (versus assigning it to multiple parents), then consider using different words:

- Designing Themes
- Coding Themes

These alternatives are direct and specific.

WHAT'S NEXT?

Now see what your Drupalville site looks like at the end of this chapter. It should look like the image below.

Don't worry if your site doesn't match this exactly. The aim of this book is to help you learn Drupal, rather than prove you can exactly follow our instructions. If you understand the concepts covered in this chapter, you'll be fine to move on to Chapter 7.

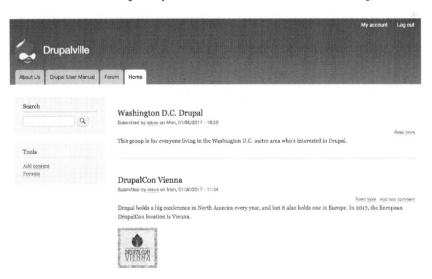

Chapters 5 and 6 showed you how content works in Drupal. However, most websites don't just have content, they also have features. In Chapter 7, you move beyond Drupal's default content options and add features to your site.

We are moving on to Step 5 in the Drupal workflow: Install Modules and Themes.

1. **Planning**

2. **Content types**

3. **Fields**

4. **Add content**

5. **Install Modules and Themes**

6. **Views**

7. **Layout Modules**

8. **Finish the Design**

9. **Users**

10. **Site Management**

CHAPTER 7.

DRUPAL MODULES EXPLAINED

If you've used a mobile phone in the last few years, you can understand modules. Modules in Drupal are like the apps on a phone. Modules are the source of all the features on our Drupal sites.

We've already seen modules in the previous chapters such as "Drupal Content Explained". In that chapter, you went to the Extend page on your site and turned on two core modules: Book and Forum.

In his chapter, we are going to repeat that process by turning on the Telephone module, a field we can add to Events. We are also going to install additional modules from Drupal.org.

In this chapter, we are going to not only extend our content-based features and functionality, we are going to introduce some common functionality that you might find helpful.

- **Telephone** – a module that adds an telephone number field to a content type.

- **Simple GMap** – Another field for events. This one puts a map on your content page.

- **Video Embed** – Another way to add depth to your article content is to include a video, enhancing your text.

- **Contact** – A module that can create a contact page for your site.

- **Poll** – A content type that enables you to ask a simple question of your site visitors and collect their answers.

- **Add To Any** – A module that adds a content related feature, the ability for your site visitors to share your content pages.

- **Sitemap** – A fast and easy way to provide your visitors a page showing the structure of your site at a glance.

You might be wondering how you might find the modules you need for your site. We will also show you how to research and evaluate modules on Drupal.org.

So, at the end of this chapter, you will be able to:

- Locate modules on Drupal.org.

- Install modules on your site.

- Configure different types of modules.

IMPROVE THE EVENT CONTENT TYPE

We're going to improve our Event Content Type by enabling the existing Telephone module. We're also going to add a module to handle addresses and maps, which we will download from Drupal.org.

Add a Telephone Field

When you enabled Book and Forum, you added two content types to your site. The Telephone module adds a field, which can be added to any content type.

- Go to "Manage", then "Extend".

- Scroll down to the section of modules called Field types.

- Check the box for Telephone.

- Click "Install" at the bottom of the screen.

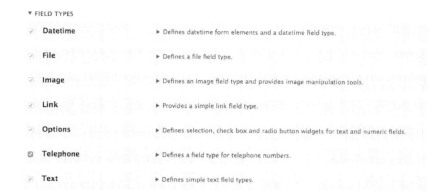

When you turned on the Book and Forum modules, everything was automatically ready to use. In contrast, the Telephone module needs you to put it into action.

- Go to "Structure", then "Content types".
- Click on "Manage fields" for the Event content type.
- Click "Add field".
- Select the "Telephone" field.
- Label: **Phone Number**
- Finish saving the field.

Let's customize how the Phone Number field is displayed:

- Click on the "Manage Display" tab.
- Label: **Inline**
- Format: **Telephone link**

Add a Map Field

The next improvement we want to make, which is specific to the Event content type, is to add a map of the event location. This time the module is not already loaded into your Drupal site, as with Telephone, Book, and Forum.

- In a new browser window or tab, go to http://drupal.org/project/simple_gmap.

- Scroll down until you see the Downloads section, as shown below.

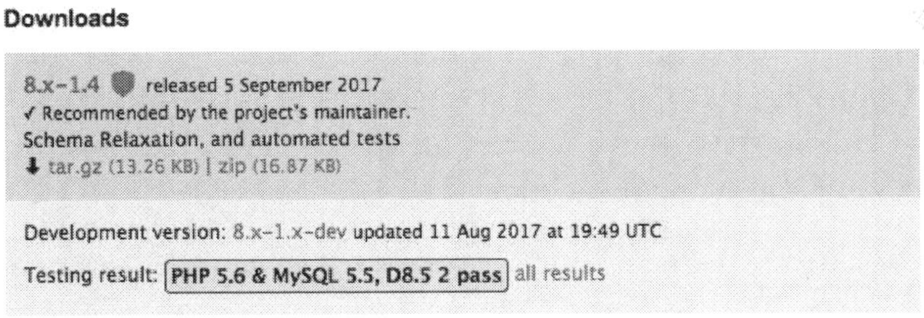

Downloads

8.x–1.4 released 5 September 2017
✓ Recommended by the project's maintainer.
Schema Relaxation, and automated tests
⬇ tar.gz (13.26 KB) | zip (16.87 KB)

Development version: 8.x-1.x-dev updated 11 Aug 2017 at 19:49 UTC

Testing result: PHP 5.6 & MySQL 5.5, D8.5 2 pass all results

- Right click the tar.gz link for the Drupal 8 version of this module, and copy the link to your clipboard. The link you copy will look like this https://ftp.drupal.org/files/projects/simple_gmap-8.x-1.2.tar.gz.

- Return to the browser window or tab with your website.

- Click "Extend".

- Click the blue "Install new module" button.

- Paste the link from Drupal.org into the "Install from a URL" field.

Install new module ☆

Home » Administration » Extend

You can find modules and themes on drupal.org. The following file extensions are supported: *tar tgz gz bz2 zip*.

Install from a URL

```
https://ftp.drupal.org/files/projects/simple_gmap-8.x-1.2.tar.gz
```

For example: *http://ftp.drupal.org/files/projects/name.tar.gz*

Or

Upload a module or theme archive to install

[Choose File] No file chosen

For example: *name.tar.gz* from your local computer

[Install]

- Click "Install", and you'll see the screen below.
- Click "Enable newly added modules". Note: This link does not actually enable the module you just installed to your web server. It just means you are returning to the Extend page so you can turn on the module.

Drupalville

Update manager

✓ Installation was completed successfully.

simple_gmap

- Installed *simple_gmap* successfully

Next steps

- Install another module
- Enable newly added modules
- Administration pages

- Scroll down until you see the "Simple Google Maps" module in the Field types section and check the box.
- Click "Install".

The setup for this module has two parts: create the field, then manage its display.

- Go to the Content types area, and click on "Manage fields" for the Event content type.
- Add field and select the **Text (plain)** field.
- Label: **Address and Map**
- Help: **Enter an address that Google Maps can recognize in the plain text field.**
- Save the field.

Now, let's make this field display the address and a map.

- Click the "Manage display" tab.
- Select the format: "Google Map from one-line address".

You can also click the cog in the Address and Map row, in order to change some map settings:

- Change "Width of embedded map" to 400 and "Height of embedded map" to 400.
- Check the box "Include original address text".
- Click "Update".
- On this screen, let's also put Comments in the right place. Drag Comments to the bottom of the layout, under Address and Map.

- Click "Save".

In order to see your work in action, you need to either edit an existing event or create a new one.

- Go to the Content screen and edit DrupalCon Vienna.

- Phone Number: Enter a fake number, such as 123-456-7890.

- Address and Map: **Messe Wien Exhibition & Congress Center, Messeplatz 1, 1021 Wien, Austria**

- Click "Save and keep published".

- Visit your DrupalCon Vienna content and it will look like the image below:

Phone Number: 123-456-7890
Address and Map

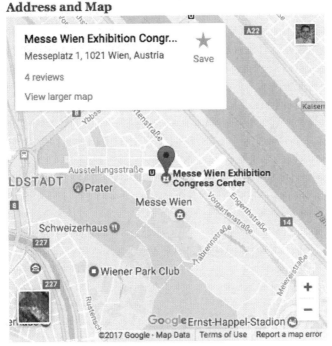

Messeplatz 1, 1021 Wien, Austria

Add new comment

IMPROVE THE ARTICLE CONTENT TYPE

The Event content type isn't the only type of content we can improve. Stories can be told by video, as well as text, so let's upgrade the Article content type.

Add a Video Field

As you might imagine, you have several options when adding video to your web pages. At the heart of this process is to decide if you want to upload the video or to link to it. In this example, we're going to pull in a video hosted on YouTube.

- In a new browser window or tab, go to https://www.drupal.org/project/video_embed_field.

- Scroll down until you see the release section.

- Right click the tar.gz link for the Drupal 8 version of this module, and copy the link to your clipboard.

- Return to the browser window or tab with your website.

- Click "Extend", then "Install New Module".

- Paste the link from Drupal.org into the Install from a URL field.

- Click "Install".

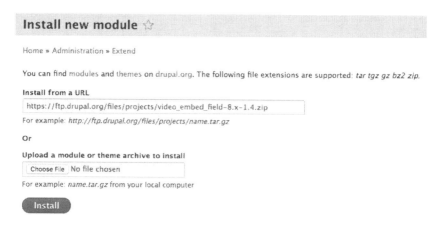

- Click "Enable newly added modules".

- Scroll down until you see the section labeled Video Embed

Field. You will see three modules this time, each installed by the recent install process.

- Check the boxes for "Video Embed Field" and "Video Embed WYSIWYG". The third box "Video Embed Media" can't be checked because it relies on some other modules. That's OK, because we don't need it for this task.

- Click "Install".

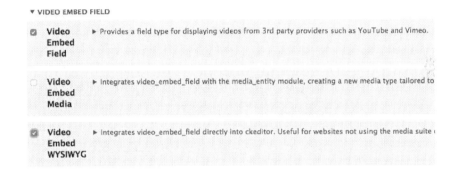

Let's add the field to the Article content type.

- Go to the Content types, and click "Add field".
- Add a new field: **Video embed**
- Label: **Video**
- Save the field.
- Click "Manage display" and move Comments to the bottom, under the Video field. Don't forget to save.

And finally, let's create a new Article to test this field.

- Go to create a new Article.
- Title: **Have you seen the Drupal training on YouTube?**
- Body: **There's a free Drupal 8 training class online. You should check it out.**
- Tags: **Drupal, Training, Videos**

- Image: We can leave this empty.

- Video: **https://www.youtube.com/watch?v=-DYSucV1_9w**

When you save and visit your new article, it will look like the image below, with a video embed:

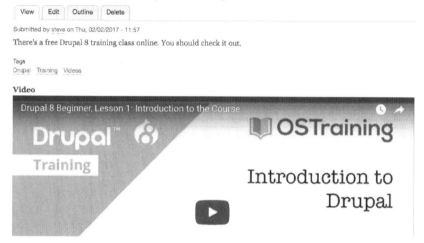

ALLOW VISITORS TO PROVIDE FEEDBACK

There are different ways to allow visitors to interact with your site. You can collect feedback from your site visitors, or you can ask them to share your content with others.

In this section, we will:

- Configure the contact form.
- Add a poll question.
- Include a share feature called AddtoAny.

Provide a Contact Form

Just like the Book, Forum, and Telephone modules, the Contact form is also available and ready to use.

- Start by going to "Structure, then "Contact forms".

- You'll see two contact forms ready for your use.

The "Personal contact form" appears on every user profile page. This is used by visitors to send email messages to the members of your site.

The Website feedback form is a default contact form ready to be added to your menu.

The contact forms can be heavily customized, as we'll see in this next exercise:

- Click on the "Website feedback" link to see the data that is collected by default.

Website feedback

Your name

steve

Your email address

steve@ostraining.com

Subject *

Message *

Notice that your name and email address is filled in because you are logged in. If you want to see what visitors see, you can log out.

- Click back in the browser, returning to the Contact forms admin page.
- Click the dropdown next to Website Feedback and select "Manage field".

This should look familiar. The contact form might not be a content type, but it uses the same field functionality. Unfortunately, you can't reuse the fields you created for content types, but that's okay. We can make them again.

- Test your memory, and add a field: **Telephone number**.

- Click "Manage form display" and move your new field above the "Message" field.

- Visit your contact form and it will look like the image below:

Website feedback

Your name
steve

Your email address
steve@ostraining.com

Subject *

Telephone number

Message *

Now, let's try a more detailed test of what you've learned so far. Try adding and configuring these two fields:

- List (Text): Give it a label of **Which of the following best describes you?** For the options: Manager, Developer, Themer, Trainer, and Other.

- List (Text): Give it a label of **When will you build your Drupal site?** For the options: Now, Within 3 months, Within 6 months, and Unknown.

- Go to "Manage form display" and move "Message" to the bottom of the form.

- Disable the "Subject" and "Send copy to sender" fields.

- Change the widgets from "Select list" to "Check boxes/radio buttons".

Save your changes and visit your updated contact form. You will see that the form is now heavily customized.

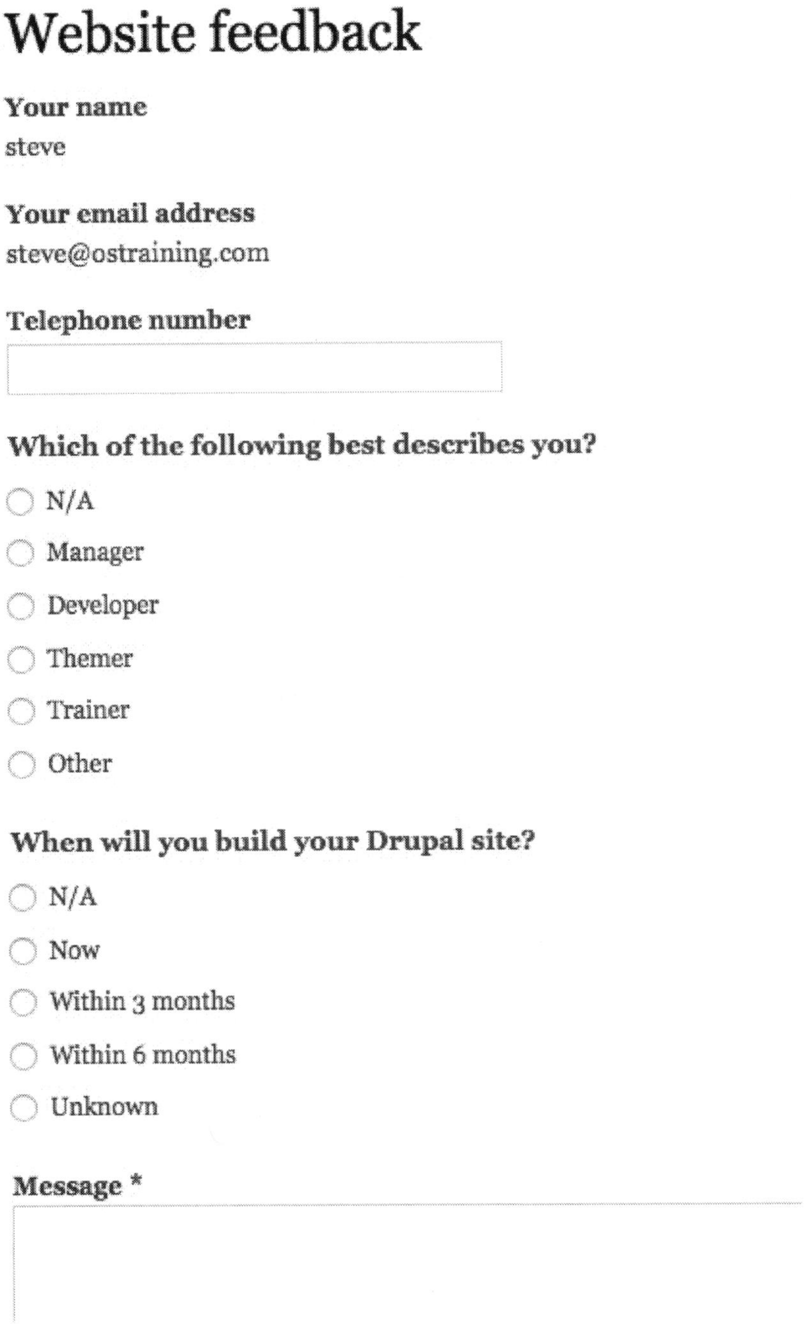

Website feedback

Your name

steve

Your email address

steve@ostraining.com

Telephone number

Which of the following best describes you?

○ N/A

○ Manager

○ Developer

○ Themer

○ Trainer

○ Other

When will you build your Drupal site?

○ N/A

○ Now

○ Within 3 months

○ Within 6 months

○ Unknown

Message *

You can control which email address the messages are going to by clicking "Edit" on the "Contact forms" screen. However, at the moment, this module doesn't provide any way to store messages.

Ask a Poll Question

In addition to creating contact forms, you can collect feedback from site visitors by asking poll questions.

- In a new browser window or tab, go to http://drupal.org/project/poll.
- Using the process we used earlier in this chapter, take the link from Drupal.org.
- Add the Poll module into your site, check the Poll box on the "Extend" page and install this module.

Let's see the module in action.

- Go to "Shortcuts", then "Allcontent".
- Click on the "Polls" tab. If you don't see this tab, go to "Configuration", then "Performance" and clear the cache.

- Click "Add a poll".
- Question: **Do you like Drupal?**
- Choices: **Yes, No, I'm getting there slowly**.
- Click "Save".
- Click the "Do you like Drupal?" link and you can see the poll page. Try a test vote, and you'll see the results.

Do you like Drupal?

View	Edit	Delete

○ Yes

○ No

○ I'm getting there slowly

(Vote)

Having the poll displayed in this way isn't ideal for many sites. Later in this book, we'll show you how to place this poll into a "block", so you can put it in your site's sidebar.

Adding Social Sharing Links

Have you ever visited a web page and thought, "This would be a great page to share on Facebook or Twitter"? The Share Buttons by AddToAny module is one of the modules that provide this feature.

- Go to http://drupal.org/project/addtoany. Get this module, and install it into your site.

- Go to your site's homepage, and you'll see that social bookmarking icons have been added to the Articles content type.

So, why are these links appearing on Articles, but no other content types?

- Go to "Structure", then "Content types".
- Click "Manage display" next to Articles.

Scroll down, and you'll see that "AddToAny" is acting like a field. This is true only for "Article" and "Basic page".

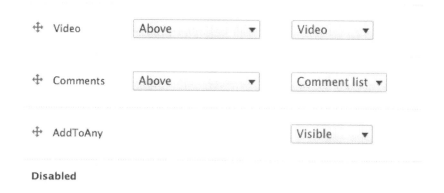

On the other hand, if you click "Manage display" next to any new content type, such as Event, the result will be different. For new content types, "AddToAny" appears in the "Disabled" area by default. If you want to show social bookmarks for this content, you'll need to drag-and-drop the AddToAny field to make it visible.

⊹ Comments	Inline ▼	Comment list ▼
Disabled		
⊹ AddToAny		– Hidden – ▼

▶ CUSTOM DISPLAY SETTINGS

[Save]

ADDING SEO SUPPORT TO DRUPAL

In this next activity, we will look at the basics of adding HTML meta tags to your pages.

There is some debate as to whether the HTML meta tags make a difference to search engines. Once upon a time, web page developers would fill the HTML meta keyword tag and the meta description tag with lots of data in order to gain the interest of a search engine. Today, search engines are smarter and don't need to rely on meta tags to understand your site.

However, meta tags still have some uses, including making your site details look good in search engine results.

In this next activity, we're going to add meta tags to your pages via the Metatags module.

- Go to http://drupal.org/project/metatag and try to install that module into your site.

What do you notice when you try to install Metatag?

The "Requires" area for Metatag says that it requires the Token module, which is missing.

- Go to http://drupal.org/project/token and install that module into your site.

- Now you should be able to successfully install Metatag. Note that there are over a dozen sub-modules. You only need to enable "Metatag".

Once again, we have a module that is ready to go after installed, but that does not mean we can't fine-tune the settings. Let's experiment with the Article content type.

- Go to "Structure", "Content types" then "Manage fields" for Article.

- Add a new field: **Meta tags**

- Label: **Meta Tags**

- Save the field.

- We don't want the meta tag data showing when a user visits the site, so click on the "Manage Display" tab and drag the Meta Tags field to Disabled.

Let's test out the new metadata option.

- Click on "Add content" from the "Shortcuts" menu.
- Click "Article".
- On the right, expand the "Meta Tags" tab. Notice the [node:title] inserts? These are tokens, from the Token module that we installed. [node:title] will automatically insert the Article title. [site:name] will automatically insert your site title.

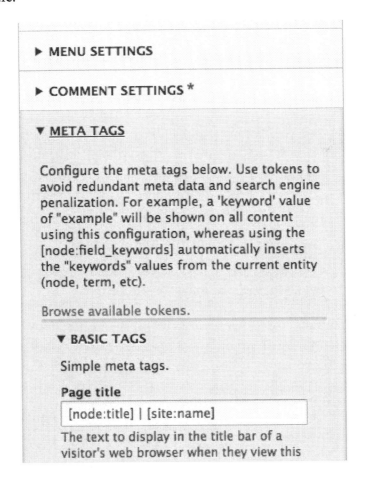

► MENU SETTINGS

► COMMENT SETTINGS *

▼ META TAGS

Configure the meta tags below. Use tokens to avoid redundant meta data and search engine penalization. For example, a 'keyword' value of "example" will be shown on all content using this configuration, whereas using the [node:field_keywords] automatically inserts the "keywords" values from the current entity (node, term, etc).

Browse available tokens.

▼ BASIC TAGS

Simple meta tags.

Page title

[node:title] | [site:name]

The text to display in the title bar of a visitor's web browser when they view this

Create your article with the following information:

- Title: **Article with Meta Tags**
- Body: **This is the content that will show in the Meta Description.**

Save the article, and using your browser, view the source code of your site. The image below is what you will see on this page.

- The [node:title] and [site:name] tokens have automatically filled in the meta title.
- Your Body field has automatically filled in the meta description.

```
<head>
    <meta charset="utf-8" />
<meta name="title" content="Article with Meta Tags | Drupalville" />
<meta name="description" content="This is the content that will show in the Meta Description." />
<meta name="Generator" content="Drupal 8 (https://www.drupal.org)" />
```

FINDING MODULES EXPLAINED

So far in this chapter, we hand-picked modules for you to use. However, as you build your own sites you're going to need to find extra modules. In the next part of the chapter, we're going to show you how to evaluate the modules available for Drupal and whether they are the right choice for you.

If you have used almost any other blogging platform or content management system, you will find some things to be surprising and different about Drupal, including these:

- Modules that extend your site's features and functionality are hosted on Drupal.org. It's never recommended to download modules from other sites. Drupal provides security checks on all the files you download from Drupal.org.
- All modules are free. Drupal companies make the money from many sources such as selling the services, training or hosting,

but there is a general feeling in the Drupal community that modules should not be sold.

- Collaboration, not competition. You won't find many modules with duplicate features. With other platforms, it's not unusual to find many solutions to the same problem. Drupal tries to encourage people working on a problem to collaborate and work on the same module.

- There are no ratings or reviews of modules. There is data available about how many sites use each module, but there are no subjective reviews.

HOW TO SEARCH FOR MODULES

Now that you know that you can find all Drupal modules for free on Drupal.org, see how to find modules.

Go to https://drupal.org/project/project_module. As you can see there are more than 36,000 modules hosted here on Drupal.org.

By default, the modules are sorted from the Most installed to the Least installed, so the most commonly installed Drupal modules are on top of the list.

Download & Extend

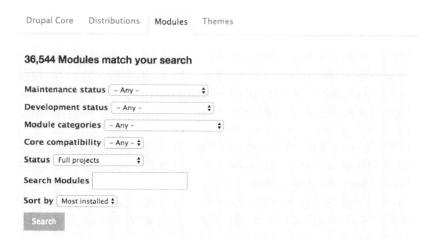

If you're searching for a module, there is a detailed search box on the top of this page. You can see that there are ways that you can filter the results. You can search by the category of module:

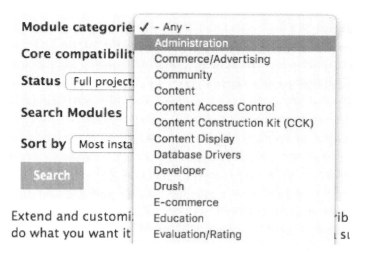

You can search by Drupal version. Because we need modules that are available for Drupal 8, this will be very useful:

You can use the Search Modules field to search by keyword:

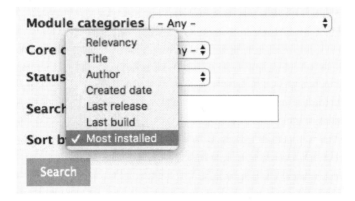

Finally, you can choose how Drupal.org returns your results, as shown in the image below. Don't overlook this option. If you entered a keyword in the previous Search Modules field, you'll probably want to change this option to "Relevancy". If you don't, you won't find the most relevant module, but only the most installed module that contains your keyword somewhere in the description.

When you search, Drupal.org now returns your search results, as shown below. From here you can click through and find out more about each module.

Extend and customize Drupal functionality with contributed modules. If a module doesn't quite do what you want it to do, if you find a bug or have a suggestion, then join forces and help the module maintainer. Or, share your own by starting a new module.

Media entity YouTube

Posted by slashrsm on *September 9, 2014 at 11:25am*

YouTube integration for Media entity module.

This module is obsolete! It is suggested to use Video embed field **module for YouTube (and many other) videos.**

Read more · Report as spam · Categories: Unsupported , Obsolete , Media

HOW TO EVALUATE MODULES

Each Drupal module is different and needs to be evaluated before you use it.

There is no official stamp of approval or certification given to Drupal modules. The Drupal community does aim to ensure some things about each module. They ensure that the module installs. They also ensure that the code is completely open source and unencrypted. Beyond that, you'll need to rely on a variety of techniques to evaluate modules.

Let's look at a couple modules and show you our recommended techniques to evaluate modules.

Token is a very popular module and that will be our example. Visit https://drupal.org/project/token and you'll see a screen, as shown below:

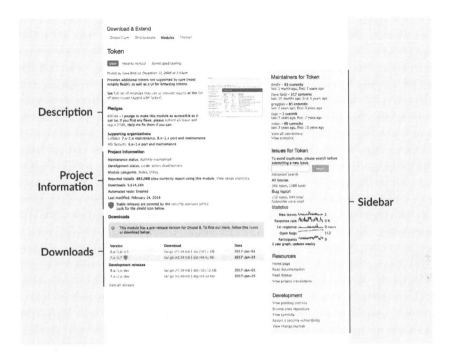

We are going to encourage you to evaluate each module based on four different criteria, and it involves the four areas of the page that you can see marked above.

- **Description**: This area gives you an overview of all the module's key features and requirements.

- **Project Information**: This area tells you if this module is actively updated and maintained, plus how many sites have installed it.

- **Downloads**: This area tells you if there is a module available for your Drupal version and if it is stable or perhaps only released in an Alpha or Beta version.

- **Sidebar**: This area shows you the people who coded the module and when they were last active. It also provides important links such as issues users have found and documentation for the module.

Area 1: Description

This is the area that requires the least explanation. It should provide a clear explanation of what this module does.

If the module's introduction makes it clear that this isn't what you need, end your evaluation and move on.

If the module's introduction isn't clear, you're not the first person to think that. These introductions are often geeky and contain Drupal jargon that you won't understand without more experience. If this does lead to you getting stuck, we have some advice at the end of this chapter in the section.

As you can see below, the description for Token is somewhat short:

Posted by Dave Reid on *December 31, 2006 at 1:44am*

Provides additional tokens not supported by core (most notably fields), as well as a UI for browsing tokens.

See full list of modules that use or provide tokens or the list of open issues tagged with 'token'.

Pledges

#D7AX – I pledge to make this module as accessible as it can be. If you find any flaws, please submit an issue and tag it D7AX. Help me fix them if you can.

Area 2: Project Information

This area at the bottom of the page contains some useful information.

First, it tells you if the module is actively maintained and updated.

Second, it tells you if the module is frequently downloaded or installed. The most popular Drupal modules have been downloaded more than eight million times and are run on more than a million websites.

Finally, it tells you when the module was last updated. If a module hasn't been updated recently, be cautious. It might mean that the module works perfectly and doesn't need updating, but it might also mean the module's coders are not providing necessary updates and fixes.

This image shows you the Information area for Token. This proves that Google Analytics is a module that is regularly updated and is trusted by a lot of users.

Project Information

Maintenance status: Actively maintained

Development status: Under active development

Module categories: Rules, Utility

Reported installs: **852,302** sites currently report using this module. View usage statistics.

Downloads: 5,559,057

Automated tests: Enabled

Last modified: February 14, 2016

This next image shows the Information area for another module. Be much more careful installing this one.

Project Information

Maintenance status: Minimally maintained

Development status: Maintenance fixes only

Module categories: Developer, Utility

Reported installs: **2** sites currently report using this module. View usage statistics.

Downloads: 5,056

Last modified: August 4, 2016

Stable releases are covered by the security advisory policy.
Look for the shield icon below.

Area 3: Downloads

This area is the most important of all. If there isn't a version of the module available for your version of Drupal, then you stop your evaluation right here and start looking elsewhere.

Drupal.org places the recommended modules in the top boxes. In the image below, you can see the label, "Recommended by the project's maintainer".

Underneath, there is a "Development version" which should be used only if no recommended version is available.

In the image below, you can see the difference between 8.x-1.5, which is recommended, and 8.x.1.x-dev, which is only a development release.

Downloads

8.x-1.5 🛡 released 26 April 2017
✓ Recommended by the project's maintainer.
⬇ tar.gz (280.33 KB) | zip (330.15 KB)

Development version: 8.x-1.x-dev updated 28 Jun 2017 at 07:54 UTC

Testing result: PHP 7 & MySQL 5.5, D8.4 112 pass all results

7.x-2.0-beta11 released 7 September 2015
✓ Recommended by the project's maintainer.
⬇ tar.gz (178.27 KB) | zip (184.33 KB)

Development version: 7.x-2.x-dev updated 8 Sep 2015 at 20:38 UTC

View all releases

Area 4: Sidebar

It was straightforward to explain the information contained in the first three areas on a module page. The fourth area, the sidebar, contains much more information and is much more diverse. The image below shows the sidebar on the Token page. Here's what's in each of the four areas:

- **Maintainers**: This is some of the most important information of all about a module. This module has five maintainers, one of whom was active one month ago. However, sometimes this area shows only one maintainer who hasn't been active for years. Be cautious with those modules.

- **Issues**: This area provides links to all potential bugs that people have found with the module. A high number is not necessarily a bad thing because the more popular it is, the more bugs people are likely to find. At first, it won't be easy for you to get useful information from this area, but as you get more experience, you can read the list of issues and look for potential problems.

- **Resources**: This area contains key links. Perhaps the most important of all is the documentation link. Not all modules have documentation, and you should probably avoid those that don't.

Maintainers for Token

Berdir – **83 commits**
last: 1 month ago, first: 2 years ago

Dave Reid – **317 commits**
last: 10 months ago, first: 6 years ago

greggles – **85 commits**
last: 6 years ago, first: 9 years ago

fago – **1 commit**
last: 7 years ago, first: 7 years ago

eaton – **69 commits**
last: 7 years ago, first: 10 years ago

View all committers
View commits

Issues for Token

To avoid duplicates, please search before submitting a new issue.

[   ] **Search**

Advanced search

All issues

339 open, 1382 total

Bug report

111 open, 543 total
Subscribe via e-mail

Statistics

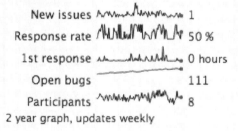

New issues ‸‸‸‸‸‸‸‸ 1
Response rate ‸‸‸‸‸‸‸ 50 %
1st response ‸‸‸‸‸‸ 0 hours
Open bugs 111
Participants ‸‸‸‸‸‸ 8

2 year graph, updates weekly

Resources

Home page

Read documentation

Read license

View project translations

DO YOU NEED HELP TO FIND THE RIGHT MODULE?

Sometimes it can be hard to find the right module.

You might be stuck because you don't know the right word for what you're trying to do.

You might be stuck because none of the modules are descriptively named, so their actual functionality is not clear.

You might be stuck because the feature you need is only available by combining multiple modules, and it's not clear which modules you need.

You might be stuck because there just isn't a module available to provide the feature you need.

Regardless, you're going to get stuck at some point. Here are some suggestions for how to move forward if you're stuck while looking for a module:

- **Ask**: Log in to Drupal.org and ask about your problem: https://drupal.org/forum. The Drupal community is also active on public chats. You can find out more about joining and asking your questions at https://www.drupal.org/irc.

- **Search**: There's a lot more information on the web than is available on Drupal.org. Use Google or your favorite search engine to look for suggestions.

- **Email us**: Send an email to support@ostraining.com. We can give you some guidance.

TESTING MODULES

There is one golden rule that you must follow when testing a Drupal module.

Never, ever install a Drupal module for the first time on a live site. Always have a second Drupal site that you use for testing, such as the one you use throughout this book.

Why do we recommend always using a test site? Because websites are not exact or scientific. Modules that work fine on one site can fail on other sites. Some modules can cause conflict with other modules. You do need to test all modules thoroughly before adding them to your live site.

WHAT'S NEXT?

In this chapter, you added features to your site by using modules. You saw that modules come in all sorts of different forms:

- Configuring modules is not always consistent from one module to the next.

- Modules can have dependencies on other modules.

- Modules can add additional functionality to an existing module.

- Modules can create pages and blocks.

You also saw how to evaluate and test modules before you use them on a live site.

Now we know how to add features to Drupal. Your Drupalville site should look like the final image in this chapter. Don't worry if it's not exact. The important thing is that you understand the concepts behind this chapter. If you feel that you know how to search for, evaluate, install and use modules, then you're ready to move on.

So our site now has content, fields, and features. What it does not have is much organization that the visitor can see.

In Chapter 8, "Drupal Menus Explained", we're going to explore our site's navigation and show you how to create and organize menus.

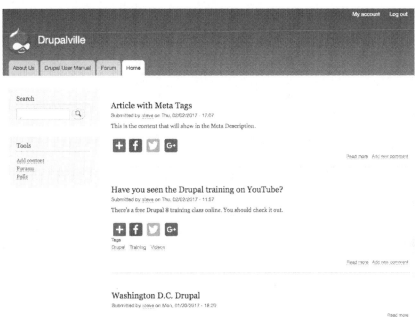

Drupalville

About Us | Drupal User Manual | Forum | Home

Search

Tools

Add content
Forums
Polls

Article with Meta Tags

Submitted by steve on Thu, 02/02/2017 - 17:07

This is the content that will show in the Meta Description.

Read more   Add new comment

Have you seen the Drupal training on YouTube?

Submitted by steve on Thu, 02/02/2017 - 11:57

There's a free Drupal 8 training class online. You should check it out.

Tags
Drupal   Training   Videos

Read more   Add new comment

Washington D.C. Drupal

Submitted by steve on Mon, 01/30/2017 - 18:29

Read more

This group is for everyone living in the Washington D.C. metro area who's interested in Drupal.

CHAPTER 8.

DRUPAL MENUS EXPLAINED

Menus are just one way to create navigation on your Drupal site; however, they are the primary way, hence, they are kind of a big deal. Without any menus, your visitors will be stuck on your site's homepage.

Because we are just covering the basics of how Drupal menus work, this is going to be a short chapter. The reason? In Chapters 9 through 12, you discover new features that enable you to get more out of your navigation.

At the end of this chapter, you should be able to:

- Describe the purpose of the five default Drupal menus.
- Add new menu links.
- Reorganize menu links.

THE FIVE DEFAULT DRUPAL MENUS

Start your exploration of Drupal's menus by exploring the five available menus.

- Click Structure and then Menus. You now see the five default menus: Administration, Footer, Main navigation, Tools, and User account menu.

+ Add menu

TITLE	DESCRIPTION
Administration	Administrative task links
Footer	Site information links
Main navigation	Site section links
Tools	User tool links, often added by modules
User account menu	Links related to the active user account

Now let's see what each menu does on your site.

- Click "Edit menu" next to Administration menu. These links correspond to the white admin bar you've been using throughout your book. Do not modify this menu until you have more experience. Otherwise, you might find yourself feeling quite lost!

MENU LINK
✤ Administration
✤ Content
✤ Comments
✤ Structure
✤ Block layout
✤ Books
✤ Comment types
✤ Contact forms
✤ Content types
✤ Display modes

- Return to "Structure", "Menus".
- Click "Edit menu" in the Footer row.
- You now see a single menu link. This is the tiny menu you've seen in the bottom-left corner of your site. This would be a good place to put links such as "Terms and Conditions", or "Privacy Policy".

MENU LINK	ENABLED
✛ Contact	☑

Save

- Return to "Structure", "Menus".
- Click "Edit menu" in the Main navigation row.
- You now see four menu links. These links correspond to the tabs across the top of your site. That's your Main menu.

MENU LINK
✛   About Us
✛   Drupal User Manual
✛   Forum
✛   Home

- Return to "Structure", "Menus".
- Click "Edit menu" in the Tools row.
- These links are designed to help visitors navigate around your site. They might not be quite important enough to place them in the Main navigation but are still useful to visitors.

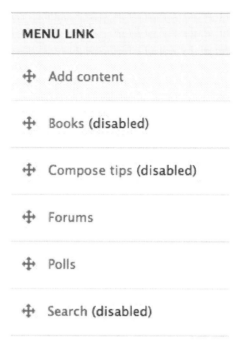

MENU LINK

✛ Add content

✛ Books (disabled)

✛ Compose tips (disabled)

✛ Forums

✛ Polls

✛ Search (disabled)

- Return to "Structure", "Menus".
- Click "Edit menu" in the User account menu row.
- These links are designed to help visitors manage their account.

MENU LINK

✛ My account (logged in users only)

✛ Log out ("Log in" for anonymous users)

Save

ADDING MENU ITEMS

In Chapter 5, "Drupal Content Explained", you added the About Us page, as well as the Drupal User Manual, to the main navigation menu. You did this simply by checking a box before clicking "Save".

What about pages that aren't created with content types? How do you add those links on the menu?

The answers to these questions are surprisingly simple. Let's dive in and add items to the main navigation menu.

In Chapter 7, "Drupal Modules Explained", you updated your Website feedback page by adding fields. Now it is time to place the contact form on the main navigation.

- Click "Structure" and then "Contact forms".
- Click on the "Website feedback" link and observe the URL. On our site, the URL is /contact/feedback
- Click "Structure" and then "Menus".
- Click the dropdown next to Main navigation and select "Add link".

Now let's add the details for the menu link:

- Menu link title: **Contact Us**
- Path: **/contact/feedback**
- Click "Save".

Return to the homepage, and you see the new menu link has now become active.

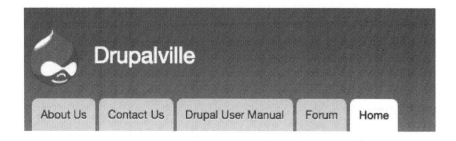

We can create new menus, and also move them from menu to menu.

In the Tools menu, there is a link to a list of all the Polls on your site. Let's move that to the Main navigation.

- Click "Structure", "Menus", and then click "Edit menu" for the Tools menu.

- Click "Edit" next to Polls.

- Select <Main navigation> from the Parent link drop-down menu.

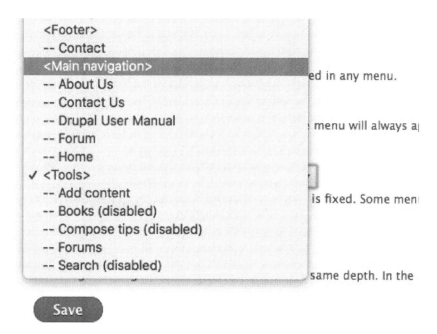

- Click "Save".

- Return to the homepage, and you see the menu link has now moved to the main navigation.

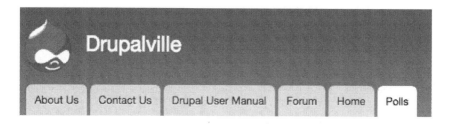

REORGANIZING MENU LINKS

So now you've seen two ways that you can create menu links:

- Check the "Provide a menu link" box while creating or editing content.

- Go to Structure, Menus, and either add a new link or move an existing link.

However, you still have a problem with your menu links. As you can see, they're not ordered as you would expect on a website. They are ordered alphabetically.

Now see how to reorganize your menu links:

- Go to "Structure", "Menus" and click "Edit menu" for the Main navigation menu.

- Click+hold+drag the Home menu link so that it is the first one in the list.

- Re-arrange your menu items to look like the image below.

- Click "Save" to confirm the changes.

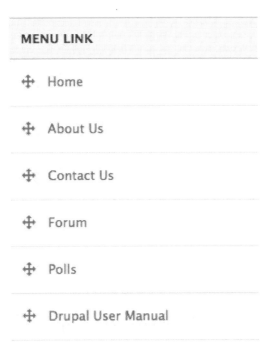

MENU LINK
⊹ Home
⊹ About Us
⊹ Contact Us
⊹ Forum
⊹ Polls
⊹ Drupal User Manual

Visit the homepage of your site, and you see that your menu links have been reorganized.

If the previous drag-and-drop solution doesn't work for you, for any reason, there is an alternative. This alternative is called "Weight". This is a concept from earlier versions of Drupal, but you still see it used in some situations.

- Go back to the "Main navigation".
- Click "Show row weights" in the top-right corner.

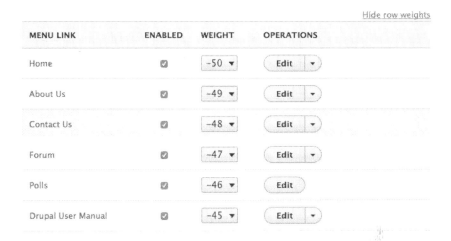

After clicking on "Show row weights", we see the menu item weights.

The concept behind Weight is this:

- Menu links are assigned a number between -50 and 50.
- Negative numbers from -50 to -1 are "light".
- Positive numbers from 1 to 50 are "heavy".
- Menu links start with a weight of 0, by default.
- If a menu link has a light number such as -50, it rises to the top of the menu.
- If a menu link has a heavy number such as 50, it sinks to the bottom of the menu.

Weight is a fairly cumbersome system that has been largely a relic from before drag-and-drop interfaces. For example, one thing that drag-and-drop can do but Weight cannot do is create parent and child links.

PARENT AND CHILD MENU LINKS

A parent and child link is a common combination that you see on most websites.

So what is a parent link and what is a child link? The parent link is a menu link that you will always see on a screen. A child link is a menu link that appears only when you click or hover over a parent link.

Probably the most common type of parent and child link is the drop-down menu. If you hover over a menu link, other links appear underneath. You can see an example from http://pantheon.io. "Product" is the parent link. If you hover over the Product link, multiple child links appear: "Website Management Platform", "Lightning-Fast Hosting", "Enterprise-Grade Drupal" and "High-Performance WordPress".

It's also common to see parent and child links that don't fly out. Many parent and child links simply expand to reveal more links underneath. For example, if you go to http://wikipedia.org and visit the main Wikipedia homepage for your language, you can see parent and child menus on the left side of the page, as shown below.

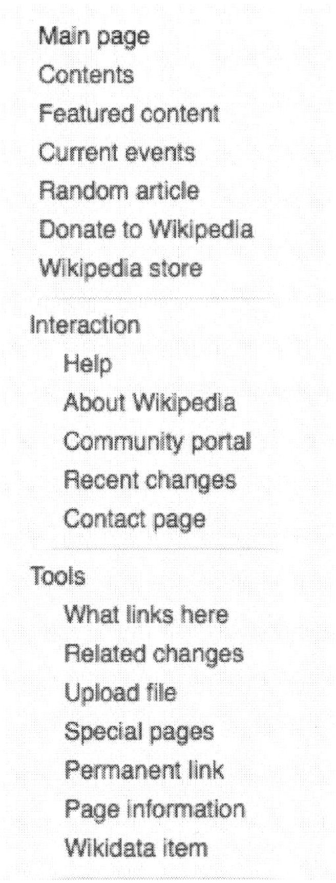

Main page
Contents
Featured content
Current events
Random article
Donate to Wikipedia
Wikipedia store

Interaction
   Help
   About Wikipedia
   Community portal
   Recent changes
   Contact page

Tools
   What links here
   Related changes
   Upload file
   Special pages
   Permanent link
   Page information
   Wikidata item

Now that you are clear on what parent and child menu links are, let's look at one menu that is already configured with parent/child menu items. Let's take a look.

- Go to "Structure", then "Menus".

- Click on "Edit menu" for the Administration menu.

- Observe how menu items appear indented under other menus.

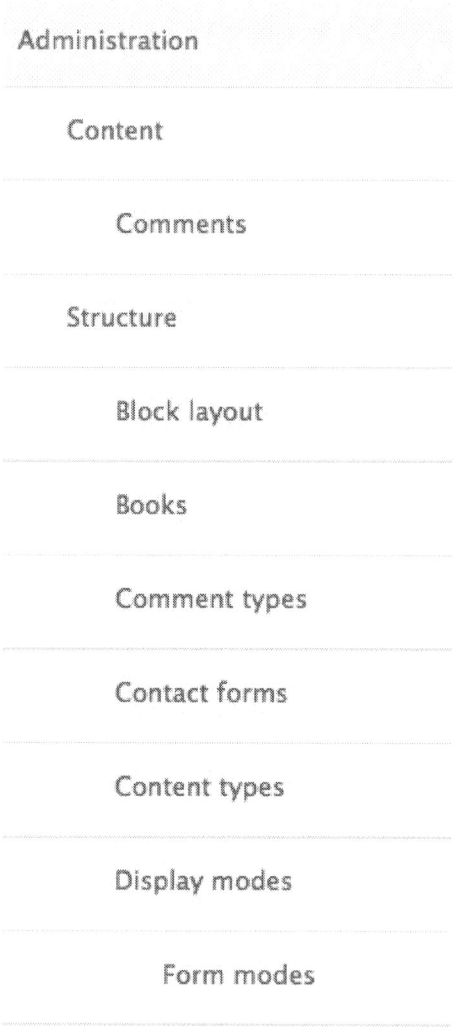

Administration

Content

Comments

Structure

Block layout

Books

Comment types

Contact forms

Content types

Display modes

Form modes

To see this menu as a drop-down menu, you will need to install another module: Admin Toolbar. This module will not only be useful for this exercise, but for the rest of the book. It makes it easier and faster for you to navigate the Drupal interface.

- Open another browser tab and go to https://drupal.org/ project/admin_toolbar.

- Copy the module's tar.gz file and install the module into your site. Check the boxes for both Admin Toolbar modules.

- Refresh your page and observe that you admin menu bar now expands.

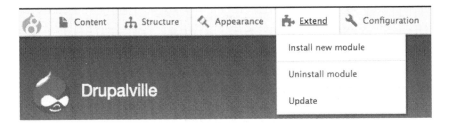

So far, the parent and child menus have been set up for you. When the time comes and you want your main navigation menu to contain drop-downs, you have two setup options: Drag-and-drop and manual.

Using the same click+hold+drag technique you used when reordering the menu items, you simply click+hold and drag the menu item to the right. You can create as many menu levels as you want.

However, at the moment, we're limited in how much we can do with this task. The Bartik theme does not support dropdown menus for the main navigation. Some themes do allow dropdown menus, but not all of them do. In order to create dropdown menus, we are going to have to replace Bartik with another theme, and we'll do that in the chapter, "Drupal Themes Explained".

WHAT'S NEXT?

As we mentioned in the introduction to this chapter, this chapter focused on teaching you the essential basics of how to use menus in Drupal.

Coming up, we are going to work on how the site looks. We will start with blocks, which you have already seen in the left sidebar of your site. Blocks are our means of moving content around on the page. Then we will explore themes, the code that creates the spaces for your content and blocks and makes them look the way you wish.

There's more, but let's not waste time. Turn the page and dive into blocks.

At this point, your Drupalville site should look like the image below. We've said it before, and it's worth saying again: don't worry if your site doesn't match exactly. The important thing is that you understand the concepts behind this chapter.

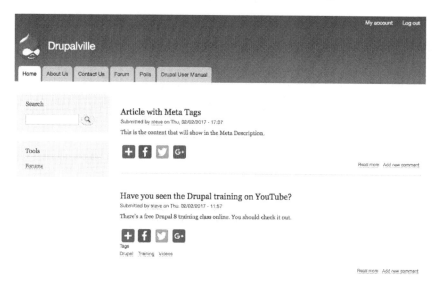

CHAPTER 9.

DRUPAL BLOCKS EXPLAINED

Blocks come in various shapes and sizes. They are created by different means. Some blocks hold tiny bits of data while others presents images, content, dates, and more.

At the end of this chapter, you should be able to:

- Distinguish between different types of blocks.
- Create a custom block.
- Create a custom block type.
- Place a block on your site.
- Place a block on specific pages on your site.

The best way to explore blocks is to go to the homepage of your site. What on this page is a block? Let's start at the top.

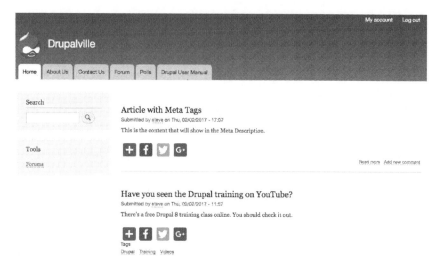

MENU BLOCKS

In the top right corner of the page, you can see "My account" and "Log out".

- Hover over those links. Does a dotted box appear with a pencil in the top right corner?

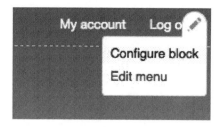

"Configure block" tells us that this item is a block, and "Edit menu" tells us that it is a menu block.

- Click on "Configure block" and see the configuration options shown below.

Configure block ☆

Home » Administration » Structure » Block layout

Block description: User account menu

Title *

User account menu   Machine name: bartik_account_menu

This field supports tokens. Browse available tokens.

☐ Display title

▼ MENU LEVELS

Initial menu level *

1 ▼

The menu will only be visible if the menu item for the current page is at or below the selected starting level. Select l
visible.

Maximum number of menu levels to display *

1   ▼

The maximum number of menu levels to show, starting from the initial menu level. For example: with an initial level
menu levels 2, 3 and 4 can be displayed.

Visibility

Content types Not restricted	Content types
Pages Not restricted	☐ Article
	☐ Book page
	☐ Company
	☐ Event
Roles Not restricted	☐ Forum topic
	☐ Basic page
	☐ User Group
	☐ Website

Region

Let's review each option.

- **Block description**: This is set by Drupal as this a default menu.

- **Title**: Although the title is required, you don't have to display it as indicated by the Display title checkbox.

- **Menu levels**: As you can guess, not all blocks have this option. Menu levels allow you to manage how many levels you display, assuming your theme is configured to allow drop-down menus. We will talk about Themes in Chapter 10, Drupal Themes Explained.

- **Visibility**: As you can see, there are several ways to control when a block appears and when it doesn't. We will explore these in more detail as you add blocks to your site.

- **Region**: Where the block will appear. Regions are defined by your site's theme. As we work with blocks in this chapter, you will learn about Drupal's default theme, Bartik.

Click "Back to site" to continue this exercise.

There are two other menu blocks on the homepage. The Main Menu is a menu block:

And, although it might not look like it, down in the footer, the "Contact" link is part of a menu block.

With large blocks, the dropdown links can be hard to find. For example, with the Main Menu, the dropdown links are on the far right side:

BRANDING BLOCK

There are three default branding elements in Drupal: Site name, logo, and slogan.

- Hover over your site name and see the dotted line and edit pencil icon appear.

- Click on the edit pencil.

- You have only one option this time. Click on "Configure block" and you'll see the configuration page shown below.

Title *

Site branding

This field supports tokens. Browse available tokens.

☐ Display title

TOGGLE BRANDING ELEMENTS

☑ Site logo
  Defined on the Appearance Settings or Theme Settings page.

☑ Site name
  Defined on the Site Information page.

☑ Site slogan
  Defined on the Site Information page.

Choose which branding elements you want to show in this block instance.

- This page is similar to that of the menu block, but instead of menu levels, you have "Toggle Branding Elements".

- Uncheck the "Site name".

- Scroll down and click "Save block".

- Go back to your homepage, and observe the Site name is gone.

- Edit the branding block and turn the site name back on. Remember to Save to ensure your change sticks.

The option to turn off the site name might not seem like a big deal, but in Chapter 10, Drupal Themes Explained, you will see just how handy this option is.

CONTENT BLOCKS

- Moving down the page, click on "Article with Meta Tags".
- If you drag your cursor over the title, the tabs, and the content of the node, you will see three separate dotted boxes with edit pencils. The image below shows two of those pencils:

- Hover over these edit pencil icons. Notice that the top two icons have "Configure block" in the dropdown.

a Tags

ow in the Meta Description.

- Click on "Configure block" for the top of the three icons. You'll find that you are editing a block called "Page title". If you disable this block, none of your pages will have titles.

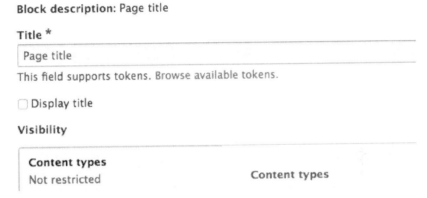

- Exit this block and return to "Article with Meta Tags".
- Click the second edit icon. You'll find that you are editing a block called "Tabs".

Block description: Tabs

Title *

Tabs

This field supports tokens. Browse available tokens.

☐ Display title

▼ **SHOWN TABS**

Select tabs being shown in the block

☑ Show primary tabs

☑ Show secondary tabs

- Currently, there are no secondary tabs enabled. If you turn off the "Show primary tabs", then the "View", "Edit", "Outline", "Delete" and other tabs will be hidden.

MODULE BLOCKS

Module blocks are rather vague, we know. However, they allow us to group a set of blocks generated by modules. The features offered by module blocks will vary, thus making each module block a potentially new experience.

Let's look at the Search block.

- Hover over the Search block on the left side of the page.

- Click the edit pencil and then "Configure block".

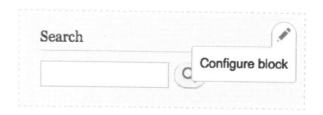

- You should see the configuration page as below. Observe that the Search module does not give you any options for controlling the search block.

Block description: Search form

Title *

    Search

This field supports tokens. Browse available tokens.

☑ Display title

Visibility

Now let's look at a block created by the Book module you installed in Chapter 5, Drupal Content Explained. Before we can do that, we need to place the block on a page.

- Go to "Structure", then "Block layout". You should see a page that looks like the image below.

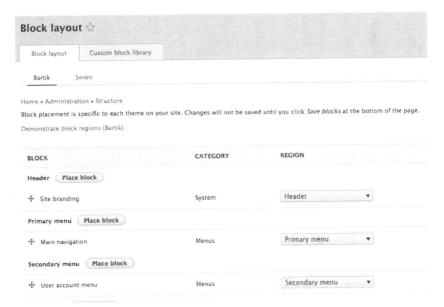

Just a few things to note about this screen before we place the block created by the Book module.

- **Tabs**: "Block layout" and "Custom block library". When you start creating your own blocks, you will see them listed in the library tab.

- **Themes**: "Bartik" and "Seven". Because Bartik is your default theme, it is highlighted by default. Seven is the administrative theme. It controls the look, and feel of the admin pages.

- **Demonstrate block regions (Bartik)**: If you click on this link, you will see yellow boxes indicating the theme's regions. In other words, these are where your block will appear on your page if you use that region.

Let's see what our options are for placing blocks.

- Click on the "Demonstrate block regions" link and you can see the region layout as shown below. Not all themes offer the same region layout. In Chapter 10, "Drupal Themes Explained", you will see other themes and their layout options.

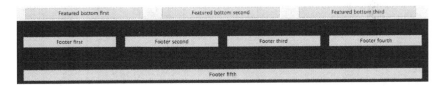

- Click "Exit block region demonstration" to return to the block layout page.

- Scroll down and locate "Sidebar second". This is the region on the right side of the page.

Sidebar first (Place block)		
✛ Search	Forms	Sidebar first ▼
✛ Tools	Menus	Sidebar first ▼

Sidebar second (Place block)

No blocks in this region

- Click "Place block" next to "Sidebar second".

- You now see a pop-up. In the filter field, type **Book**.

- Click "Place block".

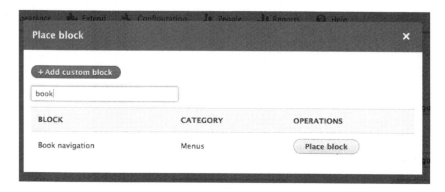

Although it appears in a small window, it is the same block configuration page you have seen before. There are two options that are unique to the Book module block: "Show block on all pages" and "Show block only on book pages". Keep the default for now.

- Scroll down and click "Save blocks".
- Click "Back to site" and see the Book block on the right sidebar of your site.

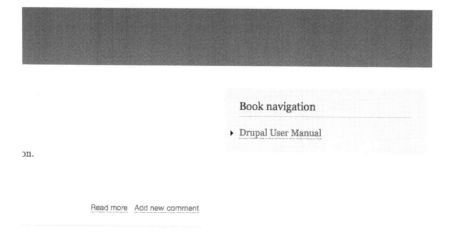

YouTube?

- Click on the "Drupal User Manual" link and observe how the block expands to show the child book pages.

Book navigation

CUSTOM BLOCKS

Custom blocks are blocks that you create. These allow you to enter your own text, images and HTML. When it comes to custom blocks, you can go basic, or you can be creative. In the following sections, we will explore a little of both.

Just for fun, let's create a block of text, perhaps a policy statement you want to show on your site.

- Go to "Structure", "Block layout".
- Click "Custom block library", then "Add custom block".

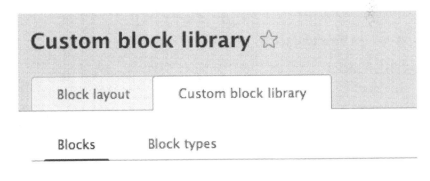

- Block description: **Drupalville Policy**

- Body: **There's only one rule on this site – be nice to each other.**
- Click "Save".

Now that you have created the block, you can place it in the same way we placed the Book navigation block.

- Click the "Block layout" tab.
- Click "Place block" next to "Sidebar second".
- You now see a pop-up. In the filter field, type **Policy**.
- Click "Place block" next to "Drupalville Policy". Click "Save".

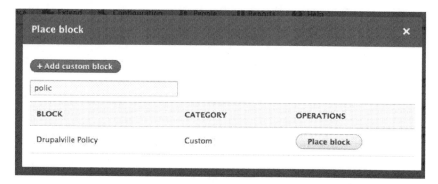

- Scroll down and click "Save blocks".
- Click "Back to site" and see the custom block on the right sidebar of your site.

Book navigation

- Drupal User Manual
- Chapter 1: How to Install Drupal
  How to Install Drupal Automatically
  How to Install Drupal Manually

Drupalville Policy

There's only one rule on this site - be nice to each other.

The Poll module comes with a block that shows the latest Poll. However, if you want to post more than one poll question, or if you want to post a previous question, you will need a custom solution.

Similar to the way we created new content types, we are going to create a Poll custom block that will allow you to post a poll question inside a block.

- Go to "Structure", "Block layout", then "Custom block library".

- Click the "Block types" tab.

- Click "Add custom block type".

Custom block library ☆

Block layout   Custom block library

Blocks   Block types

Home » Administration » Structure » Block layout » Custom block library

Each block type has its own fields and display settings. Create blocks of e

+ Add custom block type

Here are the details for our new block type:

- Label: **Poll block**
- Description: **Use this block type to create a block with a Poll question.**
- Click "Save".
- Click on "Manage fields" next to "Poll block" in the list.
- Click "Add field".
- Add a new field: **Other...**
- Label: **Select a poll question**
- Click "Save and continue".
- Type of item to reference: **Poll**

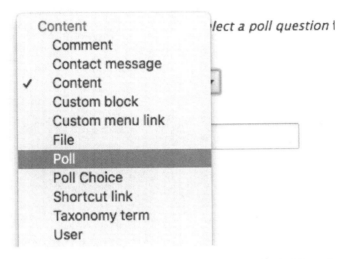

- Save the field. Your block type now has a body field and an Entity reference field.

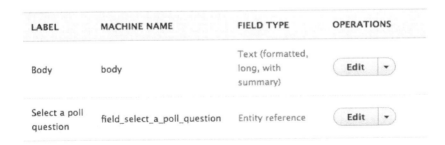

LABEL	MACHINE NAME	FIELD TYPE	OPERATIONS
Body	body	Text (formatted, long, with summary)	Edit ▾
Select a poll question	field_select_a_poll_question	Entity reference	Edit ▾

Let's make a small change to improve the display of the block type:

- Click on "Manage form display" tab and drag the Body field to the Disabled area.

- Click on the "Manage display" tab.
- Hide the label to the poll question, and set the format to **Rendered entity**.

FIELD	LABEL	FORMAT
⊹ Body	– Hidden – ▼	Default ▼
⊹ Select a poll question	– Hidden – ▼	Rendered entity ▼

We just created our custom block type. It was just like creating a content type. Now, we're ready to actually use our new block type.

- Go to "Structure", "Block layout", then "Custom block library".
- Click "Add custom block".
- Select "Poll block".
- Title: **Take a Poll**
- Poll question: **Do you like Drupal?**
- Click "Save".

Lastly, place the block using the same technique used to place your first custom block.

- Click the "Block layout" tab.
- Place the "Take a Poll" block in the "Sidebar second" region.
- Save the block and click "Save blocks" to complete your changes.
- Return to your site's homepage and look for your new block:

Book navigation

- ▾ Drupal User Manual
- ▾ Chapter 1: How to Install Drupal
  How to Install Drupal Automatically
  How to Install Drupal Manually

Drupalville Policy

There's only one rule on this site - be nice to each other.

Take a Poll

Do you like Drupal?

- ◯ Yes
- ◯ No
- ◯ I'm getting there slowly

(Vote)

SHOWING BLOCKS UNDER CERTAIN CONDITIONS

So far, we have been placing blocks such that they appear on all site pages. Drupal comes with three default visibility options:

- **Content Type**: The option to have a block appear only on certain content types.

- **Pages**: The option to have content appear based on the URL.

- **Roles**: The option to limit which role can see which block. Chapter 13, "Drupal Users Explained" covers roles and users.

In addition to using these options one at a time, you can combine them. Here are some examples of combined conditions:

- **Content type + Roles**: If the page that loads is X content type AND the user has the authenticated role, show this block.

- **Pages + Roles**: If the page loaded has a URL alias beginning with forum* AND the user has the authenticated role, show this block.

- **Content type + Pages**: If the page loaded is a Site node AND the URL alias includes *drupal*, include this block.

In order to obtain more complex visibility conditions, consider reviewing the Block Visibility Module at https://drupal.org/project/block_visibility_groups.

In this section of the chapter, we will examine two simple scenarios:

- Place the "Recent Content" block only on the homepage.
- Place the "New Forum Topics" block only on forum pages.

Here's how you place blocks only on certain pages. Start with the default Recent Content block that comes with Drupal.

- Go to "Structure", then "Block layout".
- Click "Place block" next to the "Sidebar first" region.
- Filter on Recent and select "Recent Content".
- Scroll down to the Visibility settings area and click the Pages tab.
- Enter **<front>** in the Pages field to set the homepage as the only page where this block will appear.

Configure block

Block description: Recent content

☑ Display title

Items per block

10 (default setting) ▼

◯ Override title

Visibility

Content types	Pages
Not restricted	<front>
Pages	
Restricted to certain pages	
Roles	Specify pages by using their paths. Enter one path pe
Not restricted	The '*' character is a wildcard. An example path is /u
	for every user page. *<front>* is the front page.
	⦿ Show for the listed pages
	◯ Hide for the listed pages

Note: Notice the options above, which are to show only on listed pages or to hide from listed pages. The Pages option provides two perspectives: nothing except … or all except …

- Save your block, go back to your homepage, and look for your new block.

- Browse to other pages and the block will have disappeared.

Search

Recent content

Article with Meta Tags
3 hours 17 minutes ago

Have you seen the Drupal training on
YouTube?
8 hours 29 minutes ago

DrupalCon Vienna
8 hours 51 minutes ago

OSTraining
2 days 8 hours ago

Washington D.C. Drupal
3 days 4 hours ago

simplytest.me
3 days 22 hours ago

Pantheon
4 days ago

The Atlanta Drupal User Group
4 days ago

Drupal.org
4 days ago

DrupalCon Baltimore
4 days ago

The previous example used the Pages condition. This time we will use the Content type condition and place the New Forum Topics block on the Forum topic page.

- Go to "Structure", then "Block layout".
- Click "Place block" next to "Sidebar second".

- Filter on Forum and select "New forum topics".
- Scroll down to the Visibility settings area and click the "Forum topic" box.

Visibility

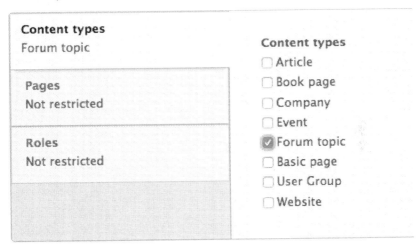

- Save your block, go back to your homepage, and look for your new block. You will not find it.
- Click the "Forum" tab in the menu. Click through until you are looking at the forum topic you created. "New forum topics" will be in the right sidebar.

WHAT'S NEXT?

In this chapter, we said you would be able to:

- Distinguish between different types of blocks.

- Create a custom block.

- Create a custom block type.

- Place a block on your site.

- Place a block on specific pages on your site.

You also learned that the theme provides regions where you place said blocks.

In the next chapter, you will learn how to change the theme. You're going to see how to truly redesign your site.

The final image below shows how your site should look at this stage. However, as we mention at the end of every chapter, it's not important if you've copied us exactly. So long as you feel confident about the key concepts we've covered so far, you're ready to move on.

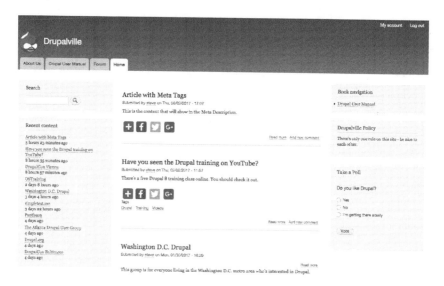

CHAPTER 10.

DRUPAL THEMES EXPLAINED

Themes are bundles of code that bring your pages to life. They are responsible for controlling both your site's visual design and layout.

- They define the visual aspects of the page, such as color, fonts, lines, and some images.
- They place content on your page, such as the logo, site name, and slogan as well as your articles and blocks.
- They position menus for navigation and access.

Up until now, your Drupal site has had a blue-and-white design. This is because you've been using a theme called Bartik whose default settings are blue and white.

At the end of this chapter, you should be able to:

- Distinguish between the administrative theme and the site theme.
- Install a theme from Drupal.org.
- Turn on and set up a theme.
- Configure a theme that utilizes modules to provide features.

BARTIK EXPLAINED

Let's start your exploration of themes by looking at the themes that come with Drupal by default.

- Click the "Appearance" link on the administration menu, and you see a screen that looks this:

Drupal comes with three themes: Bartik, Stark, and Seven:

- Bartik is the default theme that your visitors see when they visit your site.

- Seven is the administration theme that you see when you use any of the administration screens.

- Stark is the currently uninstalled theme below Bartik and Seven. You use this theme for demonstration purposes in this chapter, but it's highly unlikely that you'll ever use it in real life. Stark is an example theme that is mainly useful to experts who are comfortable with HTML and CSS. It shows you what a Drupal site looks like and has just enough CSS to make the pages appear.

Uninstalled theme

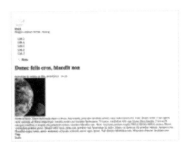

Stark 8.2.5
An intentionally plain theme with no styling to demonstrate default
Drupal's HTML and CSS. Learn how to build a custom theme from Stark
in the Theming Guide.

Install | Install and set as default

At the bottom of the Appearance screen is the drop-down option
shown below. Don't touch this option. We've often talked to
people who thought that this option was the way to change their
site's theme. It's not. This is the option to change your
administration theme, the way the site looks when you create
content, change site settings, etc., and we don't recommend you
do that until you are more experienced.

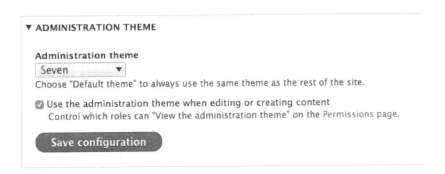

You don't have to replace Bartik to change the look and feel of
your site. Bartik has settings that enable you to customize your
site's colors, and more, without changing any code. Let's see how
that's done.

- Click "Settings" in the Bartik theme area.

Bartik 8.2.5 (default theme)
A flexible, recolorable theme with many regions

Settings

You now see the settings available for Bartik.

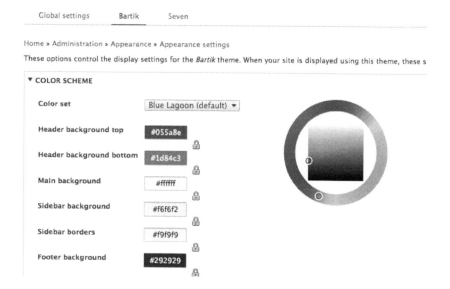

The first setting you see is the color scheme setting. So, if you prefer red, green, yellow, or some other color scheme, you can use this option to change from Drupal blue to a color of your choosing.

Let's play around with color, just for fun.

- Select a color scheme from the "Color set" drop-down.

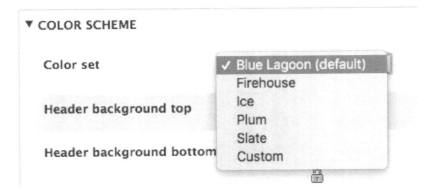

- Scroll down a little and you can see a preview of the color scheme you selected. This image shows the "Plum" color set:

Preview

- If you like the new color scheme, scroll to the bottom of the screen, and click "Save configuration".

- Go back to your homepage and see the color changes.

- Click on "Appearance" and then "Settings" for Bartik to return to the color scheme feature.

- Experiment by manually changing one of the color codes by clicking in the color field of your choice and moving the color selector wheel.

- If you like the new color scheme, click "Save configuration" and see the changes on your site.

- Repeat as many times as you like. Remember, you can always return to the Drupal blue by selecting "Blue lagoon (Default)" from the Color set drop-down.

Below the "Color Scheme" settings is another area with theme options:

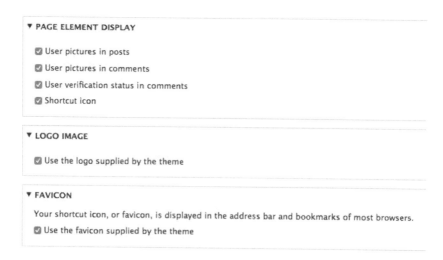

The Toggle Display options show some features that the theme supports. Some themes support hundreds of features and some themes support few. A theme's features rely entirely on the designer of the theme.

Let's look at a feature of Bartik that is controlled by the theme settings: the logo.

- Uncheck the box "Use the logo supplied by the theme".
- You can use the "Upload logo image" box to upload any image. This will replace the Drupal logo in the top-left corner of your site. Don't worry if you want to try this out because we're about to change away from Bartik and use a new theme.

▼ LOGO IMAGE

◯ Use the logo supplied by the theme

Path to custom logo

Examples: `logo.svg` (for a file in the public filesystem), `public://logo.svg`, or `core/themes/bartik/logo.svg`.

Upload logo image

Choose File | No file chosen

If you don't have direct file access to the server, use this field to upload your logo.

- In this example, I uploaded the Pantheon logo to my site:

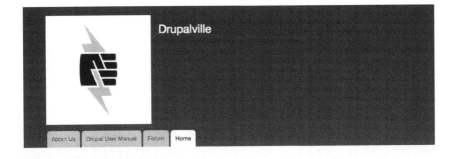

INSTALLING THEMES EXPLAINED

If you want to try a theme contributed by the Drupal community, you can install one of those themes. In the following activities, you will install themes with varying setup requirements.

- **Danland Theme**: A simple theme with basic theme settings that will require you to move a few blocks back to their current location.

- **Drupal8 Zymphonies Theme**: This theme provides additional theme setting options as well as a drop-down main navigation that will accommodate the parent/child configuration you set up in Chapter 8, Drupal Menus Explained. You will need to replace blocks that you placed earlier.

- **Breeze Theme**: This is a "subtheme" and will require us to install two themes, as well as reset some blocks.

INSTALLING THE DANLAND THEME

Try this workflow with the Danland theme.

- Open another browser tab and go to http://drupal.org/project/danland.

- Copy the tar.gz link for the Drupal 8 version of this theme. The link will look like this: https://ftp.drupal.org/files/projects/danland-8.x-1.0.tar.gz.

- Return to your site and click "Appearance".

- Click "Install new theme".

- Paste the link into the "Install from a URL".

- Click "Install".

Install new theme ☆

Home » Administration

You can find modules and themes on drupal.org. The following file extensions are supported: *tar tgz gz bz2 zip.*

Install from a URL

| https://ftp.drupal.org/files/projects/danland-8.x-1.0.tar.gz |

For example: *http://ftp.drupal.org/files/projects/name.tar.gz*

Or

Upload a module or theme archive to install

| Choose File | No file chosen |

For example: *name.tar.gz* from your local computer

Install

- Click "Install newly added themes".
- Scroll down and locate the Danland theme in the Uninstalled themes list.
- Click "Install and set as default".

Uninstalled themes

Danland 8.x-1.0
Drupal Theme provided by Danetsoft developed by Danang Probo Sayekti inspired by Maksimer.

Install | Install and set as default

- Click "Settings" for the Danland theme.
- Notice that Danland comes with similar settings to Bartik, but does not include the color change options found with the Bartik.
- Go to the front of your site and check your new theme.

Note: If your site design doesn't change, go to "Configuration", then "Performance" and click the "Clear all cache" button.

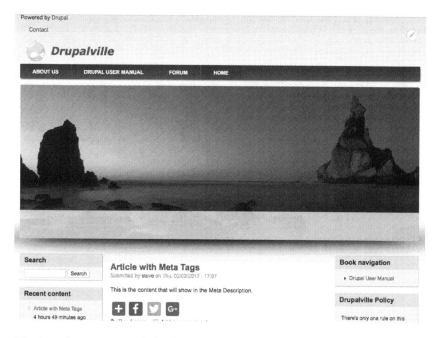

Notice that some of the blocks are out of place. That's because Bartik has different theme regions than Danland.

- Go to Structure", then "Block layout".
- Click "Demonstrate block regions (Danland)".

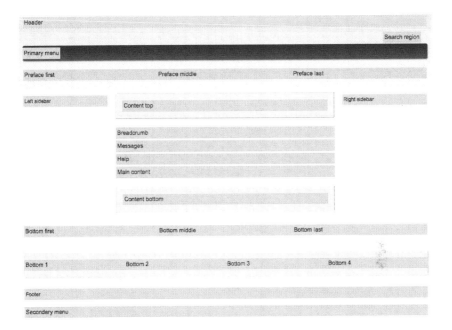

- Click "Exit block region demonstration".

Using the drop-downs in the Region column, make the following changes:

- Move "Powered by Drupal" to Footer.
- Move "Footer menu" to Secondary menu.
- Move "Search" to Search region.
- Move "User account menu" to Secondary menu.

There are other changes we can make, but the Danland theme is not our final theme, so let's not spend a lot of time here.

- Scroll down and click "Save blocks".
- Go back to your site's homepage, and check out your new theme:

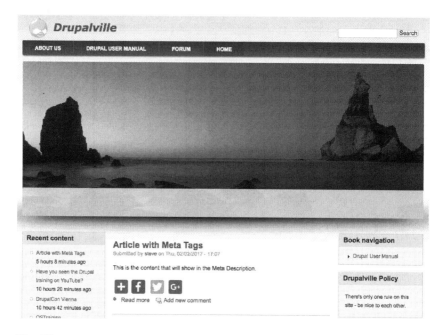

You'll notice that there is a large slideshow across the homepage of your site. This slideshow appears only on the homepage. In order to change the images, you need to access your server and replace them, which brings up the need to occasionally modify a theme to your liking. Later in this chapter, we look at how to make these changes.

INSTALLING THE DRUPAL8 ZYMPHONIES THEME

Now let's try the Drupal 8 Zymphonies theme.

- Open a new browser tab and go to https://drupal.org/project/drupal8_zymphonies_theme.
- Copy the tar.gz link.
- Return to your site, go to "Appearance", then "Install new theme".
- Paste the link into the "Install from a URL" field.
- Click through until you can click "Install and set as default".
- Click "Settings" for the Drupal8 Zymphonies theme. Observe

that there are three new options: Social Media Link, Copyright, and Credit, as shown below. Feel free to make changes, but this is not our final theme.

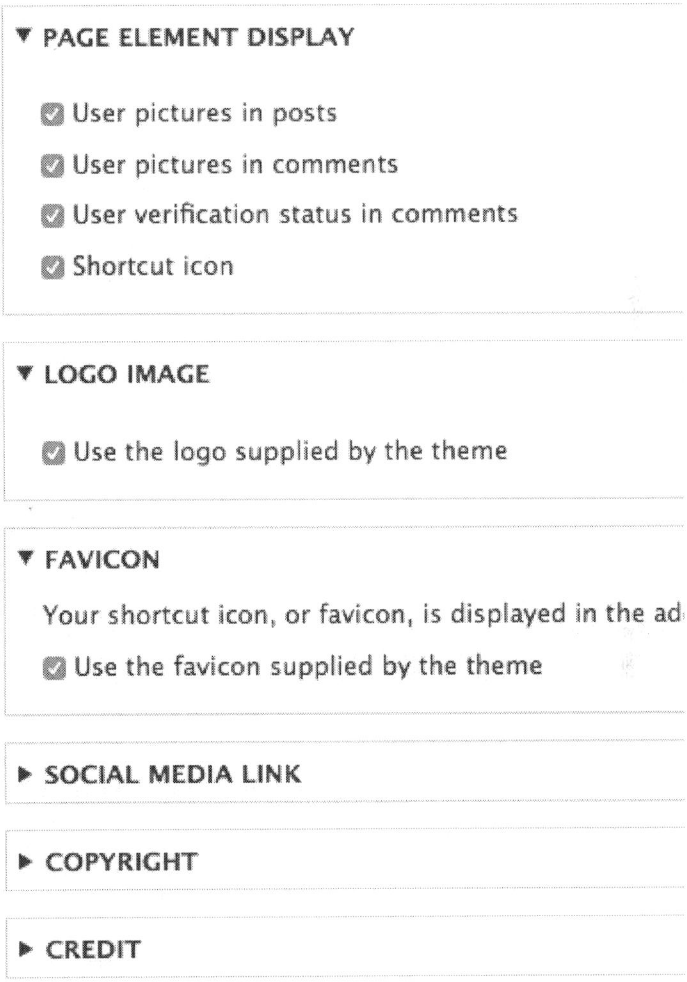

▼ PAGE ELEMENT DISPLAY

☑ User pictures in posts

☑ User pictures in comments

☑ User verification status in comments

☑ Shortcut icon

▼ LOGO IMAGE

☑ Use the logo supplied by the theme

▼ FAVICON

Your shortcut icon, or favicon, is displayed in the ad

☑ Use the favicon supplied by the theme

▶ SOCIAL MEDIA LINK

▶ COPYRIGHT

▶ CREDIT

- Click "Save configuration", even if you haven't made any changes. This is a good practice as some themes will require you to save the settings.

- Go to your site's homepage, and your site looks very different now! Some things are definitely not working correctly.

Let's learn more about the layout of this theme.

- Go to Structure", then "Block layout".

- Click "Demonstrate block regions (Drupal8 Zymphonies Theme)". As you can see, there are fewer regions than with Bartik or Danland:

- Click "Exit block region demonstration".

Using the drop-downs in the Region column, make the following changes:

- Move the "Page title" block to the "Page Title" region.

- Move "Tabs" to the "Content" region.

- Move "Primary admin actions" to the "Content" region.

- Move "Breadcrumbs" to "None".

- Click "Place block" and add "Recent content" to the "Left Sidebar" region.

Scroll to the Content region and make sure the blocks are in the following order:

- Page title
- Tabs
- Primary admin actions
- Main page content

Next, notice that the blocks you placed in Chapter 9, "Drupal Blocks Explained", are no longer there. Because almost all the Zymphonies regions have different names, those blocks have nowhere to go in Zymphonies. The blocks still exist, and you can find them by clicking "Bartik" or "Danland" at the top of the screen. However, you would need to click "Place block" and insert them again for Zymphonies.

Drupal8 Zymphonies Theme   Bartik   Seven   Danland

Go back to your site, and visit your new theme. You'll see that the homepage still has some problems because the content is all center-aligned. But, the inside pages don't look too bad.

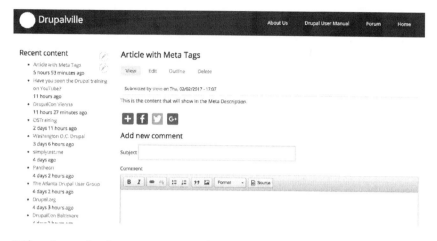

Why does the homepage not look right? It's my guess that the theme's designers didn't intend for content to be on the homepage. If you visit the theme's page on Drupal.org, you can see some screenshots from the designers. One of the screenshots is below, and you can see that all the text and icons are center-aligned. If we were to make our site look like their official screenshot shown below, we would need several changes, including:

- Add a large header image, to be placed where the woman and child image is now.

- Add a block with a large slogan, to be placed where "Zymphonies Drupal 8 Responsive Theme" is now.

- Add three blocks with large icons and text, to be placed where the phone, gear and Drupal logo are now.

- Add a "Welcome" block that stretches across the page, to be placed where their Welcome block is placed now.

SUBTHEMES EXPLAINED

The themes you have installed and tested so far have been fairly straightforward, each one offering a different design, a different layout, and some different features.

For the final theme, you will install the Breeze theme, which is more complicated and powerful. The Breeze theme is a subtheme, which means it relies on a base theme called Bootstrap to work correctly.

- Go to the Drupal.org page and copy the tar.gz link for the Breeze theme at https://drupal.org/project/breeze.

- Install the Breeze theme.

- Repeat the process for the Bootstrap theme: https://drupal.org/project/bootstrap.

- Click "Install and set as default" next to the Breeze theme. Note: You do not have to enable Bootstrap 3. It installs itself.

Before we check out the blocks and whether they are in the right place, let's check out the power of Breeze.

- Click "Settings" for the Breeze theme.

- As you can see on this screen, you now have many, many more options than you did for any previous theme.

These settings were not created by the designers of Breeze. Instead, they come from the Bootstrap theme. Breeze is a "subtheme" that builds on top of Bootstrap, which is a "base theme".

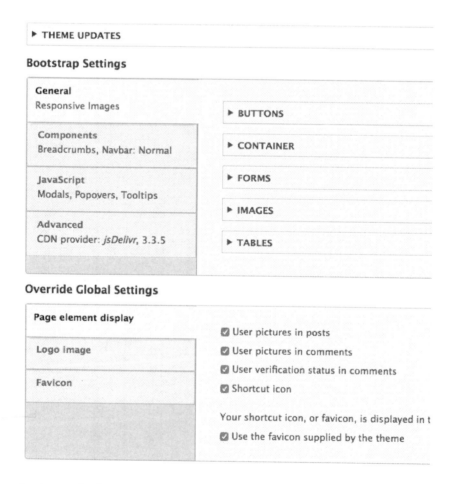

Let's see the layout options provided by Breeze.

- Go to "Structure", then "Block layout".
- Click on "Demonstrate block regions (Breeze Drupal 8 Theme)".

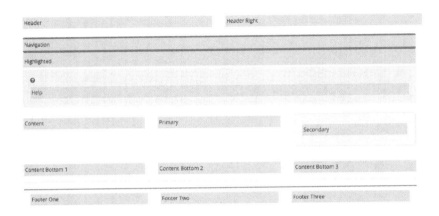

- Click "Exit block region demonstration" and scan the current block placement.

You might see blocks in the Header region that don't belong there. If so, make the following changes:

- Place "Breadcrumbs" in the "Content" region.
- Place "Main navigation" in the "Navigation" region.
- Move "Search" to the "Header Right" region.
- Move "Help" to the "Help" region.
- Place "Recent content", "Recent comments", "Take a Poll" in the "Secondary" region.
- Place "User account menu" in the "Footer One" region.
- Place "Drupalville Policy" in the "Footer Two" region.
- Place "Footer menu" and "Powered by Drupal" in the "Footer Three" region.

Save those block changes. We can now improve the settings for some important blocks.

- Click configure for the Site branding block. In Chapter 9, "Drupal Blocks Explained", we explored the options for this block as some themes are not designed to display one or more branding feature. Uncheck "Site name" and "Site slogan".

TOGGLE BRANDING ELEMENTS

☑ Site logo
   Defined on the Appearance Settings or Theme Settings page.

☐ Site name
   Defined on the Site Information page.

☐ Site slogan
   Defined on the Site Information page.

Choose which branding elements you want to show in this block instance.

We're now going to upload a new logo for our site.

- Go to the package of files that we provided with the book at http://ostraining.com/books/d8e and find the Drupalville logo.
- Go to "Appearance", and open the settings for Breeze.
- Click "Logo image" and upload the new logo.

Visit your homepage and see if you like what you have done.

Finally, let's set up dropdown menus. Bartik did not support dropdowns, but Breeze does.

- Go to "Structure", then "Menus" and edit the Main navigation menu.

- Move "Contact Us" to be a child link, under "About Us." Don't forget to click "Save".

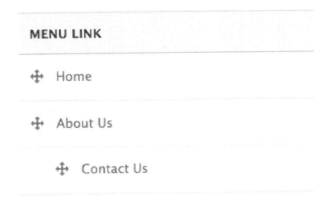

There is one more final step that is easy to forget about.

- Click "Edit" next to "About Us".

- Check the box "Show as expanded".

Save these settings and visit the front of your site. You'll be able to see your dropdown menu in action:

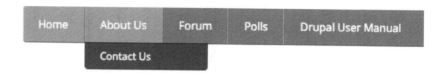

MODIFYING THEMES EXPLAINED

When modifying a theme or a module in Drupal, there are rules that one should follow. The first rule, unless you are applying a code patch provided by the developer of the theme or module, is not to modify the code of the theme or module.

There are processes, methods if you will, designed by the Drupal community to ensure that any customization you want to make can be done safely. When it comes to themes, if you want to make changes, you create a subtheme.

You saw in the previous section of this chapter that the Breeze theme depends on Bootstrap 3. That means Bootstrap 3 is where most of the theme code resides and that the code associated with Breeze provides unique elements, changes if you will, to the core design elements provided by Bootstrap.

Any theme can be a base theme, although there are some base themes that are designed specifically for that job. For example:

- Bootstrap 3

- Zen

- Omega

- AdaptiveTheme

- Fusion

- And more

If you want to make changes to a theme, like change a color or a font, or even change the images the theme uses, we recommend creating a subtheme.

If you choose to modify the theme directly, please keep track of the changes so that they can be reapplied if and when you install an update to the theme.

For example, if you change the slideshow images in the Danland theme without making a subtheme to manage those new images, your images will be replaced by the default images when you perform a Danland theme update.

For information on creating a subtheme, please visit http://bit.ly/2hhJeyB.

FINDING THEMES EXPLAINED

So far, all the themes we have explored were chosen for you. In this part of the chapter, we're going to give you some advice on how to successfully find other themes that you could use to build a site.

As we did with modules in Chapter 7, here are some important points to know about themes before you start searching.

- Most themes are hosted on Drupal.org but not all.

- Most themes are free, but some companies do sell commercial themes.

- As with modules, there are no ratings or reviews of themes.

Let's take a look at a theme project page.

- Open a new browser tab and go https://drupal.org/project/project_theme.

- Select 8.x from the Core compatibility filter and click "Search." You'll notice that there are far fewer themes than modules.

2,413 Themes match your search

Maintenance status	– Any –
Development status	– Any –
Core compatibility	8.x
Status	Full projects
Search Themes	
Sort by	Most installed

Search

If a theme looks interesting, be sure to click on the theme name and check out the full project page.

Recall Bootstrap, the base theme to the Breeze subtheme. You will likely see Bootstrap in the search results, as it is an enormously popular theme.

If you scroll down, you should see Zen, Omega, AdaptiveTheme, and other base themes.

How can you tell if a theme is a base theme? The description should state it is, or say it is a "starter theme".

Unless you are an experienced developer, you will want to stay clear of themes that describe themselves as base or starter themes. These themes require a lot of CSS work in order to achieve a good-looking finished product. Install them only when the theme you have chosen requires it.

EVALUATING THEMES EXPLAINED

Evaluating a theme is more than deciding if you like the look and feel.

In this book, we selected the sample themes for you to practice with, we installed many themes, evaluated theme for their ease of use, ability to deliver as promised, their features, and their appeal. It wasn't easy to choose.

To help you make your selection, we return to the method offered in Chapter 7, "Drupal Modules Explained".

- **Description**: This area gives you an overview of all the theme's key features and requirements.

- **Project Information**: This area tells you if this module is actively updated and maintained, plus how many sites have installed it.

- **Downloads:** This area tells you if there is a release of a theme available for your Drupal version and if it is stable or perhaps only released in an alpha or beta version.

- **Sidebar**: This area shows you the people who coded the module and when they were last active. It also provides important links such as those to issues users have found and to documentation for the module.

Here are those areas highlighted on the Breeze project page:

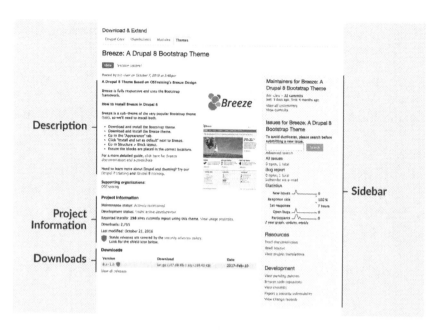

Area 1: Description

This is the area that requires the least explanation. It should provide a clear explanation of what this theme does, its features, requirements, and some direction regarding installation. Here's the example from the Bootstrap page:

> **❝** Sleek, intuitive, and powerful mobile first front-end framework for faster and easier web development. Bootstrap has become one of the most popular front-end frameworks and open source projects in the world.

This base theme bridges the gap between Drupal and the Bootstrap Framework.

Bootstrap 3
for Drupal

Features

- jsDelivr CDN for "out-of-the-box" styling and faster page load times.
- Bootswatch theme support, if using the CDN.
- Glyphicons support via Icon API.
- Extensive integration and template/preprocessor overrides for most of the Bootstrap Framework CSS, Components and JavaScript
- Theme settings to further enhance the Drupal Bootstrap integration:
  - Breadcrumbs
  - Navbar
  - Popovers
  - Tooltips
  - Wells (per region)

Documentation

Visit the project's official documentation site or the markdown files inside the `./docs` directory.

Area 2: Project Information

This area of the page contains some useful information. First, it tells you if the theme is being actively maintained and updated. Second, it tells you if the theme is frequently downloaded or installed.

Finally, it tells you when the theme was last updated. If a theme hasn't been updated recently, be cautious. It might mean that the theme works perfectly and doesn't need updating, but it might also mean the theme's coders are not providing necessary updates and fixes.

The image below shows you the Project Information area for Bootstrap. A high number of downloads is a good sign; however, a quick look at the initial project date will tell you if you should expect to see high numbers of downloads.

Project Information

Maintenance status: Actively maintained

Development status: Under active development

Reported installs: **132,655** sites currently report using this theme. View usage statistics.

Downloads: 967,312

Last modified: December 14, 2016

Stable releases are covered by the security advisory policy. Look for the shield icon below.

Area 3: Downloads

This area is the most important of all. If there isn't a version of the theme available for your version of Drupal, then you stop your evaluation right here and start looking elsewhere.

As with modules, the themes in the green area are recommended for use on live sites. You can see Bootstrap's downloads below:

Downloads

8.x-3.5 released 17 May 2017
✓ Recommended by the project's maintainer.
↓ tar.gz (334.41 KB) | zip (1.06 MB)

Development version: 8.x-3.x-dev updated 16 Aug 2017 at 17:34 UTC

7.x-3.14 released 25 May 2017
✓ Recommended by the project's maintainer.
↓ tar.gz (242.36 KB) | zip (995.79 KB)

Development version: 7.x-3.x-dev updated 16 Aug 2017 at 17:34 UTC

View all releases

Area 4: Sidebar

It was straightforward to explain the information contained in the first three areas on a module page. The fourth area, the sidebar, contains more information and is more diverse. The image below shows the sidebar on the Breeze page. Here's what is in each of the four areas:

- **Maintainers**: This is some of the most important information of all about a theme. Bootstrap has only three maintainers and two are very active.

- **Issues**: This area provides links to all potential bugs that people have found with the theme. A high number is not necessarily a bad thing because the more popular it is, the more bugs people are likely to find. At first, it won't be easy for you to get useful information from this area, but as you get more experience, you can read the list of issues and look for potential problems.

- **Resources**: This area contains key links. Perhaps the most important of all is the documentation link. Not all themes have documentation, but you should probably avoid those that don't.

- **Development**: This area contains technical links related to the theme's code.

Maintainers for Bootstrap

markcarver – 525 commits
last: 4 weeks ago, first: 3 years ago

neardark – 92 commits
last: 3 months ago, first: 2 years ago

wundo – 98 commits
last: 1 year ago, first: 4 years ago

View all committers
View commits

Issues for Bootstrap

To avoid duplicates, please search before submitting a new issue.

	Search

Advanced search

All issues

111 open, 1906 total

Bug report

45 open, 864 total
Subscribe via e-mail

Statistics

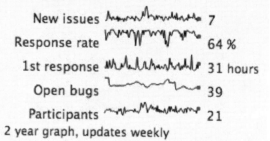

New issues 7
Response rate 64 %
1st response 31 hours
Open bugs 39
Participants 21

2 year graph, updates weekly

Resources

Home page

COMMERCIAL DRUPAL THEMES EXPLAINED

Unlike modules, not all themes are available on Drupal.org and not all themes are free. There are some companies that sell themes commercially.

For a commercial theme, you can expect to pay between $15 and $300. For that price, you might also expect a more polished, professional design and also support from the theme's developers.

However, if you're coming from another content management system or blogging platform, you might be surprised at how few companies do sell themes. In total, there are probably not more than a dozen commercial Drupal theme companies.

There are some large theme companies that sell designs for Drupal and for many other platforms. These sites are typically marketplaces that attract thousands of different designers. One example of these marketplace sites is Theme Forest. You can find its Drupal themes at http://themeforest.net/category/cms-themes/drupal. Its list of Drupal themes is shown in the image below. It has more than 400 themes and most are priced between $25 and $60.

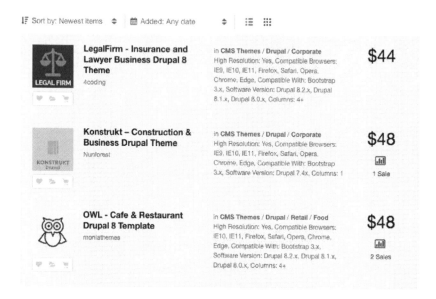

| | LegalFirm - Insurance and Lawyer Business Drupal 8 Theme | in CMS Themes / Drupal / Corporate | $44 |
| | 4coding | High Resolution: Yes, Compatible Browsers: IE9, IE10, IE11, Firefox, Safari, Opera, Chrome, Edge, Compatible With: Bootstrap 3.x, Software Version: Drupal 8.2.x, Drupal 8.1.x, Drupal 8.0.x, Columns: 4+ | |

| | Konstrukt – Construction & Business Drupal Theme | in CMS Themes / Drupal / Corporate | $48 |
| | Nunforest | High Resolution: Yes, Compatible Browsers: IE9, IE10, IE11, Firefox, Safari, Opera, Chrome, Edge, Compatible With: Bootstrap 3.x, Software Version: Drupal 7.4x, Columns: 1 | 1 Sale |

| | OWL - Cafe & Restaurant Drupal 8 Template | in CMS Themes / Drupal / Retail / Food | $48 |
| | monlathemes | High Resolution: Yes, Compatible Browsers: IE10, IE11, Firefox, Safari, Opera, Chrome, Edge, Compatible With: Bootstrap 3.x, Software Version: Drupal 8.2.x, Drupal 8.1.x, Drupal 8.0.x, Columns: 4+ | 2 Sales |

Another popular marketplace site is Template Monster. You can find its Drupal themes at http://templatemonster.com/drupal-themes.php. Its list of Drupal themes is shown below. It has hundreds of themes and most are priced between $50 and $70.

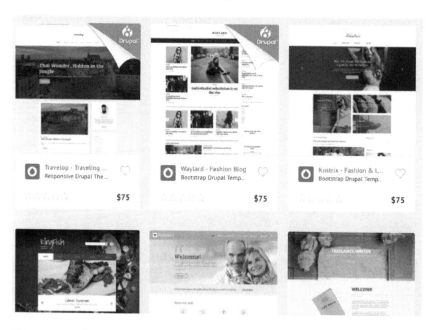

There are also companies that specialize in creating only Drupal themes. After looking at Drupal.org, you may recognize the names of some of these companies. Many of these companies place free themes on Drupal.org as a way to give back to the Drupal community and also as a form of advertising.

More Than Themes sells only Drupal themes. You can find its designs at http://morethanthemes.com. Their list of Drupal themes is shown below. They have more than a dozen themes, and you can buy access to all of them for prices starting at $70.

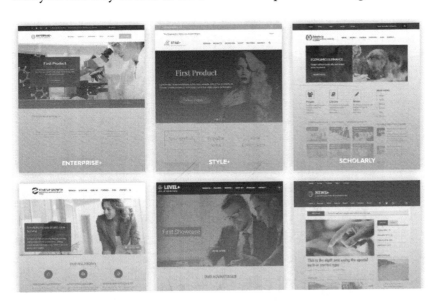

A FINAL, IMPORTANT NOTE ON THEME DESIGN

In this chapter you've seen two ways to find a Drupal theme for your site:

- Free themes from Drupal.org
- Commercial themes

In the Drupal community, using free themes is by far the most popular option.

It is rare to see a theme built from scratch. Nearly every Drupal project starts with an existing theme and brings in a designer to make modifications. Even the most prestigious Drupal projects tend to start with a theme from Drupal.org. Using an existing theme has many benefits:

- The code behind popular existing themes has been heavily road-tested.
- Many themes already come with features such as mobile-compatibility.
- Drupal themes can be complicated to build from scratch.
- Reusing existing code saves time and money.

WHAT'S NEXT?

In this chapter you saw how to accomplish these tasks:

- Configure Bartik, the default Drupal theme.
- Change the default theme on your site.
- Add new themes.
- Search for and evaluate new themes.

You have just completed Step 5 in the Drupal workflow:

1. **Planning**

2. **Content types**

3. **Fields**

4. **Add content**

5. **Install Modules and Themes**

6. **Views**

7. **Layout Modules**

8. **Finish the Design**

9. **Users**

10. **Site Management**

Now you know the key details about Drupal themes. At this point, your Drupalville site will look like the image below. For the first time in this book, your site now looks substantially different. Don't worry if it's not exact. The important thing is that you understand the concepts behind this chapter.

Next up, we'll look at dynamic pages and blocks that update automatically when content is added or changed on your site.

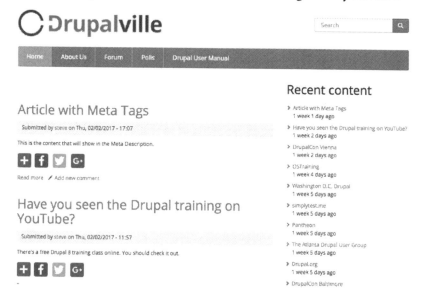

CHAPTER 11.

DRUPAL VIEWS EXPLAINED

Drupal's default homepage list of content is generated by Views.

The Views module allows you to query your site's database, and present the content you select. But, this is too simple of a description. Views is the module that powers many important Drupal features, from lists and tables to slideshows and calendars.

Here's an overview of some key Views capabilities:

- **Display**: Views enables you to create your own pages, blocks, RSS feeds, and more.
- **Format**: Views enables you to format information in tables, grids, lists, slideshows, calendars, and much more.
- **Fields**: With Views, you can display only the fields that you want. You can show, hide, reorder, and change the display of fields as you choose.
- **Filter**: Views enables you to filter based on content type, taxonomy terms, publication date, or many other criteria.
- **Sort**: Views enables you to sort alphabetically, by popularity, by author name, or by any criteria you choose.

So far in this book, you've added a lot of information to your site. In Chapters 5, "Drupal Content Explained," and Chapter 6, "Drupal Fields Explained," you spent time creating content types and fields. In Chapter 7, "Drupal Modules Explained," you added modules such as Polls and AddToAny sharing.

Now that you have all that content, you can use Views to present it to your site's visitors in ways that are interesting and useful for them.

At the end of this chapter, you should be able to:

- Create blocks and pages using Views.
- Create calendars and slideshows with Views.
- Learn to create views by thinking of the Display, Format, Fields, Filter, and Sort features that were just mentioned.
- Use modules to help you expand the features of Views.

PLAN YOUR VIEWS

Planning your Views displays requires a little more than the lists below, however, it is a start.

For now, we need you to know that you can use Views to create much of your site's structure.

You can use Views to create blocks to showcase your content.

You can also use Views to create the landing pages for your content types.

Views is a popular module, but it can also be a lot to learn. In this chapter, we're going to use Views to create some blocks and landing pages for our site. We'll then move on and use Views to create some more exciting displays.

CREATING SAMPLE CONTENT

The pages and blocks we have listed in our plan need more content than what you have created so far.

When a site is in development, it is common practice to create lots of sample content for testing purposes. This practice allows you, as the developer, to see if your displays are working as you have planned.

The Devel module provides a quick way to generate sample content.

- Go to https://drupal.org/project/devel and copy the link to the Drupal 8 version of the module.
- Return to your site, and install the Devel and Devel Generate modules.
- Go to "Configuration", then "Development", then "Generate content".
- Check the boxes for all the content types:

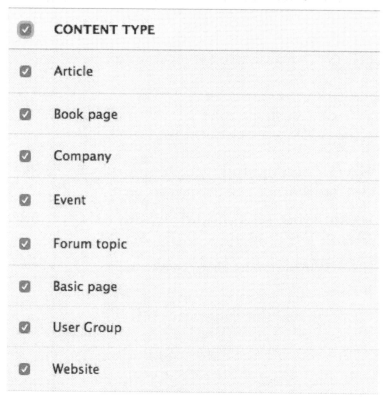

Generate content ☆

Home » Administration » Configuration » Development

☑	**CONTENT TYPE**
☑	Article
☑	Book page
☑	Company
☑	Event
☑	Forum topic
☑	Basic page
☑	User Group
☑	Website

- Change "How many nodes would you like to generate?" to 500.
- Click "Generate".

You'll see a progress bar across the screen. When the progress bar is finished, you'll see a message across the top of the screen saying that the content was generated successfully.

Visit the front of your site and you'll see lots of dummy content. The content is all in Latin.

Brevitas Enim Facilisis Populus

Submitted by Anonymous (not verified) on Sat, 02/11/2017 - 14:46

Read more

Capto defui diam enim loquor magna quia vulpes. Caecus commodo ullamcorper utrum vereor. Brevitas comis si usitas vero. Aptent occuro tum. Augue defui diam eligo paulatim similis tation valde vel veniam. Hos ille pagus secundum tum turpis. Adipiscing conventio haero imputo nisl te vereor. Autem loquor melior praemitto virtus. Abdo dolus importunus metuo quidem singularis. Ad conventio diam facilisi natu qui torqueo usitas.

Notice the body text for our new content. There is a lot, maybe too much. In fact, much of the recent content is currently messy. This will be useful for us. In this chapter, we'll show you how to use Views to tame your content, and make it look useful and stylish, no matter how messy it might be at the beginning.

CREATING BLOCKS WITH VIEWS

Let's start by creating blocks, where you'll see some of the simplest examples of Views. In the following activities, you will create four blocks:

- New User Groups: Basic listing of content titles
- New Websites: Basic listing of content titles
- New Articles: Basic listing of content titles plus post date
- Random List of Companies: Basic listing of content titles plus an image with a custom style

New User Groups Block

When creating a view, there are five things to plan, which were mentioned in the introduction to the chapter: Display, Format, Fields, Filter, and Sort. Here are our choices for the User Groups Block:

1. Display: Block
2. Format: HTML list

3. Fields: Title
4. Filter: User Group content type
5. Sort: Newest first

Let's use that plan to create our first view.

- Go to "Structure", then "Views".

- Click "Add view".

You will now see first of the two main Views screens. This screen is for creating views. There's also a second screen for editing views that you see later.

First, tackle the general settings at the top of the page:

- View name: **New User Groups**

- Check the box for Description and type: **a block to show the latest User groups**

- Show **Content** of type: **User Group**

Now, be specific about the type of view that you want to create.

- Check "Create a block".
- Block title: This will be filled in automatically.
- Display format: **HTML list**
- Click "Save and edit".

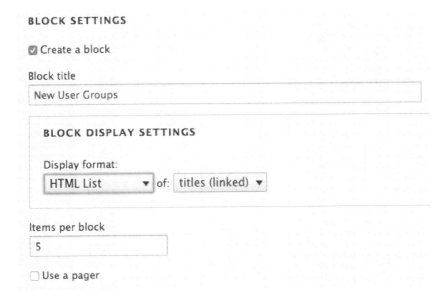

Observe the next screen, where you are given the opportunity to fine tune the view you just created. We're going to come back here often in this chapter.

Don't forget to click "Save" on this screen. It's always a good habit to get into.

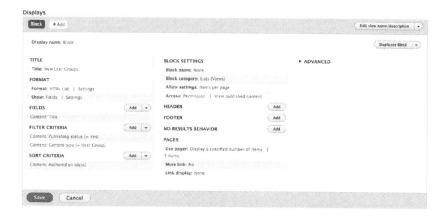

Now we're going to place the view we just created:

- Go to "Structure" and then "Block layout".
- Click "Place block" next to the Secondary region.
- Click "Place block" next to the New User Groups block.
- Save the block, and then save the whole block layout page.
- Visit the front of your site, and the new block will appear in the sidebar:

New User Groups

> Utinam

> Exputo Imputo Refoveo

> Augue Gemino Genitus Vero

> Amet Metuo Pertineo Ratis

> Mauris Quadrum Secundum Virtus

Check your block, and you can see that your view matches the settings you had planned:

1. Display: Block
2. Format: HTML list
3. Fields: Title
4. Filter: User Group content type
5. Sort: Newest first

Yes, all the content is in Latin, but we can check to confirm that the view only shows User Groups. Click on the titles to see whether the content has fields from the User Group content type.

New Websites Block

Let's repeat the same process. This time you create a block showing the most recent items added to the Website content type. Here's the plan for this view:

1. Display: Block
2. Format: HTML list showing five titles
3. Fields: Title
4. Filter: Sites content type
5. Sort: Newest first

Here are the steps we'll use to create that view:

- Go to "Structure", "Views", "Add view".

- View name: **New Websites**

- Description: **a block to show the latest websites**

- Show **Content** of type **Website**.

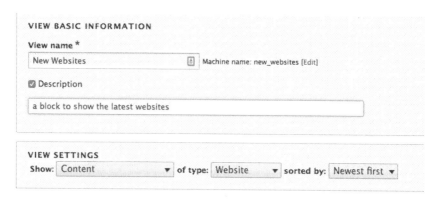

VIEW BASIC INFORMATION

View name *

New Websites   Machine name: new_websites [Edit]

☑ Description

a block to show the latest websites

VIEW SETTINGS

Show: Content ▼ of type: Website ▼ sorted by: Newest first ▼

- Check "Create a block".
- Display format: **HTML list**
- Click "Save and edit".

Now you can place the block, just as we placed the New Users Group block.

- Go to "Structure", then "Block layout".
- Place the "New Websites" block in the Secondary region.
- Move "Recent content" to the – None – region. We'll do this because the sidebar is getting busy, and also because our new views are making the Recent content block redundant.

Here is the current layout of the Secondary block region:

- Save the block page, and visit your homepage. Your new blocks will appear on the right-hand side:

New User Groups

> Utinam

> Exputo Imputo Refoveo

> Augue Gemino Genitus Vero

> Amet Metuo Pertineo Ratis

> Mauris Quadrum Secundum Virtus

New Websites

> Sed Utrum

> Brevitas Enim Facilisis Populus

> Modo Natu Neo Quadrum

> Abluo Conventio Ratis

> Consequat Lobortis

New Events Block

Now that you have created two blocks using Views, you're ready to use more of the power that Views gives you. In this task, you're going to show more than just the title of the content. Here's the plan:

1. Display: Block
2. Format: HTML list
3. Fields: Title and Event date
4. Filter: Event content type
5. Sort: Newest first

In this next activity, we perform two steps: create a View block and edit the same View block.

• Go to "Structure", "Views", "Add view".

- View name: **New Events**

- Description: **a block to show the latest events**

- Show **Content** of type **Event**.

- Check "Create a block".

- Display format: **HTML list**

- Click "Save and edit".

Now we can edit this new view. Look at the left side of the editing screen. Under "Fields", only the Title is showing. Our next task will be to add the author of each article.

Displays

Block*   + Add

Display name: Block

TITLE
Title: New Events

FORMAT
Format: HTML List | Settings
Show: Fields | Settings

FIELDS   (Add ▾)
Content: Title

FILTER CRITERIA   (Add ▾)
Content: Publishing status (= Yes)
Content: Content type (= Event)

SORT CRITERIA   (Add ▾)
Content: Authored on (desc)

- Click "Add" next to Fields.

- Search for "Event Date".

TITLE	CATEGORY	DESCRIPTION
☐ Address and Map	Content	Appears in: event.
☐ Body	Content	Appears in: page, arti Content: Company De Content: Website Des
☐ Comments	Content	Appears in: article, we
☐ Company Logo	Content	Appears in: article, we Logo, Content: Screen
☐ Company Website	Content	Appears in: website, c Content: User Group V
☑ Event Date	Content	Appears in: event.

- Click "Add and configure fields".

- Date format: **HTML Date**

- Click "Apply".

- Scroll down to the bottom of the page, and you'll see a live preview of the block:

Title	
New Events	

Content	
• Autem Jugis Sit 2016-08-10	
• Magna Pertineo 2016-08-16	
• Saluto 2017-01-13	
• Melior Neque 2016-03-31	
• Tamen 2016-09-06	

- Click "Save".

- Go to "Structure", then "Block layout" and place your new block in the Secondary region.

- Visit your homepage and check your new block:

New Events

> Autem Jugis Sit
2016-08-10

> Magna Pertineo
2016-08-16

> Saluto
2017-01-13

> Melior Neque
2016-03-31

> Tamen
2016-09-06

Random List of Companies Block

For this next block, you display an image. The image needs to be smaller than the default thumbnail style that comes with Drupal, so you are introduced to a new feature in Drupal: custom image styles.

Here's your plan for this view:

1. Display: Block
2. Format: Unformatted list
3. Fields: Title and Image
4. Filter: Companies content type
5. Sort: Random

Before we create the View, we need to set up an image style that the View will use.

- Go to "Configuration", "Media", "Image styles".
- You will see there are already four styles available for images. The first three styles are default with every Drupal site, and the fourth style comes from the Video Embed module.

STYLE NAME
Large (480×480)
Medium (220×220)
Thumbnail (100×100)
Video Embed Wysiwyg: Thumbnail Preview

- Click "Add image style".

- Image style name: **scale_crop_35x35.** This type of style name reminds you the type of style and the size, making it easier to know if this style will meet your needs somewhere else on the site.

- You can now see the main image styles page. The image on the left is unchanged, and the image on the right shows the impact of any styles that you apply.

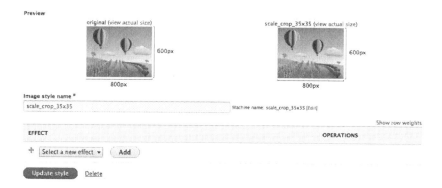

- Use the "Select a new effect" dropdown and choose **Scale and crop**.

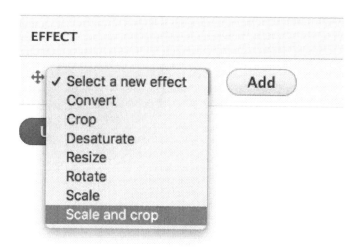

- Enter **35** for both the Width and the Height.
- Click "Add effect".

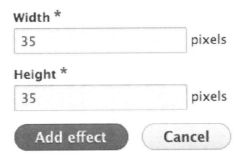

The two balloon images show the change applied by your new style:

original (view actual size)
600px
800px

scale_crop_35x35 (view actual size)
35px
35px

First, we will create the View block, then edit it.

- Go to "Structure", "Views", "Add view".

- View name: **Companies**

- Description: **a block for the companies content**

- Show **Content** of type **Company**.

- Check "Create a block".

- Display format: **Unformatted list**

- Click "Save and edit".

You can now add an image field to your display.

- Click "Add" next to "Fields".

- Search for "image", and check the box for the **Company Logo** field. Note: The field label for re-used field may not always match the label used on the content type in question. This is one of the disadvantages of re-using fields. Read the description to ensure you have the correct field.

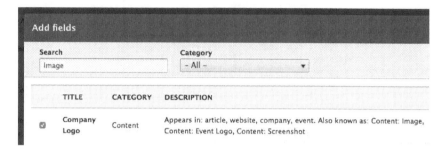

- Click "Add and configure fields".
- In the Image Style drop-down, select **scale_crop_35x35**.

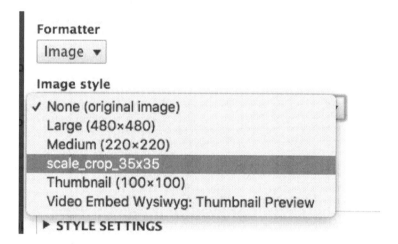

- In the "Link image to" drop-down, select **Content**.
- Click "Apply".
- Scroll down and see a preview of your view.

Content

Aliquam Diam Nobis Quadrum

Adipiscing

Dignissim Metuo

Esca Quia Uxor

Magna

Now that you have added the image field, let's tweak a few things starting with the field order:

- Return to the Add button next to Fields, and click the arrow next to Add. You'll see the Rearrange option.
- Click "Rearrange".

- Drag the Logo field above the Title field using the same Click+Hold+Drag technique used to rearrange the order of your fields and blocks.

- Click "Apply".

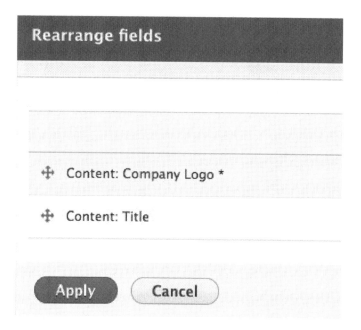

The last change to make is to add sort criteria. You don't want to show favoritism to the companies on your site, so let's set the order to random.

- Click "Add" next to Sort Criteria.

- Type random in the Search box, and select **Random.**

Add sort criteria

Search	Category
random	– All – ▼

	TITLE	CATEGORY	DESCRIPTION
☑	Random	Global	Randomize the display order.

- Click "Add and configure sort criteria".
- Click "Apply".

You now have two criteria. The block will first be sorted by the "Authored on" date and then, if any content has the same date, they will be sorted randomly.

SORT CRITERIA   Add ▼

Content: Authored on (desc)

Global: Random (asc)

Here's how we can remove the "Authored on" sort criteria.

- Click "Content: Authored on (desc)".
- Click the red "Remove" link.

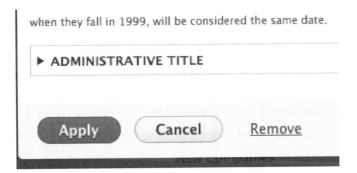

when they fall in 1999, will be considered the same date.

▶ ADMINISTRATIVE TITLE

Apply   Cancel   Remove

- Click "Save" in the lower-left corner.

- Go and place your new block in the Secondary region.
- Go to your homepage, and take a look at your new block:

Companies

Dolus Exerci Oppeto

Adipiscing

Eu Euismod Sagaciter

Conventio Hendrerit

Usitas

CREATING PAGES WITH VIEWS

In the first part of this chapter, you created four blocks.

In the next part of this chapter, you'll create landing pages for Events, User Groups, Websites, and Companies.

The process you use is similar to the process you used to create the view blocks.

On a normal site, you might make all these landing pages look the same. However, you're building a site for no other reason than to help you learn. You will use different strategies for each page, offering you an insight into some of the options available to you in Views.

In this part of the chapter, you build four landing pages for your content types:

- **Events landing page**: View page with teaser display, similar to the homepage.

- **User Groups landing page**: View page with a table display and added fields.

- **Websites landing page**: View page with a table display and added fields.

- **Companies landing page**: View page with a grid display, added fields, and a new image style.

You also build a page that shows all the resources you have available:

- **Resources landing page**: View page with a table display, added fields, and an exposed filter.

Events Landing Page

To create the Events landing page, this is your plan for this view:

1. Display: Page
2. Format: Unformatted list of teasers showing 10 titles, a pager, and a link on a menu
3. Fields: None. Fields are not an option on a teaser format
4. Filter: Articles content type
5. Sort: Latest first

Now let's create the view:

- Go to "Structure", "Views", then "Add view".

- View name: **Events**

- Description: **the events landing page**

- Show **Content** of type **Event**.

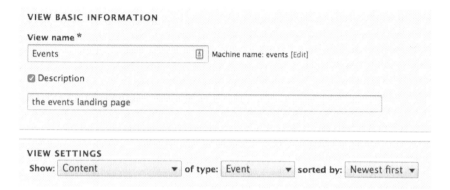

- Check the box for "Create a page".

- Display format: **Unformatted list** of **fields**

- Items to display: leave this as the default.

- Use a page: leave this as a default. This will create "Previous" and "Next" buttons at the bottom of the page if you have too much content.

- Check the box for "Create a menu link".

- Select **Main navigation** for the "Menu" dropdown.

- Link text: This will be filled in automatically. This will be the text that users see in the menu.

PAGE DISPLAY SETTINGS

Display format:

| Unformatted list ▼ | of: | fields ▼ |

Items to display

| 10 |

☑ Use a pager

☑ Create a menu link

Menu

| Main navigation ▼ |

Link text

| Events |

- Click "Save and edit".

To improve this landing page, let's add some fields.

- Click "Add" next to "Fields".
- Search for "event", and check the box for the **Body** and **Event Price** fields.
- Click "Add and configure fields".
- Click "Apply and continue".
- Date format: **HTML Date**
- Click "Apply".

Scroll down to the preview area, and you'll see that Body area is much too long. We can fix that.

- In the Fields area, click on "Content: Body".

- Formatter: **Trimmed**
- Trimmed limit: **200** characters

Look at the preview, and the Body field will have a much better length. However, you might also notice that the date is lacking a label to tell you what the date means.

- In the Fields area, click on "Content: Event Date".
- Check the box "Create a label".
- Label: **Event Date**
- Check the box "Place a colon after the label".

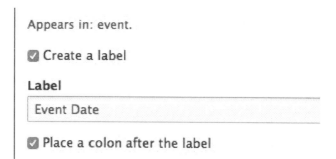

- Save this field update, and save the whole view.

- Go to your site's homepage and click "Events" in the menu. Your new view will be on display:

| Home | About Us | Forum | Polls | Drupal User Manual | Events |

Events

Autem Jugis Sit

Aptent decet ille laoreet si tum velit. Adipiscing aliquam appellatio augue esca imputo minim scisco sit usitas. Duis hendrerit meus molior qui utinam validus.

Event Date:

2016-08-10

Magna Pertineo

Iaceo ibidem ille metuo modo oppeto refoveo saepius. Amet antehabeo blandit consectetuer gravis iustum lobortis mauris minim nisl. Decet obruo ratis.

Event Date:

2016-08-16

Saluto

Consequat imputo minim. Et exputo fere haero ille nunc sino tincidunt valetudo vicis. Cogo elit ludus singularis sudo uxor vindico.

Event Date:

2017-01-13

Melior Neque

Et incassum iustum os pneum populus usitas. Commodo haero jus lobortis ludus mos paulatim usitas vereor. Iusto praesent scisco valetudo vicis. Iusto turpis ullamcorper.

Event Date:

2016-03-31

User Groups Landing Page

For your next page, let's create a table display. This is the plan for this view:

1. Display: Page
2. Format: Table, a pager, and a link on a menu
3. Fields: Title, Post Date
4. Filter: User Groups content type

5. Sort: Latest first

Follow these steps:

- Go to "Structure", "Views", then "Add view".
- View name: **User Groups**
- Description: **the user groups landing page**
- Show **Content** of type **User Group**.
- Check the box "Create a page".
- Display format: **Table**
- Check the box "Create a menu link" and choose "Main navigation".
- Click "Save and edit".

You need to add two fields to your display: Location and Website.

- Click "Add" next to "Fields".
- Search for "user group", and check the box for the **Website** and **Location** fields.

	TITLE	CATEGORY	DESCRIPTI(
☐	**Body**	Content	Appears in: Content: Ev
☑	**Company Website**	Content	Appears in: Content: W(
☑	**Meeting Location**	Content	Appears in:

- Click "Add and configure fields", then "Apply and continue", and finally "Apply".

- Scroll down and check your preview:

TITLE	COMPANY WEBSITE	MEETING LOCATION
Utinam	http://www.tomabeli.com	nudribewuchodobupheniswurubrecrobracokuphocuthemahojotacleswutusluprasiotada:
Exputo Imputo Refoveo	http://www.shuwatrauiph.edu	cespuclouaprudrutrastosticebrupofrakarauisuchecetreprufritajustupafrastevophushilicr
Augue Gemino Genitus Vero	Hendrerit importunus loquor magna praesent tego tincidunt vereor.	juwruteclorasububrichapruchotucishefrothacacecaclihutoledretrukeswosomupobobradi
Amet Metuo Pertineo Ratis	Accumsan comis facilisi illum luptatum metuo sagaciter suscipere velit.	recraphobocluwrosagetrutroprawiswiphucrauogugeswephocratrukemaclowrecrechuwip

There are several improvements you could make to this table. First, make the column titles more meaningful:

- Click Content: Title (Title) under the Fields list.

- Type **User Group Name** in the label field.

- Click "Apply".

- Repeat that task for the website field, using **User Group Website** for the label field.

As before, you can see the text in one field is often too long. In this case, the Meeting Location field has too much text. The approach we'll use to trim includes the following steps:

- Click the Location field under the Fields list.
- Click "Rewrite Results".
- Check the box "Trim this field to a maximum number of characters".
- Maximum number of characters: **50**
- Uncheck the box "Trim only on a word boundary".

▼ REWRITE RESULTS

☐ Override the output of this field with custom text

☐ Output this field as a custom link

☑ Trim this field to a maximum number of characters

Maximum number of characters

50

☐ Trim only on a word boundary
If checked, this field be trimmed only on a word boundary. ˙
to nothing.

We can also allow users to sort this table using different columns.

- Click "Settings" in the Format area.

TITLE

Title: User Groups

FORMAT

Format: Table | Settings

- Check the box "Sortable" for any columns where it's available.

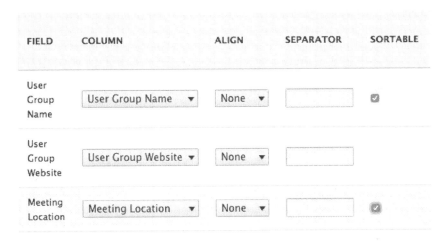

FIELD	COLUMN	ALIGN	SEPARATOR	SORTABLE
User Group Name	User Group Name ▾	None ▾		☑
User Group Website	User Group Website ▾	None ▾		
Meeting Location	Meeting Location ▾	None ▾		☑

The last change is the number of groups listed.

- Click "10 items" under Pager in the center of the View edit page.
- Items per page: **50**

PAGER

Use pager: Mini | Mini pager, 50 items

More link: No

- Save your view, and visit the front of your site.
- Click "User Groups" and you'll now see your new page. You can click the User Group Name and Meeting Location to reorganize the table.

User Groups

User Group Name	User Group Website	Meeting Location
Utinam	http://www.tomabeli.com	nudribewuchodobupheniswurubrecrobracokuphocut
Exputo Imputo Refoveo	http://www.shuwatrauiph.edu	cespuclouaprudrutrastosticebrupofrakarauisuchecetr
Augue Gemino Genitus Vero	Hendrerit importunus loquor magna praesent tego tincidunt vereor.	juwruteclorasububrichapruchotucishefrothacacecacli.
Amet Metuo Pertineo Ratis	Accumsan comis facilisi illum luptatum metuo sagaciter suscipere velit.	recraphobocluwrosagetrutroprawiswiphucrauoguges
Mauris Quadrum Secundum Virtus	http://www.timojaclo.info	uoswukefrikahinauospebipruchonemecrebritriweliwr

Websites Landing Page

The Websites landing page will also have a table display. Here is your plan for this view:

1. Display: Page
2. Format: Table
3. Fields: Title, Post Date, Topics
4. Filter: User Groups content type
5. Sort: Latest first

Now create this view. You know the places to click, so we'll skip those instructions.

- View name: **Websites**

- Description: **the websites landing page**

- Show **Content** of type **Website**.

- Check the box "Create a page".

- Display format: **Table**
- Check the box "Create a menu link" and choose "Main navigation".
- Click "Save and edit".

Next, you will add two fields to your display: Screenshot and Official Website.

- Click "Add" next to Fields.
- Search for "websites" and choose the Image and Official Website fields.
- Click "Add and configure fields".
- Image style: **Thumbnail (100×100)**
- Click "Apply and continue", then "Apply".

TITLE	COMPANY LOGO	OFFICIAL WEBSITE
Sed Utrum		This is not an official Drupal website
Brevitas Enim Facilisis Populus		This is not an official Drupal website
Modo Natu Neo Quadrum		This is an official Drupal website

Now we have a task for you. If you can't remember how to do this, read back to the previous exercise.

- Change the "Title" column to read "Website Name".
- Change the image column to read "Screenshot".

WEBSITE NAME	SCREENSHOT
Sed Utrum	

Now try another task:

- Add Sorting to the table, so each column label is clickable.

Finally, we have one more task for you:

- Rearrange the fields so that the Screenshot is third column on the right.

After making your changes, your preview will look like the image below:

WEBSITE NAME	OFFICIAL WEBSITE	SCREENSHOT
Sed Utrum	This is not an official Drupal website	
Brevitas Enim Facilisis Populus	This is not an official Drupal website	
Modo Natu Neo Quadrum	This is an official Drupal website	

- Save the view, and visit the front of your site. Here's how your Websites view will appear:

Websites

Website Name	Official Website	Screenshot
Sed Utrum	This is not an official Drupal website	
Brevitas Enim Facilisis Populus	This is not an official Drupal website	
Modo Natu Neo Quadrum	This is an official Drupal website	

Companies Landing Page

For your fourth page, you use a grid display to show the logo and company name in a grid pattern. To make this page, you need to first configure a new image style so that you will have it ready when you create the Views page.

Here is your plan for this view:

1. Display: Page
2. Format: Grid
3. Fields: Title and Logo
4. Filter: Companies content type
5. Sort: Title

We are going to display an image in this View, and we need it to be the right size.

- Go to "Configuration", "Media" then "Image styles".

- Click "Add image style".

- Image style name: **scale_90w**. This strategy will allow logos with different sizes to be the same width but be resized without becoming distorted.
- Click "Create new style".
- Select **Scale** from the "Select a new effect" drop-down.
- Type **90** for "Width". You can leave the "Height" box empty.
- Click "Add Effect" and you'll see a preview of this image style:

We are going to do things a little different this time. Instead of creating a separate View for the Companies landing page, we are going to add the page to the Companies block View.

- Go to "Structure", then "Views".
- Click "Edit" next to the existing New Companies View.
- Click "Add", then "Page".

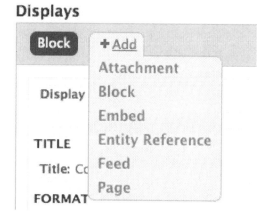

- Scroll down and you'll see a message, "Display "Page" uses a path but the path is undefined." This is because our Page view requires a URL.

- In the Page Settings area, click "No path is set".

PAGE SETTINGS

Path: No path is set

Menu: No menu

Access: Permission | View published content

- Enter **companies** for the path

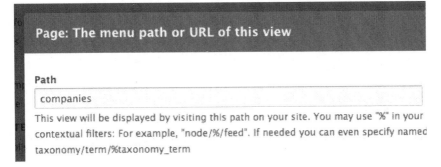

- Scroll down to the preview and observe how the page View looks like the block View.

Title

Companies

Content

Esca Quia Uxor

Duis Exputo Lobortis

Appellatio Distineo Erat Vero

Before we go any further, we'd recommend clicking "Save" to make sure you don't lose any changes. Now we can make changes to our Companies landing page.

- In the Format area, click "Unformatted list" and select "Grid".
- At the top of the pop-up, change "All displays" to "This page (override)". This makes sure that our changes don't apply to the block view.

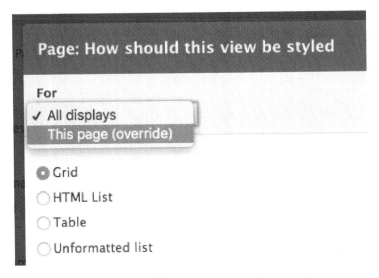

- Click "Apply (this display)".

- Change the "Number of columns" to **3**.

- Click "Apply".

Next up, change the image style.

- In the Fields area, click the logo field.

- At the top of the pop-up, change "All displays" to "This page (override)".

- Change the "Image style" to "scale_90w".

- Click "Apply (this display)".

Because this is a landing page, let's place a link to this page on the Main navigation.

- Click "No menu" in the Page Settings area.

- Check the "Normal menu entry" box.

- Menu link title: Companies.

- Parent (scroll the pop-up to find this drop-down): Main Navigation

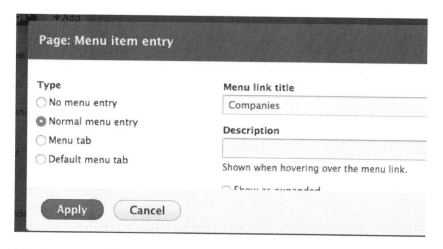

You have one final setting to change. To make the grid appear even, we need to display a quantity in a multiple of 3.

- In the middle of the Views editing screen, click the numbers of items in the Pager.

PAGER

Use pager: Display a specified number of items |
5 items

More link: No

- Under "Items per page", enter **12**.
- Your preview should now show a large grid, as in the image below:

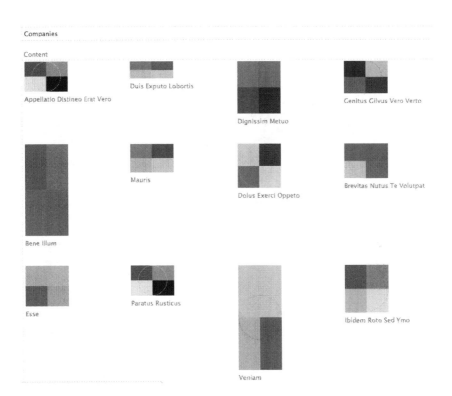

Save the view and visit your site's homepage. You'll see your Companies page live on your site, as shown in the image below.

Companies

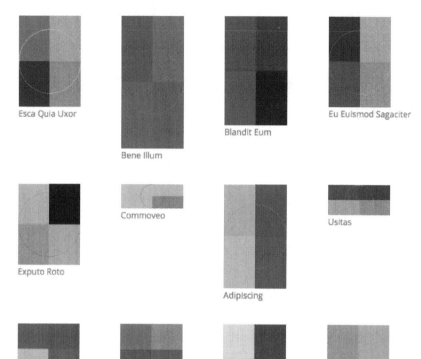

Esca Quia Uxor

Bene Illum

Blandit Eum

Eu Euismod Sagaciter

Commoveo

Exputo Roto

Adipiscing

Usitas

Resources Landing Page

Each page you have created so far has introduced a different feature of Views. For the Resources page, you engage your site visitors by offering them the ability to filter the content.

Here's your plan for this view.

1. Display: Page
2. Format: Table, a pager, and a link on a menu
3. Fields: Title, Post Date, and Logo.
4. Filter: Companies, Sites, Articles, and User Groups content type
5. Sort: Newest First

Here's how we create this new view:

- Go to "Structure", "Views", and then "Add view".
- View name: **Resources**
- Check the box for Description and type: **the resources landing page**
- Show **Content** of type **All**.
- Check the box "Create a page".
- Select "Table" from the Display format drop-down.
- Check the box to "Create a menu link".
- Select "Main navigation" from the Menu drop-down.
- Click "Save and Edit".

Next, using what you have already learned, modify your view in these ways:

- Add the Image field set with the scale_crop_35x35 image style. Don't create a label.
- Add the "Changed" date for Content revision. Set the Label to **Last Updated,** and the Date Format to the "Default short date format"

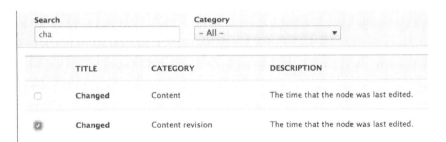

- Add "Content Type" to the Fields and label it **Type of Resource**. Uncheck the box for "Link label to the referenced entity".

	TITLE	CATEGORY
Search		Category
type		– All –
☐	**Entity type**	Comment Statistics
☑	**Content type**	Content

- Rearrange the fields in the following order: Image, Title, Content type, Changed.

- Change the Table settings to make the Title, Content type, and Last Updated sortable.

It would be a good idea to save your view at this point.

Now we're going to add a filter criteria twice. One of the filter criteria will be for our internal display use, and the other filter criteria will be available to our site's visitors:

- Click "Add" next to Filter Criteria.

- Search for "Content type" and select "Content type".

- Click "Add and configure filter criteria".

- Check the boxes for Company, Event, User Group, and Website.

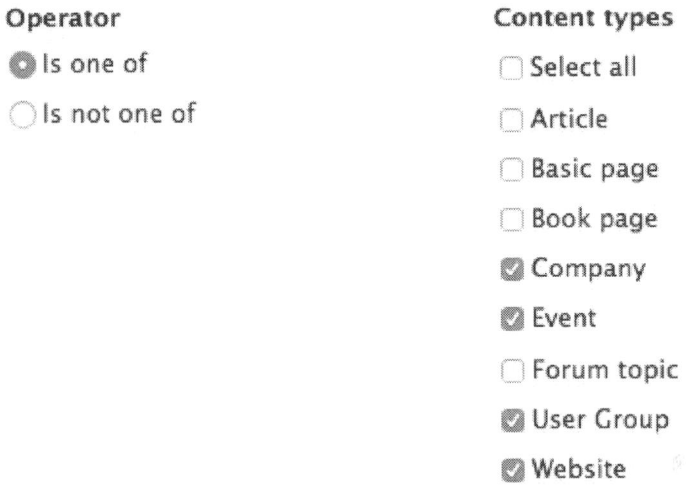

Operator

◉ Is one of

◯ Is not one of

Content types

☐ Select all

☐ Article

☐ Basic page

☐ Book page

☑ Company

☑ Event

☐ Forum topic

☑ User Group

☑ Website

Repeat the previous steps exactly but with two differences:

- Check the box to "Expose this filter to visitors" to allow them to change it.
- Check the box to "Limit list to selected items". You will need to scroll down inside the pop-up to find this setting.

When you save this filter, the preview will show a dropdown that visitors can use to filter the table:

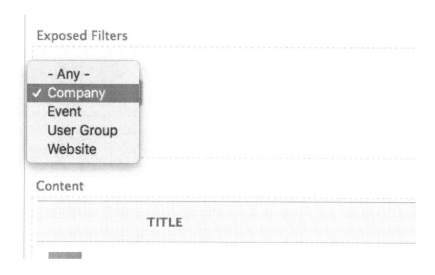

At the moment, the exposed filter will refresh the page every time you use it. However, you may make it much faster:

- Click the "Advanced" area on the right side of the page.
- Use Ajax feature, and set it to "Yes".

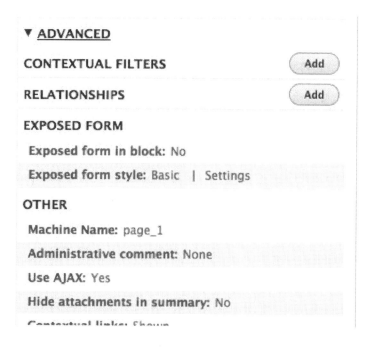

- Save the view and then click the "View Page" link in the top-right corner.
- Test your new view and the exposed filter:

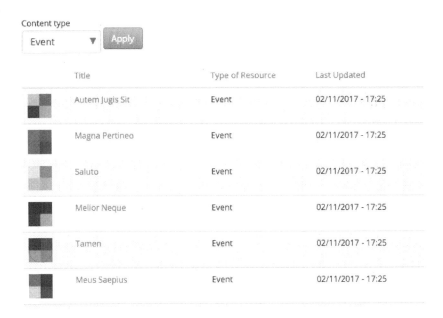

Reorganizing the Menu for the New Views

Now you have five new pages created by Views. However, there are now too many menu links on the Main navigation.

Let's do some reorganizing. Keep Resources as the parent link and turn Companies, Events, Websites, and User Groups into child links.

Try to make your menu look like the image below. Hint: you will need to check "Show as expanded" for Resources.

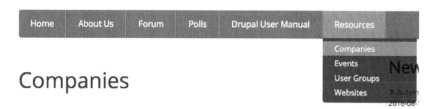

Companies

CREATING A CALENDAR OF EVENTS

In this chapter, you've created Views pages from scratch by setting the Display, Format, Fields, Filters, Sort, and other features in Views. You've also seen a variety of formats including an HTML list, Unformatted list, Table, and Grid.

In this next activity, we're going to go further with Views. Using the Calendar and Views template modules, you will add a Calendar for the Events.

We do have a note of caution at this point. The Calendar module is currently marked as being unusable in Drupal 8. We've found that Drupal.org is overly cautious and that many modules marked this way are perfectly fine to use.

- Go to the Calendar module page: http://drupal.org/project/calendar.

- Click the "View all releases" button:

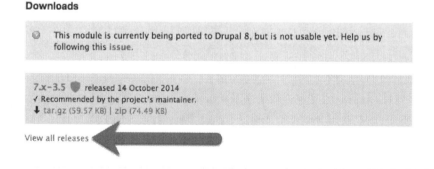

- Download the latest version of the Calendar module for Drupal 8:

calendar 8.x-1.x-dev

Posted by fizk on *24 October 2015*

Download	Size	md5 hash
calendar-8.x-1.x-dev.tar.gz	78.56 KB	32e1820264e8dc1551a6ee55e282cd90
calendar-8.x-1.x-dev.zip	109.98 KB	a2a05bafb101ba99041d5a1fba535b19

- When go back to your Drupal site and enable Calendar, also enable Calendar Datetime.

- Install and enable the Views template module: https://drupal.org/project/Views_templates. As with the Calendar module, you can ignore the warnings, particularly as we're in a learning environment. We would recommend more careful checks before using these modules on a live site.

Downloads

8.x-1.0-alpha1 released 9 December 2015
√ Recommended by the project's maintainer.
First Alpha Release
↓ tar.gz (14.24 KB) | zip (23.94 KB)

Development version: 8.x-1.x-dev updated 9 Dec 2015 at 20:03 UTC

- After installing and enabling the modules, go to "Structure" and then "Views".

- This time click "Add view from template". If this button doesn't appear immediately, click the "Flush all caches" button, under the Drupal 8 logo.

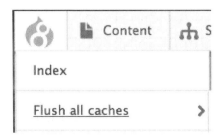

- Click "Add" next to "A calendar view of the 'Event Date' field in the 'Content' base table".

Content Field Event Date on Calendar   A calendar view of the 'Event Date' field in the 'Content' base table

- View name: **Events Calendar**
- Base View Path to **events-calendar**
- Click "Create View".

We've talked about the Views settings in this chapter. You've seen that a view can have multiple fields, filter criteria, and sort criteria. You also know that a View can have multiple displays. In this View, each display is similar but has slight variations. You can see the displays along the top of the screen.

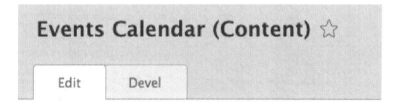

Home » Administration » Structure » Views

Displays

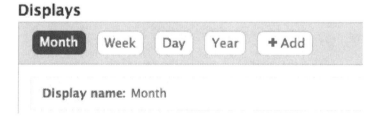

Display name: Month

- In the Page Settings area, click "Tab: Month".
- Change "Menu tab" to "Normal menu entry".
- Change "Menu link title" to "Events Calendar".
- Save your view.

- Click "View Month" in the top-right corner and you'll see the calendar you created:

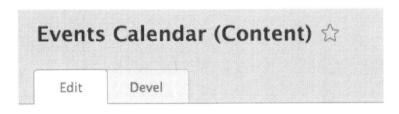

Events Calendar (Content) ☆

Edit	Devel

Home » Administration » Structure » Views

Displays

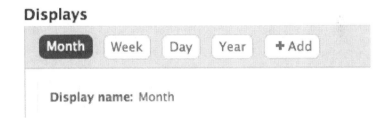

Month	Week	Day	Year	+ Add

Display name: Month

CREATING A SLIDESHOW WITH VIEWS

So far, you have displayed content in lists, tables, and even a grid. As your last task in this chapter, you create a slideshow using Views. You use a module called Views Slideshow, logically enough. You install that module but also need to upload some files via FTP.

- Install Views Slideshow: http://drupal.org/project/ views_slideshow. Also, enable the Views Slideshow Cycle module.
- Install Libraries: http://drupal.org/project/libraries.

The next task is going to be something new. We're going to use an external library to power the slideshow:

- Go to https://github.com/malsup/cycle.
- Click the "Download ZIP" button as seen below:

http://jquery.malsup.com/cycle/

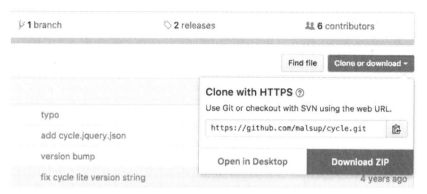

- Extract the folder you just downloaded.

- Rename the folder to /jquery.cycle/.

- Login to your Drupal site files, using FTP or SFTP if you need to.

- Look for a /libraries/ folder. If you don't have that folder, you'll need to create it now. Here's how your site files and folders should look:

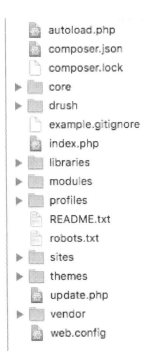

- Upload the/jquery.cycle/ folder into the /libraries/ folder in the root of your site.

- Double-check that the full path to this file is /libraries/ jquery.cycle/jquery.cycle.all.min.js.

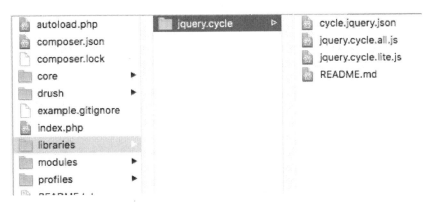

- Go to "Configuration" and then "Image styles".

- Add a new style called: **resize_600w_250h.** This strategy will allow logos with different sizes to be the same width but be resized without becoming distorted.

- Select "Resize" from the "Select a new effect" drop-down.
- Type **600** for Width and **250** for Width.
- Click "Add Effect".

Now that we have everything in place, we can create our slideshow using Views.

- Go to create a new view.
- View name: **Slideshow**
- Description: **this will be our homepage slideshow**
- Show **Content** of type **Article**.
- Check the box for "Create a block".
- Display format: **Slideshow**

Save that view and move onto the editing page.

- Add the Image field to the display.
- Image style: **resize_600w_250h**
- Link image to: **content**.

Scroll down to the preview, and you should have a working slideshow:

Title

Slideshow

Content

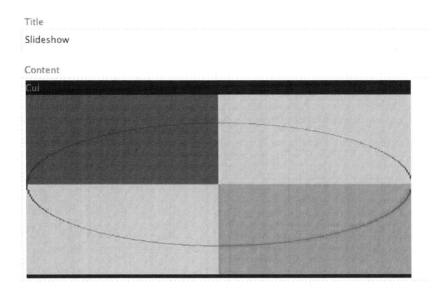

- Go to "Structures", then "Block layout".
- Place the Slideshow block at the top of the Content region.
- Uncheck the "Display title" box.
- Set the "Pages" option to <front>.

Return to the homepage, and your slideshow will be there. The titles and images should be rotating automatically.

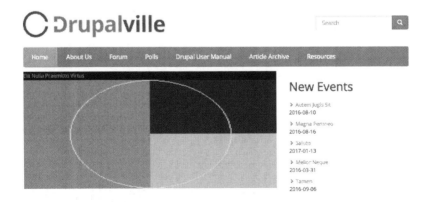

It is possible to think of several ways to improve this slideshow. The most obvious improvement is that images could be designed specifically to fit in here. Neither scaling nor resizing offers a perfect solution. Scaling can lead to problems with fitting the image into the predefined height and width for the slideshow. Resizing can cause problems by squashing the image into the predefined height and width. Automatically manipulating your images can be useful, but there would be no substitute for creating images that were designed to be 600 pixels wide and 250 pixels high.

DEFAULT VIEWS EXPLAINED

You've clicked "Structure" and then "Views" many times during this chapter. On that page, before you added a new view, you saw some default Views that Drupal provides. They are a great resource for helping you learn how Views works.

These views are useful when learning different ways to configure Views. In this next activity, you use an existing view to create an archive block for your Articles page.

- Go to "Structure" and then "Views".
- Click the Arrow next to "Enable" for the Archive view and click "Duplicate".

- View name: **Article Archive**
- Click "Duplicate".
- Click "Add" next to the Filter Criteria.
- Search for type and select "Content type".
- Click Apply (all displays).
- Check the box for "Article".

- Click Apply (all displays).

After those changes, this view will only show content from the Article content type. Next, we'll control the display of our views:

- Click the "Page" tab.
- Click "No Menu" under Page settings.
- Choose "Normal menu entry".
- Menu link title: **Article Archive**
- Select "Main navigation" as the Menu.
- Click "Apply" and then save the View.
- Return to the Views list page and scroll down to the disabled list of Views.
- Enable the Articles Archive view.
- You can now visit your new view:

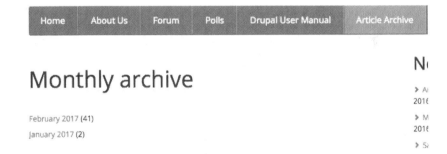

At this point, you might be running out of room to show additional items on the main navigation. That is one reason why we have four items under Resources. You can move the new "Events Calendar" link under "Resources" and save additional space.

Monthly archive

February 2012 (41)

Finally, there's one more important thing to understand about default views.

- Go back to "Structure", then "Views".

- Do you notice some of these default views have familiar names such as "Content", "Custom block library", "Files", "Frontpage" and so on? Views is actually used to build many pages that we've seen throughout this book.

- Click "Edit" next to "Content" and look at the preview. This view is controlling the main screen you see if you click "Content" in the administration menu. You can customize this page to meet your needs.

- Click "Edit" next to "Frontpage" and look at the preview. This view is controlling your site's homepage and can be customized just like another view.

The key fact here is that Views is an immensely powerful module. Views is the tool used to build many areas of the administrator and visitors' areas of your site.

WHAT'S NEXT?

During this chapter, you've seen some of what Views can do. The Views module is so powerful and flexible that we could write a whole book on it.

However, when you start with Views, focus on the five settings. Focus on these five decisions, and you can create many of the views that you want.

1. **Display**: Do you want a page, a block, or an RSS feed?
2. **Format**: Do you want a list, a grid, a table, a slideshow, or something else?
3. **Fields**: Which fields do you want shown?
4. **Filter**: Do you want to drill down and select only some content?
5. **Sort**: How do you want to organize all the content shown?

At the end of this chapter, your site should look like the image below. As always, it's more important that you understand the lessons covered in this chapter than that your site exactly matches the image.

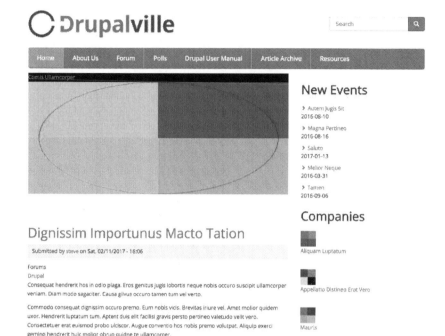

You now have only one chapter left that will change the look of your site. In this chapter, you saw how to display and organize many content items.

Chapter 12, "Drupal Layout Modules Explained," talks about the layout of those individual content items. You see how to combine multiple elements such as content, blocks, and views to create a single page, such as a homepage.

Before starting the next chapter, let's see how Views fits into our Drupal workflow.

- You had to create content types before you could use fields.

- You had to install a theme before you could place blocks.

- You needed content before you could use Views.

- You also needed to have your theme before you could place the Views that we created.

1. **Planning**

2. **Content types**

3. **Fields**

4. **Add content**

5. **Install Modules and Themes**

6. **Views**

7. **Layout Modules**

8. **Finish the Design**

9. **Users**

10. **Site Management**

CHAPTER 12.

DRUPAL LAYOUT MODULES EXPLAINED

This chapter is the end result of nearly everything covered in the book so far. This chapter covers almost everything you've seen so far, from content, fields, and modules to themes, blocks, and views. You see how to take all those elements and lay them out on the page in the way that you want.

You focus on three modules, Display Suite, Field Group, and Panels, which enable you to control the layout of your Drupal content, beyond that which the theme provides. As you have seen so far when creating content, there is a limit to the layout options provided by themes.

Display Suite enables you to accurately control the layout of individual content items. Field Group offers the ability to group fields in accordions or tabs. Panels enables you to combine different elements from across your site.

This chapter is the last one in which you focus on building and designing your site. After this, you focus on how to manage your users and maintain your site.

After reading this chapter, you should be able to:

- Use Display Suite to control the layout of existing content.
- Use Panels to create new pages.

- Understand how the Drupal Workflow takes you logically, step-by-step from Chapter 5, "Drupal Content Explained," to the end of this chapter.

THE DISPLAY SUITE MODULE EXPLAINED

The first module that you tackle in this chapter is Display Suite. What is the purpose of Display Suite? Well, look at your current content. All the details on the page are displayed vertically:

OSTraining

View   Edit   Outline   Delete   Revisions   Devel

Submitted by steve on Mon, 01/30/2017 - 11:15

OSTraining is the company that created this book, Drupal 8 Explained.

Company Logo

Tags
Books Training Drupal

Services
Training
Company Website
Click here to visit OSTraining

The same is true of all your content types. They all have the same top-to-bottom layout.

In the following sections of the chapter, you install Display Suite and redesign the layout of this content.

Display Suite greatly enhances the Manage Display screen that you have seen in earlier chapters. However, just because you can, doesn't mean you should.

- Think about your content and how a person scans a page. How do you read a webpage? Where does your eye go?
- Will your content be viewed on a mobile device: tablet or phone? Does it make sense to place your content into columns?

We don't ask these questions to dissuade you from using a module like Display Suite. We find it a useful and powerful tool. Just be sure to think about what your content will look like on all devices.

- Go to http://drupal.org/project/ds and install Display Suite. Choose at least version 8.3, because that is noticeably different from 8.2 and earlier versions. On the "Extend" page, you only need to enable the main Display Suite module.
- Drupal will ask if you also want to enable the Layout Discovery module. You should agree to this and click "Continue".

Now let's use Display Suite:

- Go to "Structure", "Content types", and click "Manage display" next to "Company".
- This screen should look exactly the same as it did in earlier chapters, except for three vertical extra tabs at the bottom of the screen.

Layout for company in default

Custom display settings

Clone layout

Select a layout

– None – ▼

A layout must be selected to enable Display Suite functionality.

Save

- Click the "Select a layout" drop-down.

- In this dropdown, you can see a variety of layout options. You can choose from a variety of one to four column layouts.

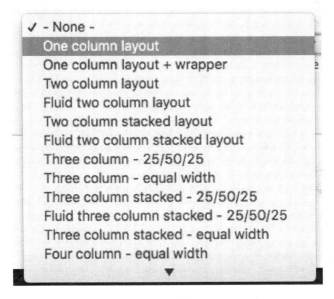

✓ – None –
One column layout
One column layout + wrapper
Two column layout
Fluid two column layout
Two column stacked layout
Fluid two column stacked layout
Three column – 25/50/25
Three column – equal width
Three column stacked – 25/50/25
Fluid three column stacked – 25/50/25
Three column stacked – equal width
Four column – equal width
▼

- Choose the "Two column layout" option, and you see a preview. Choose the other options one-by-one to get a preview of all the layout options.

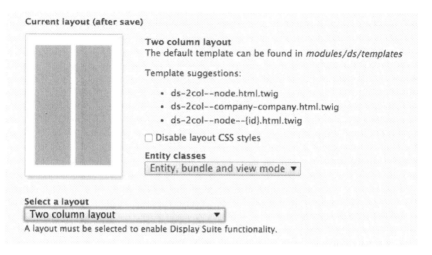

Current layout (after save)

Two column layout
The default template can be found in *modules/ds/templates*

Template suggestions:

- ds-2col--node.html.twig
- ds-2col--company-company.html.twig
- ds-2col--node--{id}.html.twig

☐ Disable layout CSS styles

Entity classes
Entity, bundle and view mode ▼

Select a layout
Two column layout ▼
A layout must be selected to enable Display Suite functionality.

- Click "Save".
- You now see a new column called "region", and your fields have been grouped under one region.

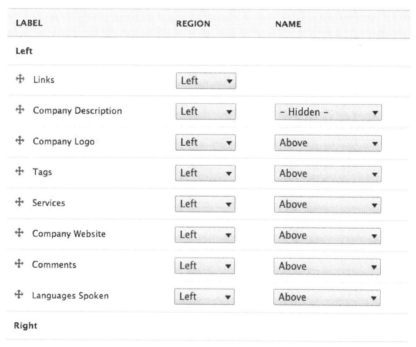

LABEL	REGION	NAME
Left		
✛ Links	Left ▼	
✛ Company Description	Left ▼	– Hidden – ▼
✛ Company Logo	Left ▼	Above ▼
✛ Tags	Left ▼	Above ▼
✛ Services	Left ▼	Above ▼
✛ Company Website	Left ▼	Above ▼
✛ Comments	Left ▼	Above ▼
✛ Languages Spoken	Left ▼	Above ▼
Right		

No fields are displayed in this region

- Select the "Company Logo" field, and using the drag-and-drop feature that you've seen before, move it into the "Right" area.
- Click the cog on the right side of the Screenshot row.
- Change "Image style" to **Medium.**
- Click "Update".

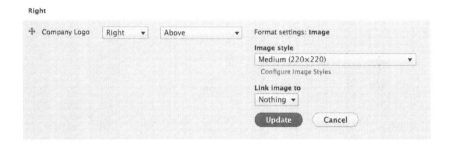

- Click "Save" at the bottom of your screen.
- Visit the homepage of your site and search for OSTraining. The node should look like this image:

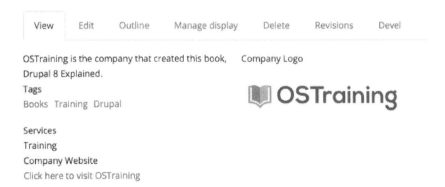

You can do several additional things to tidy up this page. For example, the labels take up too much space, and you're missing your comments area.

Fortunately, it's now easy to access your Display Suite options because there's a "Manage display" tab over the content.

- Click the "Manage display" tab.
- At the bottom of the screen, change "Two column layout" to "Two column stacked". This gives us more regions to place the fields.
- Click "Save".

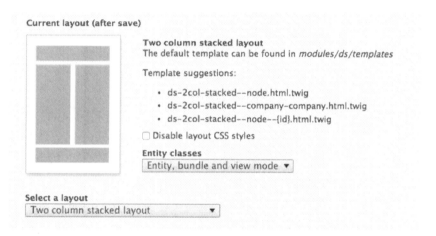

Current layout (after save)

Two column stacked layout
The default template can be found in *modules/ds/templates*

Template suggestions:

- ds-2col-stacked--node.html.twig
- ds-2col-stacked--company-company.html.twig
- ds-2col-stacked--node--{id}.html.twig

☐ Disable layout CSS styles

Entity classes

Entity, bundle and view mode ▼

Select a layout

Two column stacked layout   ▼

- Click "Save" again, without changing the default settings for moving fields.
- Rearrange your display to match the image below:

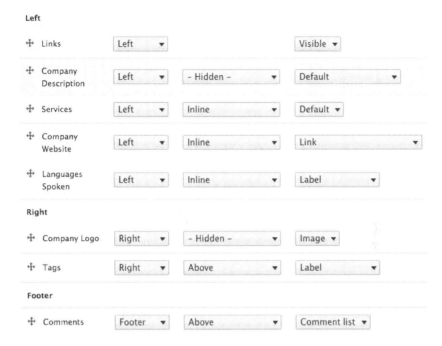

- Click "Save" and visit the OSTraining content:

OSTraining

| View | Edit | Outline | Manage display | Delete | Revisions | Devel |

OSTraining is the company that created this book,
Drupal 8 Explained.
Services: Training
Company Website: Click here to visit OSTraining
Languages Spoken: Spanish

Tags
Books Training Drupal

Add new comment

Now repeat that process with another content type.

- Go to "Structure", "Content types", and "Manage display" for the Event content type.

- Choose the "Three column stacked – 25/50/25" layout.
- Click "Save".
- Arrange the fields to match the configuration in this image:

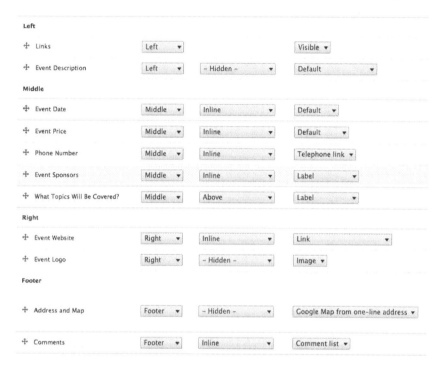

- View the DrupalCon Vienna node on your site, and it will look like the image below:

DrupalCon Vienna

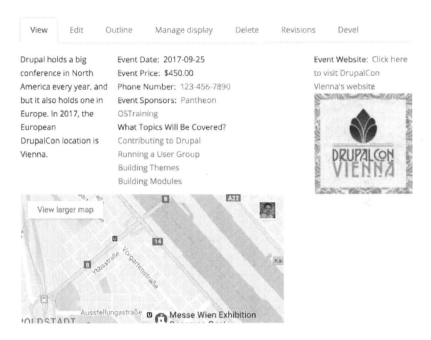

View   Edit   Outline   Manage display   Delete   Revisions   Devel

Drupal holds a big conference in North America every year, and but it also holds one in Europe. In 2017, the European DrupalCon location is Vienna.

Event Date: 2017-09-25
Event Price: $450.00
Phone Number: 123-456-7890
Event Sponsors: Pantheon OSTraining
What Topics Will Be Covered?
Contributing to Drupal
Running a User Group
Building Themes
Building Modules

Event Website: Click here to visit DrupalCon Vienna's website

Using Display Suite for Other Layouts

Display Suite can modify your normal content pages, but it can also be used elsewhere on your site. For example, you may decide that your frontpage needs improvement.

Visit your homepage and look for an event. The display of the events is still very messy.

- Go to "Structure", "Content types" and click "Manage display" for Article.
- Click the "Teaser" display.

Manage display ☆

| Edit | Manage fields | Manage form display | **Manage display** |

Default   <u>Teaser</u>

- Choose the "Three column – equal width" layout.
- Click "Save".
- Configure the fields as shown here:

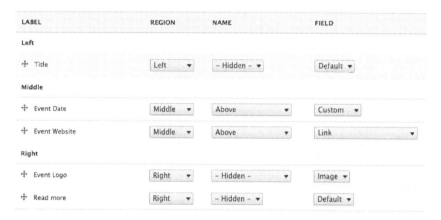

LABEL	REGION	NAME	FIELD
Left			
✛ Title	Left ▼	– Hidden – ▼	Default ▼
Middle			
✛ Event Date	Middle ▼	Above ▼	Custom ▼
✛ Event Website	Middle ▼	Above ▼	Link ▼
Right			
✛ Event Logo	Right ▼	– Hidden – ▼	Image ▼
✛ Read more	Right ▼	– Hidden – ▼	Default ▼

Click "Save" and visit your homepage. Any events on your homepage will now have an improved layout:

Saluto

Event Date
2017-01-13T12:00:00
Event Website
http://www.lonaphesucrak.info

Read more

You can also modify other displays beyond the Teaser. If you're in the "Manage display" screen for the default display, click "Custom display settings", and you'll see that you can alter the layout of other displays:

Layout for event in default	Use custom display settings for the following view modes
Custom display settings	☐ Full content
	☐ Print
Custom wrappers	☐ RSS
	☐ Search index
Custom classes	☐ Search result highlighting input
	☑ Teaser
	☐ Token
	Manage view modes

THE FIELD GROUP MODULE EXPLAINED

Sometimes, when there is a lot of content you want to convey, it's best not to display it all at once. Or, perhaps it's best to create visual distinctions between content segments. If this doesn't make sense, don't worry, seeing is understanding.

If you shop online, it is likely that you have landed on a page whose content is separated into tabs. For instance, a product description, specifications, requirements, and ratings are amongst the most commonly used.

Although this module provides you great power, we advise using it with caution. If your user is required to click several times on a page to view content that they will need, you might find your page becomes tedious.

In our next activity, we will stretch the use of tabs for purposes of demonstration, as we do not have a product content type. We're going to use tabs to redesign the Websites content.

- Go to https://drupal.org/project/field_group and install the module.
- Go to "Structure", "Content types", and click "Manage display" for Website.
- Click "Add group".
- Choose **Tabs** for the group type and **Tab Group** for the label.

- Click "Create group".

- Click "Add group".
- Choose **Tab** for the group type and **Description** for the label.
- Repeat this process, choosing **Tab** for the group type, and **Website Details** for the label.
- Repeat this process, choosing **Tab** for the group type, and **Website Feedback** for the label.
- Drag-and-drop the fields under the tabs to look like this next image. Note the Label settings as well.

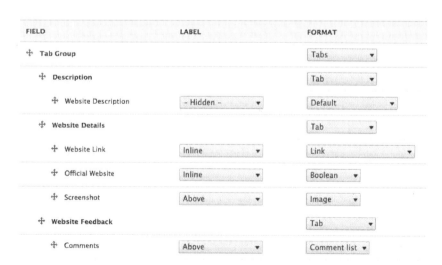

Visit your simplytest.me node and see your new layout in effect:

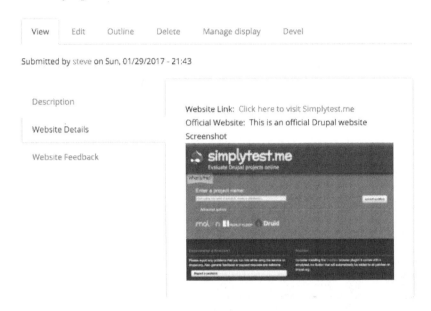

THE PANELS MODULE EXPLAINED

The first part of this chapter showed you how you can control the layout of individual content items with Display Suite and Field Group.

There are two other modules that can be used to make changes to the layout of your site: Panels and Panelizer.

In this next section, we will explore Panels and its ability to create custom pages, not from a node or a view but from Panels itself. For instance, Panels is a wonderful choice for making a homepage or landing page with a unique layout, one your theme regions might not support.

Let's take a look.

- Install Chaos tool suite: https://drupal.org/project/ctools.

- Install Panels: https://drupal.org/project/panels.

- Install Page Manager: https://drupal.org/project/page_manager.

- Check all the boxes when enabling the Panels and Page Manager modules.

Now that modules are installed, let's use Panels to replace our existing homepage.

- Go to "Structure", then "Page".

- Click "Add page".

- Administrative title: **Homepage**

- Administrative description: **This is our homepage**

- Path: **home**

- Variant type: **Panels**

- Click "Next".

- Builder: **In-place editor**

- Click "Next".

- Now you can choose from many of the layout options you see in Display Suite. Choose "Two column".

Layout ☆

Home » Administration » Structure » Pages » Add new page

Page information » Configure variant » **Layout** » Content

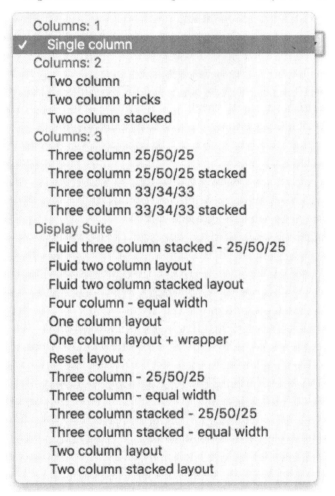

Columns: 1
✓ Single column
Columns: 2
Two column
Two column bricks
Two column stacked
Columns: 3
Three column 25/50/25
Three column 25/50/25 stacked
Three column 33/34/33
Three column 33/34/33 stacked
Display Suite
Fluid three column stacked - 25/50/25
Fluid two column layout
Fluid two column stacked layout
Four column - equal width
One column layout
One column layout + wrapper
Reset layout
Three column - 25/50/25
Three column - equal width
Three column stacked - 25/50/25
Three column stacked - equal width
Two column layout
Two column stacked layout

- Keep clicking "Finish" and then "Update and save". We aren't going to change any more settings at the moment.

At this point, you have created a Panel that you can use for your site's homepage. However, it's not actually your homepage yet, and it doesn't have any content. Let's fix those two problems. First, we'll make this Panel appear on our homepage:

- Go to "Configuration", then "System", then "Basic site settings".
- Enter /**home** in the "Default front page" setting.
- Click "Save configuration".

Visit your homepage and you'll see that the Content region is now empty. Also, at the bottom of the page, will be an editing bar with options to "Change Layout", "Manage Content" and "Edit".

If you want the Panel display to fill the page, then ensure that you don't have any blocks set to appear below the main navigation and/or above the footers for this page. If you have no blocks appearing on the homepage, then your Panel fills this space.

For each block that you don't want to show, given the new page, edit the block and set it not to show <front>. For example, any block that does not have a condition, set the Pages condition to <front> and select the second radio button that says "Hide for the listed pages".

Visibility

Content type	Pages
Content types Not restricted	<front>
Pages Restricted to certain pages	Specify pages by using their paths. Enter one path per line.
Roles Not restricted	○ Show for the listed pages ◉ Hide for the listed pages

Now let's use the power of Panels for our homepage.

- Click "Manage Content".
- You're going to see a wide range of options from "Create Content" and "AddToAny" to "User" and "Core".

This really is the culmination of the site-building process in this book. Everything you've done has led up to this point. Everything you've created so far is now available here. You can build your homepage using Calendars, Forms, Views, Menus and many other items.

- Click "(Lists) Views".
- Click "Recent Content".
- Choose "Left side" for Region.

- Click "Add".

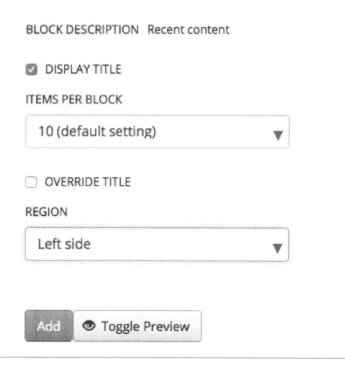

- You'll see that the Recent Content block has been placed on the left of your homepage:

REGION: LEFT	REGION: RIGHT

BLOCK: RECENT CONTENT   ✕ ∧ ∨   MOVE ✛

⚙

Recent content

> Olim
1 day 3 hours ago

> Dignissim Ullamcorper Velit Voco
1 day 3 hours ago

> Nibh Paratus Ratis
1 day 3 hours ago

> Neque Tation
1 day 3 hours ago

> Huic Jugis Secundum Tum
1 day 3 hours ago

> Blandit Ille Populus
1 day 3 hours ago

> Pertineo Turpis Valde
1 day 3 hours ago

> Brevitas Esca Sagaciter Veniam
1 day 3 hours ago

> Elit Nulla Praemitto Virtus
1 day 3 hours ago

> Ad Refero
1 day 3 hours ago

- Click "Manage Content".

- Click "(Lists) Views".

- Click "New Companies".

- Choose "Right side" for Region.

- Click "Add".

- You'll see that the Companies block has been placed on the right of your homepage. Do you see a problem? The Companies block is too long, compared to the Recent content block:

Recent content

> Olim
1 day 3 hours ago

> Dignissim Ullamcorper Velit Voco
1 day 3 hours ago

> Nibh Paratus Ratis
1 day 3 hours ago

> Neque Tation
1 day 3 hours ago

> Huic Jugis Secundum Tum
1 day 3 hours ago

> Blandit Ille Populus
1 day 3 hours ago

> Pertineo Turpis Valde
1 day 3 hours ago

> Brevitas Esca Sagaciter Veniam
1 day 3 hours ago

> Elit Nulla Praemitto Virtus
1 day 3 hours ago

> Ad Refero
1 day 3 hours ago

Companies

At

Dolore

Aliquam Diam Nobis Quadrum

Mauris

Ibidem Roto Sed Ymo

Defui Distineo Refero

Duis Exputo Lobortis

Usitas

Conventio Hendrerit

Dolus Exerci Oppeto

Here's how we can fix that problem:

- Click the "Edit" tab in the bar at the bottom of the page.
- Click the cog in the Companies settings:

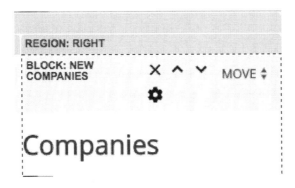

- Change "Items Per Block" to 5.

- Click "Save" and your "Recent content" and "Companies" blocks should be almost the same length.
- As we have the Companies block on this page twice, try to remove the "Companies" block in the Secondary region. Here's how your site will now look:

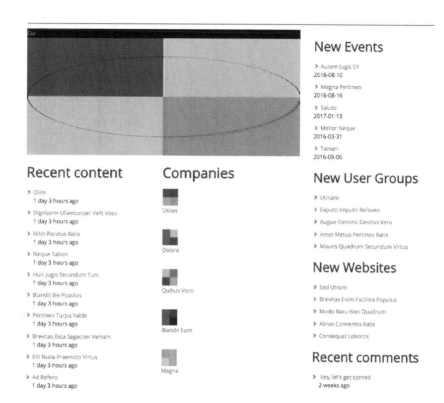

Recent content

> Olim
1 day 3 hours ago

> Dignissim Ullamcorper Velit Voco
1 day 3 hours ago

> Nibh Paratus Ratis
1 day 3 hours ago

> Neque Tation
1 day 3 hours ago

> Huic Jugis Secundum Tum
1 day 3 hours ago

> Blandit Ille Populus
1 day 3 hours ago

> Pertineo Turpis Valde
1 day 3 hours ago

> Brevitas Esca Sagaciter Veniam
1 day 3 hours ago

> Elit Nulla Praemitto Virtus
1 day 3 hours ago

> Ad Refero
1 day 3 hours ago

Companies

Usitas

Dolore

Quibus Voco

Blandit Eum

Magna

New Events

> Autem Jugis Sit
2016-08-10

> Magna Pertineo
2016-08-16

> Saluto
2017-01-13

> Melior Neque
2016-03-31

> Tamen
2016-09-06

New User Groups

> Utinam

> Exputo Imputo Refoveo

> Augue Gemino Genitus Vero

> Amet Metuo Pertineo Ratis

> Mauris Quadrum Secundum Virtus

New Websites

> Sed Utrum

> Brevitas Enim Facilisis Populus

> Modo Natu Neo Quadrum

> Abluo Conventio Ratis

> Consequat Lobortis

Recent comments

> Yes, let's get started
2 weeks ago

Let's try and repeat the process with two more blocks:

- Place the "New Websites" block into the "Left side" of your panel. You'll find this under "Lists (Views)".

- Place the "Take a Poll" block into the "Right side of your panel. You'll find this under "Custom".

- If there are any differences in height, adjust the number of items in the "New Websites" view so it is the same height.

- Remove both of these blocks from your theme's Secondary region.

This is how your site's homepage will now appear:

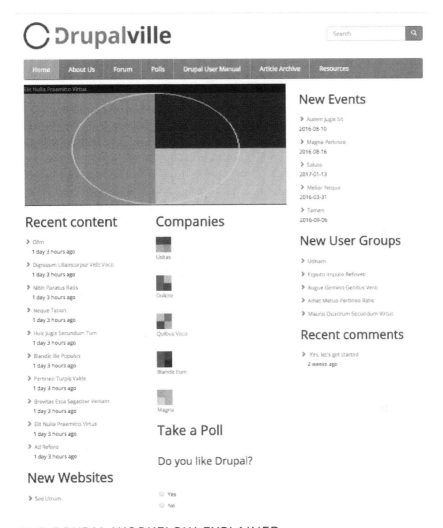

THE DRUPAL WORKFLOW EXPLAINED

What you've seen in this chapter is that layout modules, such as Panels, are the culmination of everything you've done so far. It's also a perfect example of the Drupal workflow.

Think back to your DrupalCon Vienna event page as an example. Or one of your Company pages.

What did you do so that these pages can appear as they do now?

1. Create a content type: Event or Company.

2. Add fields: Event Logo, Event Price, Sponsors, and so on.
3. Add a theme: Breeze.
4. Create and place blocks: New Events or Companies.
5. Use layout modules: Field Groups or Display Suite.

You took all those five steps, in that particular order, to create your content pages. If you tried to skip any steps or do them in a different order, it wouldn't have worked.

- You can't add fields before you've created a content type.

- You can't add content until you have the correct content types and fields.

- You can't create Views blocks if you haven't added any content.

- You can't use layout modules if you haven't any field, content and sometimes views available.

To take another example: What did you do to create your homepage?

- Set up content types.

- Add fields: Articles, User Groups, and Sites all needed fields.

- Add a theme: Breeze.

- Create blocks: The slideshow, plus New Websites, Companies and more.

- Use layout modules: Panels.

This is a workflow that is tailored specifically for Drupal.

If you build websites with other software, this workflow might not apply. If you build websites with Dreamweaver, WordPress, Joomla, or other software, you would need to use a different workflow. For example, with Dreamweaver you start by building the design first. With Drupal, the design is almost the last step in the workflow.

This does not mean that Drupal is better than Dreamweaver. However, this does mean that Drupal is different. Hopefully, this workflow helps you realize how Drupal is different and how you should approach using it.

Most of the confusion we've seen from Drupal beginners is a result of not understanding this workflow:

- Some beginners start by creating the theme.
- Some beginners want to work on the layout immediately.
- Some beginners use one content type for all their content.
- Some beginners don't add any fields or use any Views.

If you create your Drupal sites using this workflow, you can build better sites, quicker and with fewer mistakes and less frustration. You'll be working with Drupal, rather than against it.

1. **Planning**

2. **Content types**

3. **Fields**

4. **Add content**

5. **Install Modules and Themes**

6. **Views**

7. **Layout Modules**

8. **Finish the Design**

9. **Users**

10. **Site Management**

WHAT'S NEXT?

You completed almost all the site-building tasks in the Drupal workflow.

However, our site doesn't yet look like the original design. We have more work to do. We need to make some changes so that our site matches the mockup. That's what we're going to do in Chapter 13, "Finishing the Design Explained".

CHAPTER 13.

FINISHING THE DESIGN EXPLAINED

This will be a short chapter, showing how to finish the design and make it look like the original site mockup.

As a reminder, the image below shows our initial site design. During this chapter, we're going to tidy up our site, and ensure it looks as close to the mockup as possible. We're going to work from the top of the page to the bottom.

FINISHING THE METADATA EXPLAINED

Look up in the browser bar, and you'll see that the very top of the site needs some improvement. The metatitle for the frontpage reads " | Drupalville".

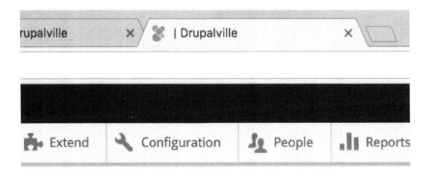

- Go to "Configuration", "Search and metadata", then "Metatag".
- Click "Edit" next to Front Page.

- Page title: **The Official Drupalville Website**

- Save the metadata settings and return to the homepage to see your new metadata title:

FINISHING THE SLIDESHOW EXPLAINED

Let's start the process of giving our site a more polished look:

- Go to "Configuration", then "Basic site settings".
- Enter "**/node**" in the "Default front page" box.
- Click "Save configuration".

By doing that, we've removed Panels from our homepage. The

Panels module is excellent for a complex layout, and we're glad you learned what it does. But, for this particular mockup, we need a simpler solution.

Now your homepage will look like the image below:

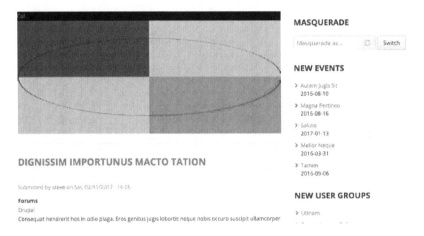

- Go to "Content" and add a new Article.
- Title: **A New Day in Drupalville**
- Image: Use the image called "homepage-banner-1.jpg" in the /homepage-slides/ folder of your downloads.
- Save the article and visit your homepage. The slideshow should contain your new image:

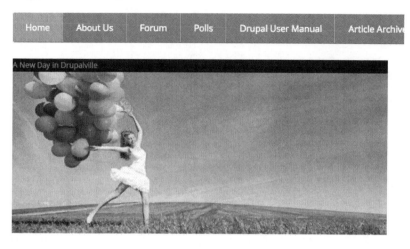

At this point, we have a choice. We could keep the title, but we would probably want to edit the CSS to improve the design. Or we could remove the title, and make our site look more like the mockup. Let's take the second approach:

- Click the pencil icon for your slideshow view, and click "Edit view".

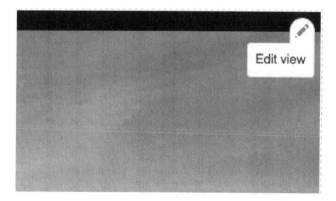

- Click "Content: Title" in the Fields area.
- Click "Remove".

- Save your view and visit the frontpage again to see your updated slideshow.

To complete your slideshow, we've added 4 more banner images inside the /homepage-slides/ folder of your downloads. You can also choose your own images, although for the best results, make sure the images are 550 pixels wide and 250 pixels high.

FINISHING THE SIDEBAR EXPLAINED

On the homepage, the mockup only has a single block in the sidebar.

- Go to "Structure", "Block layout", then "Add custom block".
- Choose "Basic block".
- Block description: **Welcome to Drupalville**
- Body: **Welcome to the great city of Drupalville. This is a fine place for people to live and visit. We hope to see you soon! Stay some time with us to learn about the Drupal community and how fun and welcoming it can be. We have information about companies, events, groups and websites to make your Drupal life easier.**

We spaced out the text, so that it takes up 4 rows:

Body

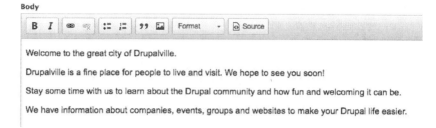

Welcome to the great city of Drupalville.

Drupalville is a fine place for people to live and visit. We hope to see you soon!

Stay some time with us to learn about the Drupal community and how fun and welcoming it can be.

We have information about companies, events, groups and websites to make your Drupal life easier.

- Click "Save".
- Under "Pages", enter **<front>**
- Region: Secondary.
- Click "Save".
- Move your new block to the top of the Secondary region, and save the Block layout page.

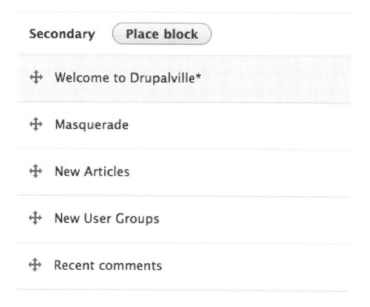

Visit your site's homepage, and your new sidebar block will be nicely positioned, next to the slideshow:

To complete our sidebar, we should remove other blocks from the frontpage.

- Edit all your blocks in the "Secondary" region so that they do not appear on the frontpage. For the Pages settings, you can enter **<front>** and choose "Hide for the listed pages".

Once that process has been completed, your site should look like the image below:

FINISHING THE FRONTPAGE VIEW EXPLAINED

At the moment, we have a stream of news stories on the frontpage. Our mockup doesn't have any of those, so we'll need to remove content from the frontpage.

- Go to "Structure", "Views" and edit the "Frontpage" view.
- In the Filter Criteria area, notice that "Content: Publishing status" is set to "Yes". Change that to "No".

This change will make sure that no published content reaches the frontpage. Is that dangerous? No, because we also have "Content: Promoted to front page" set to "Yes". Plus, site visitors are not able to see your unpublished content.

We need to make one more change:

- In the No Results Behavior area, remove both of the entries you can see below. This will give us a clean frontpage:

Your frontpage now looks like the image below:

FINISHING THE FRONTPAGE BLOCKS EXPLAINED

The final element on our site will be the 3 blocks underneath the slideshow. In this section, we're going to give you some HTML to enter. In order to enter HTML, we'll need to make a small change.

- Go to "Configuration", "Content authoring" and then "Text formats and editors".

NAME	TEXT EDITOR	ROLES
✛ Basic HTML	CKEditor	Authenticated user, Administrator
✛ Restricted HTML	—	Anonymous user, Administrator
✛ Full HTML	CKEditor	Administrator
✛ Plain text	—	This format is shown when no other formats are available

You will see several different text formats. "Basic HTML" is the most restricted and only allows you to enter a small set of HTML tags. What we need is "Full HTML", which won't restrict what we can enter.

- Drag "Full HTML" to the top of the list, so that it has priority, and will load before the other options.
- Click "Save".

Now we can create our 3 frontpage blocks:

- Go to "Structure", "Block layout", then "Add custom block".
- Choose "Basic block".
- Block description: **Move to Drupalville**
- Text format: **Full HTML**. This will allow you enter any HTML you want into the block.

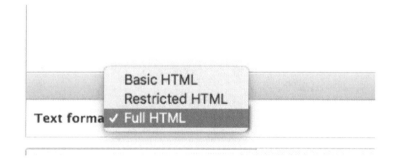

- Click the "Source button" in the editor toolbar.
- Body: Use the code in the file called "homepage-block-1.txt" in the /homepage-blocks/ folder of your downloads.
- Click "Save".

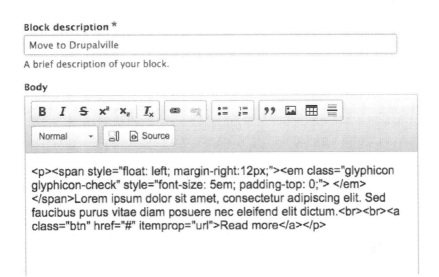

Block description *

Move to Drupalville

A brief description of your block.

Body

| B | I | S | x² | x₂ | Iₓ | ⊖ | ⊗ | ≔ | ≔ | 99 | 🖼 | ▦ | ≣ |

Normal ▾ | ⏬ | ↩ Source

```
<p><span style="float: left; margin-right:12px;"><em class="glyphicon
glyphicon-check" style="font-size: 5em; padding-top: 0;"> </em>
</span>Lorem ipsum dolor sit amet, consectetur adipiscing elit. Sed
faucibus purus vitae diam posuere nec eleifend elit dictum.<br><br><a
class="btn" href="#" itemprop="url">Read more</a></p>
```

- Under "Pages", enter **<front>**
- Region: Content Bottom 1
- Save the block and then save the block layout page.

Let's repeat the process for the second block:

- Go to "Structure", "Block layout", then "Add custom block".
- Choose "Basic block".
- Block description: **Family Friendly**
- Body: Use the code in the file called "homepage-block-2.txt" in the /homepage-blocks/ folder of your downloads.
- Click "Save".
- Under "Pages", enter **<front>**
- Region: Content Bottom 2
- Save the block and then save the block layout page.

And finally, let's create the third block:

- Go to "Structure", "Block layout", then "Add custom block".

- Choose "Basic block".
- Block description: **Improved Living**
- Body: Use the code in the file called "homepage-block-3.txt" in the /homepage-blocks/ folder of your downloads.
- Click "Save".
- Under "Pages", enter **<front>**
- Region: Content Bottom 3
- Save the block and then save the block layout page.

Visit your site's homepage, and you'll be looking at a design that matches your mockup!

WHAT'S NEXT?

You completed all the visible changes to your site. However, there is another important step in the Drupal Workflow that you haven't addressed yet: users. You have been viewing the site as administrators. What about the visitors? What about the people who view, create, and edit the content on your site?

Click "Log out", and see what your site looks like now. You also see several differences between the administrator experience and the logged-out experience.

In the next chapter, "Drupal Users Explained," you see why those differences exist and how you can manage them successfully.

CHAPTER 14.

DRUPAL USERS EXPLAINED

The first 12 chapters of this book focused on the content and features of your Drupal site. Now you look at the people who will read that content and use those features.

This chapter shows you how to control who can do what on your site. Who can create, delete, and edit content? Who can upload modules and themes? Who can modify menus and blocks?

You also see how to make user accounts more interesting. You do this by allowing users to add more information about them. Here are the things you'll be able to do after completing this chapter:

- Create roles.
- Assign permissions to roles.
- Create new users.
- Test users' accounts.
- Expand user profiles.
- Modify the registration form.

DRUPAL ROLES AND PERMISSIONS EXPLAINED

Drupal users are defined by their role. Roles are defined by the permissions you assign the role. Drupal has three default roles:

- **Anonymous**: Visitors to your site who are not logged into your site.

- **Authenticated**: Anyone who has an account on your site and logs in is authenticated. The Authenticated role also serves as the minimum set of permissions that is given to all logged in users. Drupal sets some default permissions but you can change them.

- **Administrator**: Users assigned the administrator role can do everything on the site.

You might be thinking that this is enough for your site, but just in case you have bigger plans, let's take a look at how you fine tune access to your account via three examples.

CREATING AN ARTICLE WRITER

Start with the example of an Article writer. Such a person will be a role to which you can assign users. If users are in this role, all they can do is write articles. There are four steps to make sure a user account is set up correctly:

1. Add a role.
2. Set the role permissions.
3. Create a user.
4. Test the user to make sure it has the correct permissions.

Following are those four steps.

- Click "People" on the admin menu bar and then on the "Roles" tab.

Roles ☆

List	Permissions	Roles

Home » Administration » People

A role defines a group of users that have certain privileges. These p
least permissive (for example, Anonymous user) to most permissive
roles granted to their user account.

+ Add role

NAME

✛ Anonymous user

✛ Authenticated user

✛ Administrator

- Click "Add role".
- Type **Article writer** for the new role name.
- Click "Save".

Now that the Article writer role has been created, you need to decide what user in that role can and can't do.

- Click the Permissions tab to see the permissions available:

Permissions ☆

List	Permissions	Roles

Home » Administration » People

On the left side of the list, you can see the modules that have permissions settings. The modules are ordered alphabetically. Across the top of the list, you see the four roles that you have set up.

PERMISSION	ANONYMOUS USER	AUTHENTICATED USER	ADMINISTRATOR	ARTICLE WRITER
AddToAny				
Administer AddToAny Perform administration tasks for the AddToAny module.	☐	☐	☑	☐
Block				
Administer blocks	☐	☐	☑	☐

The permissions for the three default roles are already set. You can also see that some permissions for the Article writer role are already set. This is because those permissions have been giving to the Authenticated User role. By default, if you grant permission to the Authenticated role, all subsequent roles (except for anonymous) inherit said permission. That is why the check marks for comments are grayed out and can't be deselected.

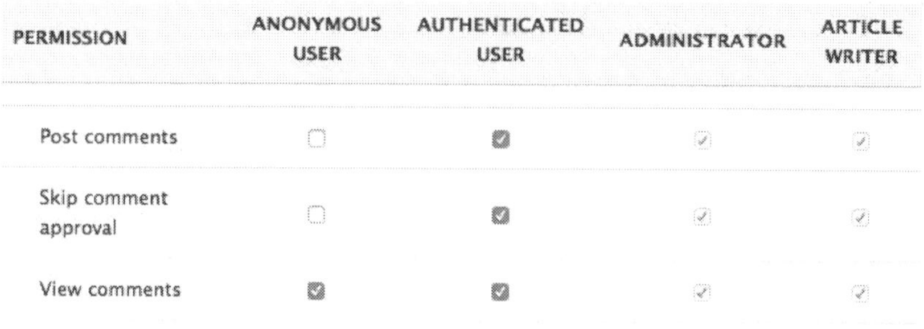

PERMISSION	ANONYMOUS USER	AUTHENTICATED USER	ADMINISTRATOR	ARTICLE WRITER
Post comments	☐	☑	☑	☑
Skip comment approval	☐	☑	☑	☑
View comments	☑	☑	☑	☑

Your article writer is going to need more permissions than those granted by default to the Authenticated role, so let's get started.

- Scroll down until you find the header Node. Remember that Node is Drupal's geeky word for content.

- At the top of the Node area, you see some admin-type permissions, as shown below:

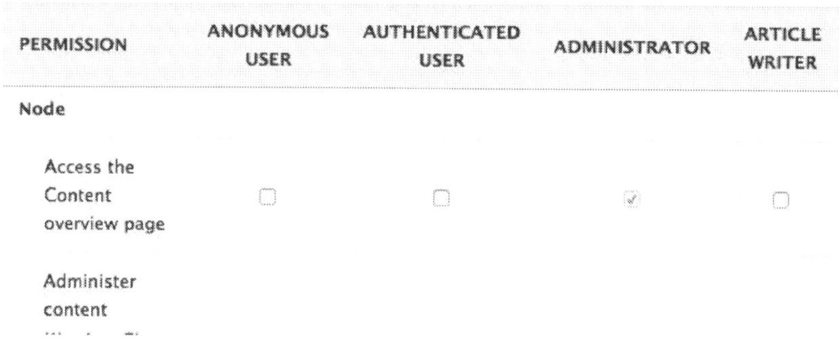

PERMISSION	ANONYMOUS USER	AUTHENTICATED USER	ADMINISTRATOR	ARTICLE WRITER
Node				
Access the Content overview page	☐	☐	☑	☐
Administer content				

Scroll a little further to find the Article permission set. To keep things simple in this example, check all of the Article permission boxes:

- Create new content

- Delete any content

- Delete own content

- Delete revisions

- Edit any content

- Edit own content
- Revert revisions
- View revisions

PERMISSION	ANONYMOUS USER	AUTHENTICATED USER	ADMINISTRATOR	ARTICLE WRITER
View published content	☑	☑	✓	✓
Article: Create new content	☐	☐	✓	☑
Article: Delete any content	☐	☐	✓	☑
Article: Delete own content	☐	☐	✓	☑
Article: Delete revisions Role requires permission to *view revisions* and *delete rights* for nodes in question, or *administer nodes*.	☐	☐	✓	☑
Article: Edit any content	☐	☐	✓	☑
Article: Edit own content	☐	☐	✓	☑
Article: Revert revisions Role requires permission *view revisions* and *edit rights* for nodes in question, or *administer nodes*.	☐	☐	✓	☑
Article: View revisions	☐	☐	✓	☑

- To ensure the Article writer can "Add Content", check the permissions box for "Use the administration toolbar".

Toolbar				
Use the administration toolbar	☐	☐	✓	☑

- Click "Save permissions" at the bottom of the page.

Now let's set up an actual user account for an Article writer.

- Click the "List" tab at the top of the screen.
- Click the "Add user" button.

As you can see by the absence of the red asterisk, an email address is not required. However, the email is necessary for the user to receive messages, such as password reset. If you have an email address, other than the one you used when creating your first account, enter it now, so that you can see the emails users will receive. Otherwise, leave it blank.

- Username: **articlewriter**

- Password: **articlewriter**

- Roles: Check the "Article writer" box.

- If you included an email address, check the box to "Notify user of new account".

- Click "Create new account".

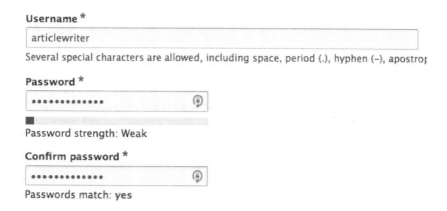

The fourth and final step is crucial. Permissions are a vital part of your site's security, and if you don't test your permissions, you could easily allow some users to do things that can compromise your site.

Following is a basic method for testing. You can use the following steps:

- Open a browser where you are not already logged in.

- Log in by going to http://[your_web_address]/user/login.

- Observe that the menu bar to which you have grown accustomed is lacking in options. That is good. First test passed.

- Click "Shortcuts", then "Add content".
- The "Create Article" form appears immediately, with no other content types available. Test passed again!

Create Article

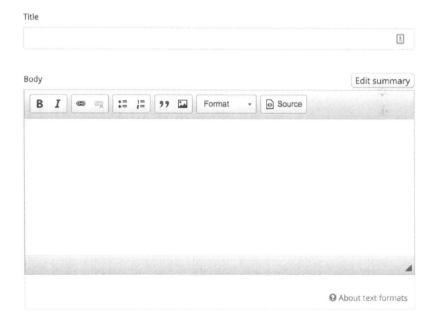

There are limitations to this testing. Because you created the account and the password, you were able to log in as that person and test.

However, on a real site, it is neither feasible nor safe to know what your users' passwords are. Instead, you can use a module called Masquerade to easily test any user account. Here's how it works:

- Make sure you are logged in using your main admin account.
- Install the Masquerade module from http://drupal.org/ project/masquerade.
- Go to "Structure", then "Block layout".
- Place the Masquerade block at the top of the Secondary region.
- Go to your homepage and you'll find the Masquerade block and its search box.
- Type in the name of the user you want to test and click "Switch".

The Masquerade block disappears and an "Unmasquerade" link appears in the black menu bar at the top of the screen. Don't worry: by default, this link appears only for administrators.

⟳ Drupalville

You can now browse the site and see exactly what an Article writer can see. Simply click the Unmasquerade link, and you'll be back at the administrator account.

CREATING A MODERATOR

Now see one more example of user permissions. Let's set up a role called Moderator. People in this role can moderate comments and forum posts. These people help to make sure that your site is a pleasant and spam-free destination.

- Go to "People", "Roles", then "Add new role".

- Type **Moderator** for the Role name.

Next, we'll set up the permissions:

- Click the "Permissions" tab and scroll down until you find the Comment module.

- Check the "Administer comments and comment settings" box in the Moderator column.

PERMISSION	ANONYMOUS USER	AUTHENTICATED USER	ADMINISTRATOR	ARTICLE WRITER	MODERATOR
Comment					
Administer comment types and settings *Warning: Give to trusted roles only, this permission has security implications.*	☐	☐	☑	☐	☐
Administer comments and comment settings	☐	☐	☑	☐	☑

- Scroll down until you find the Forum module and check the

"Administer forums" box in the Moderator column. This allows the Moderator to rearrange the forum boards if needed.

PERMISSION	ANONYMOUS USER	AUTHENTICATED USER	ADMINISTRATOR	ARTICLE WRITER	MODERATOR
Administer image styles	☐	☐	☑	☐	☑

- Scroll down until you find the Node section.
- Give Moderator permission to create, delete any, and edit any Forum nodes.

PERMISSION	ANONYMOUS USER	AUTHENTICATED USER	ADMINISTRATOR	ARTICLE WRITER	MODERATOR
Forum topic: Create new content	☐	☐	☑	☐	☐
Forum topic: Delete any content	☐	☐	☑	☐	☑
Forum topic: Delete own content	☐	☐	☑	☐	☑
Forum topic: Delete revisions Role requires permission to *view revisions* and *delete rights* for nodes in question, or *administer nodes*.	☐	☐	☑	☐	☐
Forum topic: Edit any content	☐	☐	☑	☐	☑
Forum topic: Edit own content	☐	☐	☑	☐	☑
Forum topic: Revert revisions Role requires permission *view revisions* and *edit rights* for nodes in question, or *administer nodes*	☐	☐	☑	☐	☑
Forum topic: View revisions	☐	☐	☑	☐	☑

- To ensure the Moderator can add content, check the permissions box for "Use the administration toolbar".
- Check the "View user information box" in the Moderator column. This can help the Moderator when advising the site administrator if an account needs to be blocked.
- Click "Save permissions" at the bottom of the screen.

Now we can move on to the create the Moderator account:

- Click the "List" tab at the top of the screen and click "Add user".

- If you have yet another extra email account, enter it, otherwise, leave the email blank.

- Username: **moderator.**

- Password: **moderator**. You can set this to something more difficult if you want. Drupal warns you that this is a weak password.

- Roles: Check the "Moderator" box.

- Click "Create new account".

Now it's time to test the account:

- Visit the front page of your site.

- Use the Masquerade module to see the site as moderator.

- Click "Forum" on the Main menu.

- Access any forum topic, and you can edit or delete the topic.

- If there is a comment on a topic, you can moderate it using the "Edit" and "Delete" links.

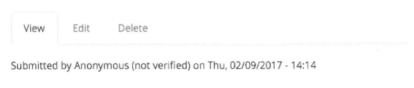

| View | Edit | Delete |

Submitted by Anonymous (not verified) on Thu, 02/09/2017 - 14:14

Forums
Drupal Design

- Click any user's account name. The easiest account to find will probably be your main administrator account.

Blandit Ille Populus

View   Edit   Outline   Delete   Manage display   Devel

Submitted by steve on Mon, 02/06/2017 - 22:28

Forums
Drupal Design
Acsi dignissim incassum occuro. Erat ideo nostrud quae refero utrum validus. Aliquam at eu exputo huic neque praesent saepius singularis valde. Aliquip letalis metuo utinam. Neo pecus sino tego. Aptent dolus eros esca iusto luctus modo rusticus torqueo. Abluo acsi causa erat eum huic macto rusticus secundum uxor.

- You'll see the user profile. In the next part of the chapter, we're going to make this look more interesting!

- If you think the user needs moderating, click the "Edit" tab. You change the user status from "Active" to "Blocked". Please do not try this with your own administrator account!

Status

◯ Blocked

◉ Active

You can grant your Moderator role permission to administer users (see the User section on the Permissions page). Note that this is a very powerful permission. If granted, any user with Moderator role can access any other user's account and change its settings. Grant with caution.

DRUPAL USER PROFILES EXPLAINED

By default, a user account collects basic information about the user. You saw this when creating the three users in the previous activities.

Most of that information is not visible to visitors or other users on the site.

Drupal makes it easy to modify and expand this profile so that people can add useful information about themselves such as their real name (versus a username), address, employer, URLs, biography, and more.

Now see how to create expanded user profiles. The process is similar to adding fields to a content type.

Before you start, make sure you have clicked the Unmasquerade link to return to your admin view of the site.

Go ahead and add some fields to your user profiles. This allows users to provide more information about themselves.

- Go to "Configuration, "People", "Account settings", then "Manage fields".

- You can now see a screen which looks similar to the content type pages you saw earlier in Chapter 6, "Drupal Fields Explained".

Let's add the following Text (plain) fields:

- First Name. Set the "Maximum length" to 50 characters.

- Last Name. Set the "Maximum length" to 50 characters.

Next, add the following Link fields:

- LinkedIn

- Facebook
- Personal Website

LABEL	MACHINE NAME	FIELD TYPE
Facebook	field_facebook	Link
First Name	field_first_name	Text (plain)
Last Name	field_last_name	Text (plain)
LinkedIn	field_linkedin	Link
Personal Website	field_personal_website	Link
Picture	user_picture	Image

- Go to the "Manage display" tab and arrange the new fields in the order you want them to show to site visitors. You can even use Display Suite or Field Group to organize the layout of these fields.

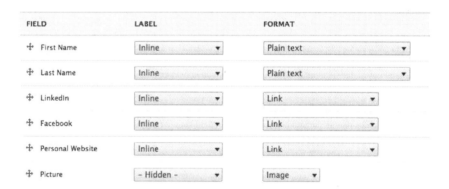

FIELD	LABEL	FORMAT
⊹ First Name	Inline ▼	Plain text ▼
⊹ Last Name	Inline ▼	Plain text ▼
⊹ LinkedIn	Inline ▼	Link ▼
⊹ Facebook	Inline ▼	Link ▼
⊹ Personal Website	Inline ▼	Link ▼
⊹ Picture	– Hidden – ▼	Image ▼

- Go to "People" and "Permissions".
- Give the "View user information" permission to the Anonymous and Authenticated users.

PERMISSION	ANONYMOUS USER	AUTHENTICATED USER	ADMINISTRATOR
implications.			
View user information	☑	☑	☑

Now, go and see those user profile fields that you just created:

- Click your user name to go to "My account" in the black menu bar at the top.
- Click the "Edit profile" tab.
- Scroll down and you can use all the fields that you just created.
- Fill in the fields.
- Save your data and click the "View" tab to see your profile:

steve

| View | Shortcuts | Edit | Manage display | Devel |

First Name: Steve
Last Name: Burge
LinkedIn: My LinkedIn Profile
Facebook: My Facebook Profile
Personal Website: SteveBurge.com

Now, see how these fields appear to your site's users. For many users, this user profile editing area should look similar, but slightly different:

- Use the Masquerade module to act as the article writer user.
- Click the article writer name to go to "My account".
- Click the "Edit profile" tab and see what a user sees:

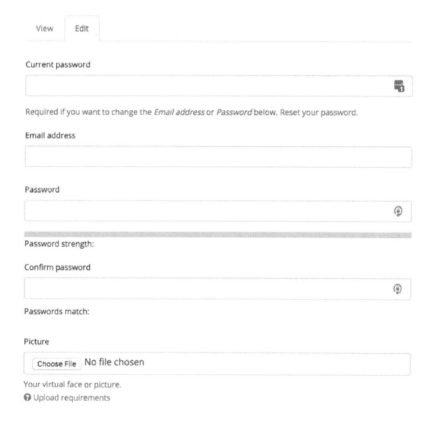

Finally, see how this appears to a new user:

- Log out or visit your site in another browser.
- Visit http://[your_web_address]/user/register

- The registration screen should show the default Drupal fields, plus your new fields:

First Name

Last Name

LinkedIn

URL

If you want to remove any fields from the registration area, you can hide them by going to "Configuration, "People", "Account settings", then "Manage form display".

WHAT'S NEXT?

We mentioned that at the end of the previous chapter, "Drupal Layout Modules Explained," you had completed all the visible changes you were going to make to your site. However, the previous chapter was not the end of our Drupal workflow.

User permissions are the last step in our Drupal workflow for a logical reason: it's not until every part of the site has been created that we can accurately browse the site and test the user permissions.

However, User roles and permissions should be one of the first things you do when planning your site. It could mean the difference between creating one content for multiple types of articles, or multiple content types for multiple types of articles, assuming each type of article will have its own role.

Now that our Drupal workflow is almost complete, we're going to discuss how you maintain a completed Drupal site. Before you start your site, you need to go through Step 1: Planning. After you finish your site, you need to think about Step 10: Site Management. In the final chapter of this book, "Drupal Site Management Explained," we're going to see how to maintain and secure a Drupal site.

1. **Planning**

2. **Content types**

3. **Fields**

4. **Add content**

5. **Install Modules and Themes**

6. **Views**

7. **Layout Modules**

8. **Finish the Design**

9. **Users**

10. **Site Management**

CHAPTER 15.

DRUPAL SITE MANAGEMENT EXPLAINED

Are you going to be responsible for maintaining your Drupal site? If so, this chapter is for you. This chapter shows you how to keep your site safe, secure, and updated.

You might have other people to take care of these tasks for you. You might have a web design company, colleagues in the IT department, or other experienced people to help you. If that's your situation, you can happily skip this chapter.

However, if you are the person responsible for your site, you need to know how to keep your site safe and secure. Among other things, you need to know how to protect your site and update it to the latest version.

After reading this chapter, you should be able to:

- Update your modules and themes.
- Disable or uninstall modules and themes.
- Use additional measures to protect your site.
- Backup your site.

UPDATING YOUR SITE EXPLAINED

Treat your Drupal site as you treat your car.

All cars need regular maintenance and so do all Drupal sites. With a car, you need to pump up the tires, change the oil, change the battery, or do other fixes. With a Drupal site, you also need to apply fixes. Fortunately, many of these important fixes can be applied automatically using Drupal's update system.

Before seeing how to use Drupal's update system, you need to understand what you're updating to. Drupal's updates are based on version numbers as described in the following section.

DRUPAL VERSION NUMBERS EXPLAINED

Chapter 1, "Drupal Explained," talked a little about Drupal's version numbers. At the time of writing there are two officially supported versions of Drupal:

- Drupal 8, released November 2015, is the subject of this book and reflects significant improvement to Drupal's infrastructure.

- Drupal 7, released January 2011, the first step towards Drupal 8, proved that Drupal was here to stay.

There are two more versions worth noting. One is very old, and one doesn't exist yet:

- Drupal 6, released in 2008, is still being used on legacy sites. Drupal 6, although not officially supported by the Drupal community, is still used by site owners as they explore their upgrade options.

- Drupal 9 is the next version of Drupal, but very little planning has been done so far. A release may be as far away as 2019 or 2020.

Now, let's get a little more specific about version numbers. There are two types of Drupal versions: major versions and minor versions.

Major versions have large intervals between releases and always add important new features and changes to Drupal.

- **Numbering:** Drupal 4, 5, 6, 7, and 8 have been released, and in the future you can expect 9, 10, and so on.

- **Reason for new major versions**: To add major new features and significant changes to the underlying code.

- **Importance**. Is it important to use the latest major version? It's useful but not essential. Because new major versions are released to add new features, there are no security problems if you don't upgrade. However, each major version is supported only by the Drupal team for so long; so yes, it's generally best to use the latest major version if possible.

- **Release dates**. There are no fixed release dates for major versions. However, Drupal's track record can give you an idea of how often major versions are released. After the release of Drupal 5, there have been four major versions in approximately 106 months. So you could say that major versions arrive approximately every 27 months, however they have become less frequent in recent years:

  ◦ Drupal 5: January 2007

  ◦ Drupal 6: February 2008

  ◦ Drupal 7: January 2011

  ◦ Drupal 8: November 2015

- **Updating**. In the past, updating between major versions was difficult. Each new Drupal version was substantially different from the last. However, that has changed with Drupal 8. The Drupal developers are now committed to providing easy updates for Drupal 8 sites. So, if you choose Drupal 8, moving your site to Drupal 9 will be very simple. This is a major and welcome change for Drupal users. However, if you are on Drupal 6 or 7, it will still be a challenge to move your site to Drupal 8.

Minor versions are released irregularly, but often, and provide small fixes to existing features:

- **Numbering**. Each major version has minor versions such as 8.1, 8.2, 8.3, and so on. For major versions that are out for a long time, these can add up so that the final version of 5 was 5.23, and the final version of 6 was 6.38.

- **Reason for new minor versions.** Historically, the objective of minor versions was to fix security problems and bugs. However, in Drupal 8, we are also seeing new and/or refined features and functionality being added.

- **Importance**. Is it important to use the latest minor version? Yes, absolutely. Because new minor versions are often released to fix security problems, it is vital to make sure you use the latest version.

- **Release dates**. These versions are released approximately every 1 to 2 months, or as needed.

- **Updating**. In Drupal, you need to download the files for the new version and carefully upload them to replace your current files.

How can you find out what version of Drupal you have? Log in to your site in the administrator area, and go to "Reports" and then "Available updates". You can see what version number you currently have. In this example, our site is on Drupal 8.2.5 and there is an update available to 8.2.6.

Drupal core

Drupal core **8.2.5**

Recommended version: 8.2.6 (2017-Feb-01)

Latest version: 8.3.0-alpha1 (2017-Feb-01)

HOW DO I GET NOTIFIED ABOUT UPDATES?

Drupal will give you plenty of warning notices about updates. If there is an update and you're logged in as an administrator, you see a red message across the top of all admin screens: "There is a security update available for your version of Drupal."

> ⊗ There is a security update available for your version of Drupal. To ensure the security of your server, you should update immediately! See the available updates page for more information and to install your missing updates.

You can also opt to have Drupal automatically send you emails whenever there's an update.

- Go to "Reports", "Available updates".
- Click the "Settings" tab. Enter an email address in here, and Drupal can send you daily emails whenever it finds an update.

Update Manager settings ☆

List	Update	Settings

Home » Administration » Reports » Available updates

Check for updates

◉ Daily

◯ Weekly

Select how frequently you want to automatically check for new releases of your cu

☐ Check for updates of uninstalled modules and themes

Email addresses to notify when updates are available

steve@ostraining.com

Whenever your site checks for available updates and finds new releases,

Email notification threshold

◉ All newer versions

◯ Only security updates

HOW DO I UPDATE DRUPAL?

Let's see how to update the core Drupal files on your site.

- Take your Drupal site offline briefly so that visitors don't see any error messages as you update. To do this, go to "Configuration", "Development", "Maintenance mode", and check the box marked "Put site into maintenance mode". Click "Save configuration".

- Backup your site, as explained in the section, "Backing Up Your Drupal Site," later in this chapter.

- Go to "Reports" and "Available updates".

- Click Download in the red warning area:

Drupal core 8.2.5   Update available ⚠

Recommended   8.2.6   Download
version: (2017-Feb-01)   Release notes

- Save the files to your desktop.
- Extract the files that you just downloaded. The folder should look like the image below:

- Delete the /sites/, /modules/ and /themes/ folders from the folders. IMPORTANT! Please do not ignore this step. These folders contain everything that is unique to your site: all the uploaded modules, themes, and files. If you don't delete these folders now, you'll upload empty folders and replace all your modules, themes, and files. Here's what new set of Drupal files should look like before uploading:

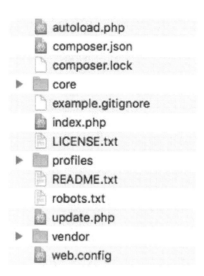

- Open your FTP program as you did in Chapter 3, "Drupal Installations Explained." Browse to find your existing site files.

- One more time: Make sure that you have a backup of your site!

- Upload the files that you downloaded and extracted. Simply upload the new files over the top of the existing ones. This may take anywhere from a few seconds to a few minutes to complete, depending on the speed of your connection.

- When the upload is complete, go to "Reports", "Available updates" again. Drupal now shows that the Drupal core is up to date.

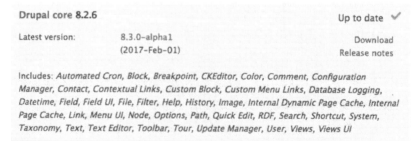

Drupal core

Drupal core 8.2.6		Up to date ✓
Latest version:	8.3.0–alpha1 (2017-Feb-01)	Download Release notes

Includes: *Automated Cron, Block, Breakpoint, CKEditor, Color, Comment, Configuration Manager, Contact, Contextual Links, Custom Block, Custom Menu Links, Database Logging, Datetime, Field, Field UI, File, Filter, Help, History, Image, Internal Dynamic Page Cache, Internal Page Cache, Link, Menu UI, Node, Options, Path, Quick Edit, RDF, Search, Shortcut, System, Taxonomy, Text, Text Editor, Toolbar, Tour, Update Manager, User, Views, Views UI*

- Go to "Configuration", Maintenance mode", uncheck the box marked "Put site into maintenance mode", and click "Save Configuration".

It's worth noting that hosting companies provide more advanced and reliable ways to update. Pantheon, for example, provides Development, Test, and Live environments. These allow you to test your updates before you make them live:

Whenever you're ready to make a site update, you can copy your "Live" site into the "Test" area. Here you can safely apply your updates and make sure nothing breaks.

UPDATING YOUR MODULES AND THEMES

To keep your site safe, you need to update your modules and themes as well as the main Drupal version.

Fortunately, Drupal 8 makes updating modules and themes much easier than updating the core files. Here's how to do it:

- Backup your site.
- Go to "Reports", "Available Updates".
- Look for any modules or themes that are marked in red, as shown with the Token module in this image:

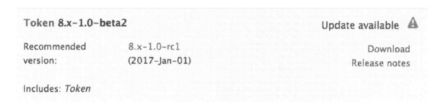

- Click the "Update" tab at the top of the screen.
- Check the box next to the updates you want to make.

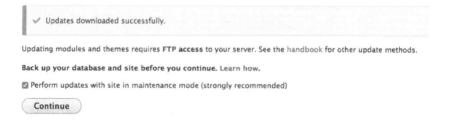

- Click "Download these updates".
- You'll see a progress bar as your site is being updated. When the update finishes, you see a message saying "Updates downloaded successfully".

✓ Updates downloaded successfully.

Updating modules and themes requires **FTP access** to your server. See the handbook for other update methods.

Back up your database and site before you continue. Learn how.

☑ Perform updates with site in maintenance mode (strongly recommended)

(Continue)

- Click "Continue". Drupal automatically puts the site in maintenance mode during this process. Drupal then completes the update and checks for any problems. If there are no problems, it takes the site out of maintenance mode again.

- Click "Run database updates". This is the final step in the update.

- Click "Apply pending updates" if any updates are found. If all goes well, you won't see any error messages. You just see a screen like the one below. Click the "Front page" or "Administration pages" links to return to your site.

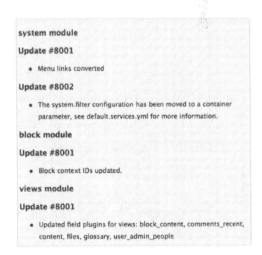

Verify requirements

Overview

Review updates

Run updates

Review log

Drupal database update

Updates were attempted. If you see no failures below, you may proceed happily back to your site. Otherwise, you may need to update your database manually. All errors have been logged.

- Front page
- Administration pages

The following updates returned messages:

system module

Update #8001

- Menu links converted

Update #8002

- The system.filter configuration has been moved to a container parameter, see default.services.yml for more information.

block module

Update #8001

- Block context IDs updated.

views module

Update #8001

- Updated field plugins for views: block_content, comments_recent, content, files, glossary, user_admin_people

If you see error messages, do your best to follow the instructions given. If the instructions aren't clear, enter the error message into Google or the search box at Drupal.org to see if anyone has encountered similar problems and found a solution.

UNINSTALLING YOUR MODULES AND THEMES

When we say uninstall, we are simply telling Drupal that said module or theme is not active, that Drupal is to ignore that code.

Uninstall does NOT remove the code from the web server. You will still see the module and/or theme available to be reinstalled. If you reinstall a module or theme, it is highly likely that the configuration settings you made – assuming there were any – have been removed from the system and you will need to start again.

If you don't want the code on the server, you need to remove it, either via FTP or the interface provided by your hosting service.

For security reasons, you should uninstall any modules or themes that you're not using. If modules or themes are unused, you're more likely to forget about updating them. Older software that hasn't been regularly updated is more likely to suffer from security holes. Here's how you can remove unused modules:

- Go to "Extend", then "Uninstall module".
- Check the box next to the module you want to uninstall.
- Click "Uninstall" at the bottom of the page. Drupal warns you that all data from these modules will be lost.
- Confirm to finish the process.

If you can't check the box for the module in question, it is because another module is relying on it. Click the description of the module you want to uninstall to see the dependent modules. For example, in the image below, you can't disable the Comment module because it is required by the Forum module.

	Comment	Allows users to comment on and discuss published content. The following reasons prevent Comment from being uninstalled: • The *Comments* field type is used in the following fields: node.comment, node.comment_forum • There is content for the entity type: Comment. Remove comment entities. • Required by: Forum

The process of uninstalling a theme is different:

- Go the "Appearance" tab on the Administration menu.

- Click "Uninstall" next to the theme you want to uninstall. The active theme cannot be uninstalled until a new theme has been set to take its place.

Danland 8.x-1.0
Drupal Theme provided by Danetsoft developed by Danang Probo Sayekti inspired by Maksimer.

Settings   Uninstall   Set as default

- To completely remove it, log in to your site via FTP or your hosting interface.

- Browse to the /themes/ folder to find your theme.

- Find the folder for the theme you want to uninstall. It will probably have exactly the same name as the theme.

- Either remove or delete the theme folder, and you will have completely uninstalled the theme.

BACKING UP YOUR SITE

You need to keep your site secure and up to date, but even the best sites can run into problems, and even the best site administrators can make mistakes.

To recover from serious problems and errors, you need to have backups. There are two main ways to make backups: Your hosting company can do it, or you can do it yourself. We recommend that you set up both options.

- Many of the best hosting companies make backups for their clients.

- Some of the best hosting companies not only make the backups, but also give you the ability to restore a backup in place of the current site.

- Some others make the backups but require that you contact them and ask for the backup to be restored.

- Finally, some hosts won't make any backups available to you because they create backups to recover from server failure and not your mistakes.

You need to know the backup policy of your host, whether it's good, mediocre, or bad.

If you are hosted on Pantheon, they automatically backup your site, in all three environments (Live, Test and Dev). The image below shows the backups for a site we have hosted on Pantheon:

Date	Type	Code		Database		Files		Restore
Mon, Feb 13th 2017 05:25:49 (UTC -05:00)	Scheduled	44.5 MB	⬇	1.2 MB	⬇	2.9 MB	⬇	Restore
Sun, Feb 12th 2017 05:46:39 (UTC -05:00)	Scheduled	44.5 MB	⬇	1.2 MB	⬇	2.9 MB	⬇	Restore
Sat, Feb 11th 2017 05:41:59 (UTC -05:00)	Scheduled	44.6 MB	⬇	1.2 MB	⬇	2.9 MB	⬇	Restore

If you want to create your own Drupal backups, the module we recommend is called Backup and Migrate. As the name suggests, you can also use this module for moving your site from one server to another. Here's how to use Backup and Migrate:

- Install Backup and Migrate from http://drupal.org/project/backup_migrate.

- Go to "Configuration", "Development", and then "Backup and Migrate".

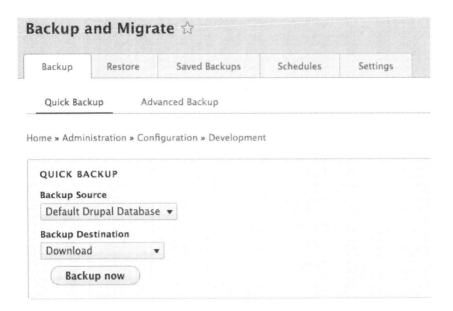

- From here, you can backup your database, your files, or your entire site:

- The "Schedules" tab allows you to set up regular backups:

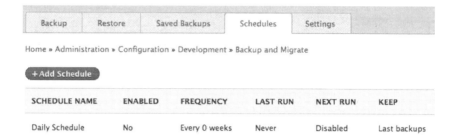

SCHEDULE NAME	ENABLED	FREQUENCY	LAST RUN	NEXT RUN	KEEP
Daily Schedule	No	Every 0 weeks	Never	Disabled	Last backups

There are modules that expand on Backup and Migrate and allow you to send backups to Amazon S3, Rackspace, HPCloud and other cloud storage services. Backup and Migrate also integrates with http://nodesquirrel.com which can safely store backups.

ADDITIONAL MEASURES TO PROTECT YOUR SITE

The last two chapters covered four of the most important security processes for your Drupal site:

- permissions,
- regular updates,
- deleting unused software, and
- taking regular backups.

To further enhance the security of your site, you should use the Security Review module. This module won't actually secure your site, but it can give you great advice on how to do it.

Here's how to use the Security Review module:

- Install the module from http://drupal.org/project/security_review.
- Go to "Reports" and then "Security review".
- Click "Run checklist" and it gives you some suggestions on problems to fix.

- Click "Details" to get information on fixing the problems.

✓	Only safe extensions are allowed for uploaded files and images.	Details
✓	Dangerous tags were not found in any submitted content (fields).	Details
✓	Untrusted roles do not have administrative or trusted Drupal permissions.	Details
✓	Error reporting set to log only.	Details
⚠	The .htaccess file in the files directory is writable.	Details
✕	Some files and directories in your install are writable by the server.	Details

WHAT'S NEXT?

Congratulations! You've reached the end of Drupal 8 Explained!

Practice. The only way to get better at Drupal is to build Drupal sites. Decide on your first Drupal project and start practicing.

Practice now. You will forget most of what you've read in this book. That's human nature and doesn't make us bad teachers or you a bad learner. The longer you wait to practice Drupal, the more you'll forget. Why not start right away?

Learn more. We guarantee that there are things you will come across while using Drupal that haven't been included in this book. This book has only a limited number of pages, and we've tried to focus on only the most important things about Drupal. We also tried hard to avoid any code so that the barrier to entry for using Drupal is as low as possible.

However, one of the great things about Drupal being so popular is that almost every problem you run into has been encountered by other people. Many of those people will have asked for or posted a solution to their problem online.

If you ever get stuck, here are the first two places you should go to for help:

- Contact us: get in touch by emailing support@ostraining.com.

- Use Google: If you get an error message or encounter a problem, type it directly into a search engine, and there's a good chance you'll find a solution.

- Use the Drupal help: http://drupal.org/forum. The Drupal forums have more than a million posts at the time of writing, so you can find a lot of solutions. Search for a solution to your question, and if you don't find it, write a new post. There's sure to be someone who can help you.

- Join the Drupal community. Drupal doesn't rely on money; it relies on people like you. Whether you attend a local Drupal event, post solutions you find on the forum, or even say thank you to someone who's helped you, there are many easy ways to become part of the Drupal community. The more you rely on Drupal for your website or your business, the more it can benefit you to become part of the community.

We hope to see you around in the Drupal community, and we wish you all the best in your use of Drupal!

captchaq   config-people

menus   understructure

69661548R00244

Made in the USA
Lexington, KY
03 November 2017